THE HOME FRONT

Archie Satterfield

THE HOME FRONT

An Oral History of

the War Years in America:

1941–45

PLAYBOY PRESS

PLAYBOY PRESS / A Division of PEI Books, Inc.

Library of Congress Cataloging in Publication Data
Satterfield, Archie.
    The home front.

    Bibliography: p.
    1. World War, 1939–1945—United States.
2. United States—History—1933–1945. I. Title.
D769.S27   940.53'73   81–80403
ISBN 0–87223–721–4   AACR2

Designed by Guy Fleming

To *Marie, Neil, Tressa, and Wayne*

CONTENTS

ACKNOWLEDGMENTS

WHILE CONDUCTING THE RESEARCH FOR THIS BOOK, I developed a network of contacts all over the nation, which began, in many instances, with a fellow journalist. They include:

John Brewer, Associated Press; Hugh Park, Atlanta *Journal*; Basil Hall, Charleston *Evening Post*; the Denver *Post*; Jonathan Yardley, Miami *Herald*; Lyn Liljeholm, Portland, Maine, *Evening Express*; *San Antonio Light*; Emmett Watson, Seattle *Post-Intelligencer*; Floy Beatty, Nashville, *Tennessean*.

Some of the material on Japanese-Americans came from the oral-history program at California State University, Fullerton, and the material on Mennonites from the oral-history program at Bethel College, North Newton, Kansas.

Ken Irwin of the Pearl Harbor Survivors Association was especially helpful, as was David Piff of the Federal Records Center, Seattle.

My friends Walter and Iris Selnak of Huntington, New York, were generous hosts during my research trip to their area and arranged for several interviews in their home and office.

The V-mail letters reprinted in the chapter headings were contributed by Julie Stewart, of Littleton, Colorado, and told me more about the war and the waiting than entire volumes.

To these people, and the 200-odd other individuals involved in the book, either through interviews or suggestions, I am very grateful.

The war came as a great relief, like a severe earthquake that in one terrible jerk shook everything disjointed, disordered, askew back into place. Japanese bombs finally brought national unity to the U.S.

Time magazine, December 15, 1941

Nobody minds a war once in a while if it doesn't last too long and isn't in your own neighborhood.

Bertrand Russell

Introduction

WITH THE BITTER EXPERIENCE of two unpopular and unfinished wars in Asia now a part of our national heritage, we have come to think of World War II as the last of the good wars and the only one we can understand. Like a short story from almost any popular magazine of that period, the war had a dramatic beginning, a middle fraught with conflict, and a happy ending. Our concept of it is not fogged by the gray areas of morality that plagued our wars in Korea and Vietnam. Nostalgia has seeped in to replace the facts of history, and many of us look back on those four years with a longing unequaled by any other period in our history.

The war years of 1941–45 are unique in our national experience: Never have we been more united with a common goal on which to focus our attention, our energies, and our hate. Unlike economic or natural disasters, World War II had a definite goal and definable enemies to overcome. So convinced were we that our cause was just that the war has become firmly lodged in our national conscience as a crusade against evil, a united effort by free people to save the world from dictatorship. It was the last of our holy wars.

Thus has nostalgia clouded our memories of a period that was not really as pleasant as we choose to remember it. We forget how many men were killed or maimed. We forget how many personal freedoms were abruptly suspended for the duration of the war, based only on race or religion and involving whole peoples who were thrust into prison or camps that today we can only call concentration camps. We forget the fear of invasion of our coasts, the panic-stricken evacuation of our far-flung territories, the loneliness of young widowed mothers, and that excruciating waiting and worrying about sons, brothers, husbands, fathers, friends, and lovers. We forget the immediate aftermath of the war when the economy was staggering under the pressure of the diversification brought on by peace. And we forget how those men who only weeks before were heroes suddenly became ordinary men let loose on the uncertain job market; heroes become anachronistic the moment war ends.

We also forget about the injustices we heaped on 4-Fs; and when we talk of our national unity at that time, we forget the draft dodgers, black marketeers, and the pious, holier-than-thou minor bureaucrats who ruled ration boards and the surly waitresses and clerks who had no fear of losing their jobs during the wartime boom. We forget how enraged we became when we heard that catchall question: "Don't you know there's a war on?" The weapon of the incompetent, the arrogant, and the smug, that question was flung in our faces anytime we complained or asked for a product or service we thought should be available.

Yet those four years were for many of us the most important years of our lives and made an indelible impression. Those years colored our concept of America and left us unprepared for brinkmanship, detente, and limited warfare. It is inconceivable that anyone could experience the intensity of that period and remain unchanged. Many of us were liberated from the prison of poverty that had been our legacy. Those who were not already poor became so during the Great Depression that occupied the entire decade of the 1930s and gave the nation despair, just as the war gave us hope. We were deeply divided by the Depression and strongly united by the war as one disaster was replaced by another. It was a special time in our history and we have never been quite the same since.

One definition of "history" might be "an anthology of personal experience," and this book was begun with that in mind. Although I was a child during World War II, I knew its impact on me and my family was enormous. Yet I found no satisfactory answers to basic questions about the era in the books I read or the people I talked to. Since I was brought up on the oral tradition of the Missouri Ozarks at a time when the only radios we could use were powered by batteries, I decided to use the oral-history approach. This seemed the only way to take the book away from policy- and opinion-makers and return history to the people who lived it. I did not want to reduce the period to the confines of an author's set of restrictions or personal viewpoint.

But after interviewing more than 200 people all across the nation, over a two-year period, I found that pure oral history with no attempt by the author to explain the background can leave gaping holes and create as many questions as it answers.

I do not pretend that this is both an oral and a formal history of the American home-front period. Instead, it is a selective history, concentrating on the events and circumstances that seemed to affect the most people. The experiences and thoughts and opinions of the individual are dominant.

I began by collecting stories without discrimination. I simply asked people what they did during the war years—and no strictly "war" stories, please. I asked newspapers around the country to run stories about the project so people could contact me, and in this manner I obtained wide geographical coverage with stories unique to particular areas. After nearly a hundred interviews had been conducted, the subject matter began to divide itself into separate categories.

Still, there were whole topics missing that I believed should be included, and I called on friends, organizations, agencies, and more newspaper editors for assistance and suggestions. In every case they responded, sometimes with information or experiences not found in any of the documents relating to the period. The subject and approach appealed to people, and almost invariably they were willing, if not anxious, to help.

Most people I interviewed were less interested in having their names published than in trying to help define this vital period of American history. Several said they hoped the book would help explain how life was back then to their children, because members of the postwar baby boom seem to find it difficult to believe war could ever have been so clear-cut and simple.

There were large areas of experience I expected to hear more stories about but did not—due in part, I suspect, to my own misunderstanding of what was considered important by those interviewed. I expected to hear from women who lost their sons or husbands in the war, but I have come to believe that most do not care to talk about those things. More than one told me there was nothing they could add beyond the bald fact that their son—or husband or lover—was killed. Also, our patriotism was whipped to such a frenzy then that it wasn't unusual for the mother of a dead soldier to tell reporters she wouldn't hesitate to send another son to the war if she had one to send. Now it is difficult for us to believe that our patriotism was so intense, and few, if any, mothers would say such things today about Korea, Vietnam, or any other war to which America sends its soldiers.

I expected to hear how we were manipulated by government propaganda, but seldom did. The fact of Pearl Harbor erased the memory of maneuverings between our government and that of Japan before the war, and there are still a few who become agitated about the possibility of our intentionally leaving our Pacific bases vulnerable to attack so the war could start on a note of deep hatred. Some believe that, but most do not. Most feel that we considered ourselves so immune to attack that absolutely nobody expected it.

Concentrating as I have on the so-called ordinary people of the country, there is very little material on some subjects, such as the death of President Roosevelt and the sudden emergence of a relatively unknown politician named Harry S. Truman. Everybody said essentially the same thing: how saddened they were by Roosevelt's death and how at first they couldn't stand the sight of Truman's eyeglasses or the sound of his voice.

Another area of interest I did not touch upon at all was the destruction of Hiroshima and Nagasaki with atomic bombs. With the exception of a Quaker I interviewed, I distrust people who speak of those bombings today as an atrocity they strongly opposed in 1945. If we are to believe what we are told, almost everyone in America was appalled that we would treat anyone that way, even though our propaganda machinery had boasted of the devastation of Dresden, Berlin, and most of Germany. Today most people who were adults during that period say they were shocked, ashamed, horrified, and strongly opposed to using the bombs.

I don't believe them. At that time virtually everyone was delighted that we dropped the bombs, not only because they shortened the war and saved thousands of American lives, but also because the "Japs" deserved it for the terrible things they had done to our boys at Pearl Harbor, Bataan, Guadalcanal, and all the way through the Pacific. Many of us today are suffering from a delayed, and perhaps unnecessary, guilt over those incidents.

Another subject I expected to yield an outpouring of complaints was rationing. I was under the impression that some people had suffered because of it. If they did, they did not tell me. The rationing system seems to have provided people with enough food, clothing, and gasoline, although the Americans' love affair with transportation made the word "enough" difficult to define. Another factor was the ability, developed over a decade, to get by, to make do, to "Hooverize." There were the usual complaints—by now expressed with good humor—about the quality of shoes and the scarcity of stockings and good cigarettes, but most admitted the system was generally fair. Part of the rationing problem was the fact that the sudden abundance of jobs and paychecks coincided with governmental restraints on spending. This led to inevitable abuses, but on a much smaller scale than one might expect. Most people believed strongly in helping the war effort and saw a direct relationship between the rationing program and the comfort and safety of loved ones fighting the war.

During the years I interviewed people for this book, the role of oral history has been questioned repeatedly. Used sparingly in the past, it has become a familiar device during the past decade. Can oral history be trusted over traditional history? Is it history or only nostalgia?

In college I was taught that interpreters of events are at least as important as the participants. Oral accounts were considered curiosities, evidence but not conclusions.

Although I have not relied totally on the oral-history approach, the book is heavily laden with information from historical eyewitnesses. As I progressed, my doubts about the accuracy of historical material gathered from eyewitnesses were eased when I found that the interviews had a way of merging, of complementing each other, until there was little room for doubt that, for example, displaced persons from Europe were roundly disliked by Americans because it was felt they didn't appreciate America enough. As one reads these accounts, one is reminded of a parent discussing an unimpressed and ungrateful child.

I also found that what might be of interest to a historian is often of little or no concern to those who experienced the events. Formal historians too often write for peer acceptance and forget the average reader. The people will tell you that their daily affairs often have their own drama, one that sometimes overshadows the headlines of the day. Thus, while men are being killed in foreign countries, women stateside may worry about that ghastly fluid they applied to their legs to simulate hose, and stateside men wonder how they are going to go on a hunting trip without sufficient gasoline and good tires.

Throughout the interviewing process I used George Orwell's dictum on autobiography as a barometer for truth: that autobiography is to be trusted only when it reveals something disgraceful; that when we give a good account of ourselves we are usually lying. I constantly watched for the Orwellian Law to be broken, and I think it only seldom was. Sometimes the disgraceful acts were concealed by an apologetic laugh, or were tossed into the conversation as jokes, but the statute of limitations on our consciences usually runs out after three decades and we are now able to discuss the sometimes shameful matters of the Second World War with only a token apology.

Early in the interviewing I wondered why people would tell a complete stranger the stories I heard from all over America. I asked some people, and their replies were varied but revealed a few basic needs on the teller's part. A major factor is that most of us are lonely and paradoxically become more so with the increase in population and mobility. Each of us is at least partially alienated from the present and we long for the virtues of the past, even though we can't always prove those virtues ever existed. Talking about the past can give it a firmer reality. Our memories are selective and the pains and joys stand above the valleys of the ordinary. We do not want our memories to die with us. Many of these memories are singular; an event or an impression will represent an entire era for us. We remember what we want to remember, and we want to share it.

At the extreme we become evangelists for the past. Some people spoke to me to explain themselves to others, and to themselves; to sort out their lives by putting them into words and into print. We do not grant interviews to absolute strangers for immortality alone. We do so to share a part of our lives and to understand it better by doing so. In such cases the printed word takes on a vivid reality that film can never duplicate.

Documents such as this must have limitations imposed by the author. Thus, I have concentrated on the people. Accounts by the powerful and the famous do not interest me, because power surely corrupts and fame usually does. Those who possess either become so accustomed to speaking through a public-relations filter that interviews with them are always suspect. They have formed the survival habits of covering their tracks and giving Orwell's good account of themselves. I wanted the defense workers, not the Henry Kaisers; the sidemen and fan-club members, not the Artie Shaws and Red Foleys; the people who voted for politicians, not the politicians themselves.

As you read these accounts of that four-year period, I think you will frequently ask yourself, as I have, whether we are any happier than we were during the Depression and the war; whether we have made any real progress in our quality of life, or whether we have simply changed our addresses and style of clothing. There is a statement near the end of the book that will always disturb me. One woman tells of the fellowship during the war and how people cared for one another, strangers helping strangers. But when the war ended, she found that people no longer cared, that we lost our humanity after the inhumanity of war was over.

Repeatedly people interrupted their narratives to offer an apology for enjoying themselves during a war. They said they did not like wars and did not like the thought of having to be at war to see the country united. World War II was different, they said. Somehow it was better.

Let's make Hitler
And Hirohito
Look as Sick
As Benito.
Buy Defense Bonds.
BURMA-SHAVE

We are the sons of the rising guns.
The U.S. will take the Nip out of the Nipponese.
Let's blast the Japs clean off the map.
Be smart—act dumb.
Loose lips sink ships.
Once a Jap, always a Jap.
Use it up, wear it out, make it do or do without.
Pay your taxes and beat the Axis.
Weed 'em and reap (Victory Gardens).
Bye-bye, Benito.

1

Remember Pearl Harbor

V-MAIL

MY DEAREST SWEETHEART:

Reporting on the first St. Louis blackout—a huge success much to everyone's surprise! The lights all over the city were off and the city looked like a big piece of barren land. The blackout extended all over nine Midwest states and was pronounced really good which just proves what we've always said, that the Midwest is in this war lots more than we know.

Last night Fred Waring dedicated his program to the P.I. Marines and played the songs they requested: "For Me and My Gal" from that last picture we saw, "Silent Night" and the Marine hymn, which made me cry with pride. You don't know how wonderful it is to tell people your husband is an officer in the Marine Corps serving overseas. They all just look at me in awe and then I show them your picture and they believe me. I'm *so* proud and so are all the folks—Dad is so busy telling everyone about us that they all think the war is all but over now that you're in action—well, so do I! Thank heaven you chose the right outfit and got your commission, too—just remember you're tops in the top outfit.

Lots and lots of love,

YESTERDAY, DECEMBER 7, 1941—A DATE THAT WILL LIVE IN INFAMY —THE UNITED STATES OF AMERICA WAS SUDDENLY AND DELIBERATELY ATTACKED BY NAVAL AND AIR FORCES OF THE EMPIRE OF JAPAN.

THE UNITED STATES *was at peace with that nation, and, at the solicitation of Japan, was still in conversation with its government and its Emperor looking toward the maintenance of peace in the Pacific.*

The attack yesterday on the Hawaiian Islands has caused severe damage to American naval and military forces. Very many American lives have been lost. In addition, American ships have been reported torpedoed on the high seas between San Francisco and Honolulu.

Yesterday the Japanese government also launched an attack against Malaya.

Last night the Japanese forces attacked Hong Kong.

Last night Japanese forces attacked Guam.

Last night Japanese forces attacked the Philippine Islands.

Last night the Japanese attacked Wake Island.

This morning the Japanese attacked Midway Island.

Japan has, therefore, undertaken a surprise offensive ex-

tending throughout the Pacific area. The facts of yesterday speak for themselves. The people of the United States have already formed their opinions and well understand the implication to the very safety and life of their nation.

I believe I interpret the will of the Congress and the people when I assert that we will not only defend ourselves to the uttermost, but will make very certain that this form of treachery shall never endanger us again.

FROM PRESIDENT FRANKLIN DELANO ROOSEVELT'S SPEECH ON RADIO, DECEMBER 8, 1941

O N THAT WINTER MORNING AMERICA, the sleeping giant so feared by cautious Japanese and Nazi officials, was slowly stirring as the thunder of distant guns and the rattling of armor grew louder and more threatening. In Europe, America's womb, the German war machine was erasing national boundaries, exterminating leaders, and trampling over lesser armies with the force and finality of a hurricane. When Hitler's Nazi party came to power in 1933 and immediately began organizing a war machine, it took less than six years to become the most powerful military force in Europe. In 1939 Germany defeated Poland in an eighteen-day war, and by 1940 Germany controlled Denmark and Norway to the north. Belgium, the Netherlands, and France followed. Then came North Africa and the bombardment of England that continued throughout the summer, fall, and winter of 1941.

To the west lay another threat, a potential enemy America did not know so well. Oriental culture was as exotic to us as an undiscovered Indian tribe in the High Andes, and Japan itself had been as insulated from Western thought as America was from the Oriental culture. This closed, remote island empire had earned a reputation for sneak attacks when on February 8, 1904, at nearly midnight, the Japanese fleet smashed the Russian navy that lay at anchor off Port Arthur, Manchuria, without benefit of formally declared war. Most Americans did not know their Asian military history, and American leaders ignored this trait so foreign to our more polite, formal methods of starting wars. Foreign wars were remote events in those days, tragedies that happened to someone else in another country. We did not care much what the Japanese, Chinese, Mongolians, and Russians did to each other. It was inconceivable that anyone in the world would attack us; and as to us attacking *them*, we didn't start wars, we only finished them.

But Japan was on the march, moving down the Asian mainland from French Indochina (which another generation of American soldiers would know as Vietnam) toward Malaysia and the islands of the Pacific. The movements were swift, unannounced, and as impersonally brutal as a tsunami. That was a problem on the far side of the world to be worked out by culturally and mentally inferior nations, we believed. No American boys would be lost in that war. We paid little attention to the reports on radio and in newspapers about the exchange of threats, deadlines, and ultimatums between the Roosevelt administration and Emperor Hirohito.

We had better things to think about. For more than a decade America's dreams and waking thoughts had been directed inward. The worst depression in our history had slowed technological and industrial growth to a crawl. There were 4 million men out of work that morning, and those with jobs were subservient to their employers. The threat of unemployment hung heavy and made men willing to swallow their pride and sacrifice self-respect in order to keep a job. There was too much truth in the old chestnut about there being at least three other men waiting for the job if you didn't like it.

A generation of younger people was growing up with no

promising future, and adults were faced with a future as bleak as their past. Opportunity hardly existed. More or less typical was a young woman, the eldest child in a family of three daughters and parents who had no jobs. Nearly four decades later she could not speak of those years without bitterness, and her life was permanently marked by injustices by her family and American society.

She was almost eighteen, a high-school senior with a year of typing and stenographic skills behind her, when one night her parents called her into the dining room. The family had $2.80 in the house and no prospects of work for the parents. She recalls:

"From the time I was fifteen I had worked for people as a housekeeper when they had money to pay me—or bedbugs to donate, which happened. My dad had been a timekeeper for the county and made seventy-two dollars a month for a family of seven. Now he had nothing.

"I had also worked for nothing. I walked two and a half miles every day after school to work for nothing for a county road district commissioner to learn secretarial skills. Once in a while his wife gave me five or ten dollars a month, but not very often. They didn't have any money either. I worked for the experience.

"So that evening while we sat around the dining-room table, I asked, 'Should I drop out of school?' and that was what they were waiting for someone else to suggest. I said I would, my dad cried and stopped hunting for a job, and we owed a big grocery bill at two stores that took me two years to pay off.

"I got a job at the WPA [Works Progress Administration]. When the man told me what I'd be making a year, I had no conception. I went out of his office into the hallway and leaned against a wall, got a piece of paper, and divided twelve into the figure he gave me as my annual salary, and came up with eighty-five dollars a month. I couldn't believe it. I went back in and said there must be a mistake because I was good at figures.

"When I cashed my first check, I got it all in one-dollar bills, took them home, and went into the kitchen. I threw them all over the kitchen and everybody grabbed those dollar bills. They hadn't seen that much money in I don't know how long. I handed my checks over to dad until 1937, when I took the bit in my teeth and left home.

"We lived thirty miles out of town and I commuted for the first six weeks, two and a half hours each way on a rinky-dink bus. When I got home I was too tired to eat. I was skinny and nervous (now I'm fat and nervous and still stupid) and I would collapse on the bed and fall asleep. My mother had to shake me awake to feed me.

"I moved to town and still sent money home. Dad figured out just how much I needed for rent, food, and occasionally some clothes. But never entertainment. So I learned to walk everywhere. I visited the morgue, the art museum, skid row, everywhere. I was never molested on those excursions. I was only molested in offices by successful businessmen and bureaucrats.

"I was the only one in the family my parents leaned on. The rest got violin lessons and baton-twirling lessons. Violins are okay—but batons? I went home one night and here's my kid sister twirling around with her baton, bought with my money, and I can't have anything for myself. That was the end of supporting my family. After that I was gone for good."

There was a bitterness across the nation that ran deeper than resentment between the haves and have-nots. There was a feeling of despair; that things were never going to improve, that there was no point in life, that the country could not care for its own and should not try to solve Europe's problems again, or get involved in a dispute between a bunch of chinks and Japs. We had already solved Europe's problems once before, during World War I, and look how much good that had done us. If they appreciated it so much, why didn't they help us during the Depression? Now they were at it again, messing up the world.

Hadn't we taken their refugees by the millions and let them flood our labor market to the point where a native-born American couldn't get a decent job? Weren't we doing enough by sending them military equipment on the Lend-Lease program? Weren't we having Bingo for Britain? Weren't women's clubs sending children's clothing to the English kids during the blitz? Stay out of it. We have enough problems of our own without getting involved in theirs. If a man in this country can't get a decent job to feed his family, what business do we have getting mixed up in that European mess?

Yet, amid this talk of isolationism, just over the horizon of history were those guns of Europe and the ships of the Orient. Something was going to happen. We could feel it as we could feel the hair on our arms prickle before a summer storm. We expected something. Change was in the air.

Few of us remember what we were doing Saturday, December 6, 1941. But that Sunday began a series of dates forever engraved in the national mind, dates when the mundane became the remarkable. We would remember that day as we would later remember the day President Franklin Delano Roosevelt died, and the day the European War ended, the day the Japanese War ended, and the day two decades later when President John Fitzgerald Kennedy was assassinated. We may have forgotten some of the exact calendar days, but not the events and emotions of those sacred days.

On that morning the children of America were reading the Sunday comics. In "Bringing up Father," Jiggs was astounded at the amount of new clothes Maggie bought for a vacation (which few Americans could afford). In "Thimble Theater," Olive bashed Popeye on the head when he tried to make her jealous. Flash Gordon was in another jam; he had stolen a seaplane from the enemy in the Pacific, but was shot down by friendly fire because they thought he was an invader. The plane's insignia was not the rising sun of the Japanese, but it was circular in design and the plane itself bore a remarkable resemblance to the Japanese patrol planes launched from ships.

Our parents read the front page, which carried a story about the Japanese fleet steaming toward the Gulf of Siam with 125,000 troops aboard. Another story told about President Roosevelt's plea to Emperor Hirohito to avoid war in the Pacific. A third story explained that Japan must be expecting something because the steamship company Nippon Yusen Kaisha had ordered its managers in Singapore and Bombay home immediately. Rear Admiral Clark H. Woodward wrote a column for the International News Service which, fortunately for all concerned, carried a disclaimer that the admiral's views were his alone and not those of the government or the newspaper. Admiral Woodward said the Nipponese navy, air force, and ground troops were inferior fighters, and that the trade restrictions imposed by America, plus the closing of the Panama Canal to Japanese shipping, would doom the tiny nation's military ambitions.

This was easy for our parents to believe. After all, Japan was such a tiny bunch of islands, its fighting men weren't much because they all wore glasses as thick as soda-bottle bottoms, their slanted eyes were crossed, they had buckteeth, and they weren't very bright. Besides, they were such little twerps.

Elsewhere in the paper our parents read with only passing interest that on the previous day England had declared war on Finland because the small nation was apparently fighting on the same side as Hitler against Russia. The Finnish president, Risto Ryti, was weary of trying to explain that they were simply fighting back against Russia (who had attacked them over disputed territory), that there wasn't much new in that, and that they didn't think much of Hitler either. President Ryti added, tiredly it seemed, that Russia's friendship with the United States and Great Britain was "a leper's handicap." It would be several years before the American public would consider his words prophetic.

Turning to the sports pages, we read that Bob Feller, the Cleveland Indians' pitching ace, had announced he was enlisting in the navy or air corps rather than be drafted into the infantry. In Washington, D.C., almost the entire government was attending the Washington Redskins–Philadelphia Eagles professional football game. In the previous day's college games, Utah had beat Arizona 12–6, Boston's amateur hockey team beat Atlantic City 5–0, the UCLA Bruins and the USC Trojans tied at 7–7, and the University of Hawaii beat Oregon's Willamette University 20–6 on their home field in Honolulu. It was the first of two games, but the second was canceled due to what one wag called weather: "East wind. Rain."

Our mothers read that King Leopold III of Belgium had taken a bride. Electrolux vacuum cleaners were selling for $15.95, all attachments included. Sears Roebuck was selling a three-piece bedroom set at its retail stores for $44.95, and sheer silk stockings were 89¢ a pair. Newspaper ads were sprinkled with militaristic jargon: A store called its book sale a "bookskreig," and an automobile agency advertised its new car as a "B-44." Most 1941 cars were selling for less than $1000, but with the average wage at just under $3000 a year, they represented a sizable investment. Still, Chevrolet, the nation's leading car, sold 930,000 that year at an average price of about $700.

The newspapers that morning were filled with cultural nonsense. "Ripley's Believe It or Not" had a mind-bender borrowed from Mark Twain that would resurface in 1947 as a hillbilly song, "I'm My Own Grandpa." Ripley, with some accuracy, called it "Confessions of a Suicide."

* * *

"I married a widow with a grown daughter. My father fell in love with my stepdaughter and married her—thus becoming my son-in-law—and my stepdaughter became my mother-in-law because she was my father's wife.

"My wife gave birth to a son, which of course was my father's brother-in-law, and my uncle for he was the brother of my stepmother.

"My father's wife became the mother of a son. He was, of course, my brother—and also my grandchild. For he was the son of my daughter.

"Accordingly, my wife was my grandmother because she was my mother's mother. I was my wife's husband and grandchild at the same time—and as the husband of a person's grandmother, is his grandfather.

"I'm my own grandfather."

In the movie gossip column there was a photograph of Brenda Joyce, whose first film role was in *The Rains Came*, and the studio publicity genius said Brenda "likes nothing better than to put on her bathing suit and play in the rain." Another woman, not a movie star, said she found fifty-three golf balls in one afternoon. The hit song of the week was selected by Benny Goodman, and he chose "Little Fool," written by a young singer named Peggy Lee.

When a ten-year-old boy in Nebraska heard the news of the attack on Pearl Harbor, it was 1:35 P.M., Central Standard Time. He was totally unimpressed. "I had never heard of Pearl Harbor, didn't care where it was, and knew that we could whip the Japs or anybody else," he says. "Then I went back to the funny papers. I doubt that I listened to another newscast that day. Who cares when you're ten? We had heard of other attacks in Europe and China for months on end, and this new one was no big deal to me at all. Our horizons were much more limited then, and if you couldn't see it from the front porch, who was to say it even existed?"

At about 2:45 P.M., Eastern Standard Time, an elderly man was walking his dog in New Jersey when a radio-station reporter conducting on-the-street interviews approached him and asked what he thought of the Japanese attack on our Pacific fleet. The elderly skeptic remembered how he had been fooled in 1938 by Orson Welles, who convinced hundreds of thousands of radio listeners that Martians had landed near New York City.

"Ha!" he snapped at the reporter. "You're not going to catch me on another of your pranks." He led his dog away.

In a small Wisconsin town Florence Rudell Marx, out of high school but still living at home because she could find no work, had eaten breakfast, gone to Sunday School and church, and was lying down for a nap before the big Sunday afternoon family dinner. Her parents were Volga Germans who had fled Europe just after World War I for freedom and opportunity. Her father had learned to speak excellent English, but her mother spent most of her time in the house with the ten children of the family and had not mastered the new language. She could understand most of what she heard, but could hardly write her own name in English. The girl's father had managed to do well in spite of the Depression. He came to America expecting to work, and had worked very hard indeed during those bad years. He built his paint-contracting business to the point where only a few months previously he had bought a new truck. His American dream was coming true. He was founding a business to pass on to his seven sons.

But his dream ended that day. The young woman, in that semiconscious state between sleeping and waking, heard her father sobbing. Instead of the Mormon Tabernacle Choir she expected to hear on the radio, she heard the voice of H. V. Kaltenborn. But she wasn't listening to Kaltenborn; she had never heard her father cry before, and she was certain it meant only one thing—that her mother had died while she napped.

She lay with her eyes closed, dreading to open them,

then heard her father saying, over and over: "My boys, my boys . . ." Then she heard the calm voice of Kaltenborn detailing the death and destruction at Pearl Harbor and the implications of the attack. Relieved, she rose and went into the parlor and found her father sitting in his favorite chair with her mother standing beside him, arms around his shoulders, her eyes dry. She was thinking of all the hardships they had survived—the hard boat trip across the Atlantic, finding a place to live among people she could not understand—all this so their children wouldn't have to fight in the wars that continually swept Europe. Now this.

Within a month of that cold winter morning, five of her seven brothers would be in various branches of the service. A sixth had lost an eye as a child, and the seventh was only ten years old.

Also on that day a Japanese-American college student from Seattle took his sister and her girl friend for a ride in the family car. It was 11:35 A.M., Pacific Standard Time, and they didn't have a radio, but they quickly became aware of cold and hostile looks wherever they drove. That was unusual. They were more accustomed to being totally ignored; most Caucasians "looked right through" them. They drove back home and found their parents gathered around a radio listening to the worst news they could expect to hear on this continent. Within an hour reporters would be driving through Little Tokyo asking citizens for their impressions of the attack. Most expressed a combination of outrage and sorrow, for all had relatives in Japan. Few Caucasians really cared what they thought, because they were convinced Orientals' emotions were different—that they didn't feel as deeply or care as much. Life was cheap in the Orient, the experts on Oriental culture said. There are millions and millions of them and they all act alike, look alike, and think alike. Get rid of one and nobody will miss him.

Thousands of miles west across the Pacific and several

hours earlier, a young navy wife, Hazel Brock, was preparing breakfast for her five-year-old son and eighteen-month-old daughter. They lived only two blocks away from the Pearl Harbor gate and were accustomed to the noises of military activity—the clatter of ship repair, whistles, vehicles, and the roar of fighter planes coming back from dawn patrols "so low they almost took the shingles off the roof." Her husband was a young officer on a cruise aboard the destroyer U.S.S. *Daubin*. She was wishing her children didn't feel it essential to be awake just because the sun was up. They were insisting that she perform the usual Sunday morning ritual of reading the comics aloud while they ate breakfast. The boy was wondering what all that noise was about.

"Finally my son pestered me so much I went up to his bedroom and looked out the window just in time to see the Japs blow up the barracks at Hickam Field. This was the first hint to me that it was not exactly practice."

Like everyone else in the officers' housing project, she ran outside to see what was happening. She saw waves of planes dropping down from behind the mountains and over Pearl Harbor so low she could see the pilots' faces, and she watched the bombs falling and exploding among the fleet that was tied up and manned by skeleton crews that weren't quite awake yet. Nearly all the ships were wide open inside for airing, giving them the flotation characteristics of a sieve once holes were blown in them below waterline. Says she:

"I ran back to the house and got the kids dressed and decided to go down to see another navy wife who was a little high-strung. I was certain she would be in hysterics and that I would have to take care of her kids. During a lull between attacks, the three of us dashed down to her house and there she was, cleaning house and giving her kids breakfast, calm as you please, as if nothing out of the ordinary was happening.

"Then we all gathered in one house. There were no bomb

shelters or anything like that and the houses weren't built worth a darn. But we all crowded into this one living room. There must have been thirty adults and that many or more kids in that one room. There was no particular reason we gathered there; it just worked out that way. I guess somebody saw a woman and kids heading in and the rest of us thought we were supposed to go there.

"The woman of the house, who also had a husband aboard the *Daubin*, was a very peculiar woman who got even more peculiar that day. At first she refused to believe we were having a real raid. Finally someone turned on a radio and she believed it. Her first words then were: 'If any of you run out of food, don't come to me.'

"One of the girls stared at her a minute, then ran next door to her house. The back doors were so close together that when a drunk came home, he never knew where he belonged. The girl came back with a bag of oranges and a bag of apples, which cost a fortune in the islands because apples don't grow there. She never said a word. She just handed them out to the kids. The woman who made that terrible remark never understood, and probably never remembered saying it.

"When the raid was over, the kids and I went back to our quarters. I didn't want to leave and didn't see any sense to it. I felt more secure there than wandering around the island. Besides, I wanted to stay and find out if my husband was dead or alive, and I wouldn't know for two days that he was fine. Ambulances and fire engines were running everywhere and people were trying to get back to the base to help, everyone scattering when the fighters came down and strafed anything they could find moving.

"Finally they talked me into evacuating. Finding an incendiary bomb near the house that hadn't exploded, and learning that a little boy had been killed across the street below us, helped convince me to head for the hills.

"My husband had bought me a portable sewing machine.

When the Japanese people on the island got married, they always got one for a wedding present. Anyway, I had been making curtains and drapes and they were all laid out on the cement floor—the house wasn't even finished yet. So I picked up the sewing machine and some clothes and some cheese and crackers and bananas, and away we went. Why I ever took that sewing machine at a time like that I'll never know. But I did.

"The other woman—the nervous one—and I loaded into her car and went down to Fort Shafter to pick up a third friend who lived just outside the gate. Then we took off down the road toward Honolulu that we called Suicide Lane because it was just like a snake. We came to a junction and there was a little Japanese Boy Scout helping direct traffic. I thought one of the women with me was going to kill him. Her Irish was up and she had had it by now. She was beginning to fall apart like a lot of people do after it is all over, and she really let go. She got out of the car and started in on that poor little boy. A soldier was there and he told her to shut up and get back in the car. She finally did and we headed for the mountains back of Honolulu.

"We went up the Kalihi Valley to a friend's house. Her husband was on the *Daubin*, too, and she was a tall gal— about six-three—a calm, easygoing nurse. Here she was having berserks. She was about twenty years older than her husband and always dressed like she was twenty years *younger* than him, which was kind of pathetic. We finally got her shut up because we had been able to keep the kids calm and didn't want them reacting to her hysterics.

"Pretty soon the sun went down, and it was one of those pitch-black nights that hit in the tropics before you know it is even late. One minute it is light, then pitch-blackness the next.

"I can't begin to tell you all the wild things that happened that night. We were all terrified, of course, and we just knew that the Japs were going to put troops ashore and that they would come storming down the mountain behind us. We were afraid our husbands were dead, and we were afraid of the black night because we couldn't have lights anywhere.

"And what did we eat that night? Pork and beans. Everybody should eat beans when they're upset. Right?

"Down the road a few yards some Chinese were having a luau. Nothing, not even war, was going to stop them from having that luau. Then about nine o'clock, when we finally had most of the kids bedded down, here comes a husband of one of the women, and he is stinking drunk. As tragic as the whole day had been for us, he was absolutely hilarious. He kept yelling in his Portuguese accent that he wanted a gun so he could fight the Japs. Nobody could quiet him down so we could sleep. Finally his wife gave him a couple of kids' toy pistols and he went outside and was shooting Japs all over the place, whooping and yelling until he got sick and passed out.

"One woman had appeared just before dark in her car, her long hair hanging down uncombed and she was wearing a dress that buttoned down the front. Only one button was holding it to her. She wore that dress, a pair of tennis shoes, and not another stitch. I asked her what on earth she was doing and she said she had gone upstairs that morning to get dressed when the attack came. She remembered looking out the window and seeing the *Arizona* take several hits, and not one thing did she remember after that. Somehow she had driven all the way, dodging shell holes, strafing planes, fought her way through traffic jams, and arrived up in the hills with us.

"When it was all over and she went back home, her husband told her that she had marched downstairs, right past him and out the front door to the car, leaving him sitting at the breakfast table in total astonishment.

"Another woman down the street had a rotten reputation she had worked very hard to earn. She had three little boys and she was as tough as nails. But the minute the bombs began falling, she knew what was happening and what needed to be done. She took the boys to her next-door neighbor and told her to take care of them and she didn't know when she would be back but goodbye. She ran all the way to the hospital in the middle of the raid and never got a wink of sleep for three days while she helped with the wounded.

"The saddest thing I knew of that day was the husband of a friend, who tried to run back to his destroyer. He never made it. They tried to tell her he was dead, but she wouldn't believe them. All they found of him was his hand. On New Year's Day they took all those bodies in gunnysacks to funeral homes and you couldn't get within blocks of the places because of the stench. They had a mass burial and each wife was given a grave number and a lei. When this woman went up to the cemetery, she couldn't find the grave of her husband. She had a number and a lei and that was all. She collapsed and they sent her back to the mainland on the first ship."

The dependents were evacuated from Hawaii as soon as possible, many aboard the luxurious Luraline vessels that had been immediately transformed into troop transports on westward journeys, and dependents' transports heading back to California. From all accounts, the evacuation was a miserable event, but through no fault of the Matson line. Officers' wives pulled rank on the enlisted men's wives, and one woman insisted that she would have stayed in Honolulu with the bombing raids, even troop landings, rather than make the voyage again with the hysterical, rank-pulling women and their undisciplined children.

Before the ships arrived in San Francisco, the women were warned against confirming or denying anything that had been reported about Pearl Harbor. But newspaper reporters had no trouble getting their stories, some wildly inaccurate because the survivors had nearly a week aboard ship to let the adventure age and grow.

Months after the war began and all the Pearl Harbor wives were back on the mainland to wait with other women for the war to run its course, Hazel Brock had moved near her parents and found a job. She recalls:

"I went down to the bus stop one morning and saw a woman moving into the house on the corner. I'd heard she was at Pearl Harbor during the attack, but hadn't had a chance to meet her. While the movers were hauling her furniture in, I went over and introduced myself and said I heard she was at Pearl. Before I had a chance to tell her I was there, too, she started in. She told me how terrible it was and how her house was hit by a bomb and that her kids couldn't sleep nights, and on and on.

"I asked her where she lived and she told me. By this time I'd had it with Pearl Harbor liars, and told her: 'That's funny. We were just down the street two blocks from you and those places weren't touched.'

"Her face got crimson and she never spoke to me again."

In Alaska another similar evacuation was being conducted from Kodiak, where a large construction project was under way at the air base there. Americans had no experience in evacuations and the wife of the construction superintendent remembers the actions of most women as disgraceful:

"I remember two things about the Pearl Harbor attack: I had to cancel a cocktail party, and the only light we had in the house that night was the tiny little light at the bottom of our Hallicraft radio.

"The military people were afraid the Japanese were going to work their way up the Aleutian Islands and into Kodiak, so they ordered an immediate evacuation of all nonessential civilians and all military dependents. They sent a cargo ship, the U.S.S. *Grant*, to evacuate us. It was the biggest mess I've ever been in. I've never seen people act so wretched before or since. Imagine, if you can, a big ship filled with nothing but women and little kids with a mixture of navy wives and civilians. The navy wives established a pecking order immediately that was terribly unfair and stupid and mean.

"They loaded us on the *Grant* to take us to Seattle, and what was ordinarily a ten-day trip took two weeks this time. We turned around twice because of submarine scares, and one time we went through a narrow passage between two islands that no ship the size of the *Grant* had ever entered. We were on a darkened ship at night and had to wear our life jackets all the time, even in bed, in case we were torpedoed. Children were constantly warned about throwing anything overboard, even gum wrappers, which might leave a trail for the Japanese. And the Japanese knew we were there. They even announced on their propaganda radio that they had sunk the *Grant*. That gave our relatives something to worry about, I'll tell you.

"They put several civilian women and enlisted men's wives and kids down in the troop quarters, which was brutal with all the darkness and seasickness. Of course the navy wives would not help or offer them their staterooms. Some of my close friends were down there, so other civilian wives and I insisted that they use our staterooms for washing and resting or to take care of the sick kids. Some of the children were seriously ill from seasickness, and some were bitten by cockroaches and bedbugs. We had a public-health nurse from Kodiak aboard, and she was very, very busy the whole two weeks.

"One young navy wife was ill and insisted she was dying. I believed her and went to the army colonel in charge. He told me to ignore her. 'She's a spoiled brat and needs a spanking. Who isn't seasick?' I had to agree.

"The longer we were aboard the ship, the worse the women became. There were a lot of spoiled, selfish, and extremely childish women married to navy officers, who were accustomed to ordering people about. It didn't work well at all with civilian wives, but the enlisted men's wives were afraid to buck them.

"All during the trip several suffered from a mild ptomaine-like poisoning that caused cramps and fever. We never did find out what caused it, but the medical people aboard knew it was not seasickness. None of us had it long, but it kept hitting people during the whole trip. Every time it hit one of those pampered officers' wives, they were convinced they were dying and would raise all kinds of trouble. Some of them I never wanted to see again."

Although most people's lives were changed the moment they heard of the Pearl Harbor attack, there were a few in scattered pockets of isolation who did not hear of it until the next day, or even the next week. Neil Satterfield was an eighteen-year-old boy in the Missouri Ozarks. He was a senior in high school, and to reach school he had to drive the family's Model A Ford about five miles to a river crossing, picking up three other students along the way, and then they rowed a boat across the river to where the school bus picked them up. He was in love with the bus driver's daughter and they would be married before another year went by.

"We didn't hear about Pearl Harbor until the next day, and even then it didn't mean much to us. But to appreciate how isolated we were, I'll tell you a little about how we lived.

"We had a small farm in the Ozarks and it was twelve miles to the nearest town, six miles to the nearest telephone, and two miles to the nearest electric light. My parents had saved enough money to buy an old Model A when I was sixteen, and I was the only one in the family who could drive it. My parents didn't learn to drive until sometime in the 1950s. The main reason they bought it was so I could go to high school; there weren't even any high-school buses that came past our farm. So every morning I picked up two other kids, who helped buy gas, and we drove down to the Norfolk River right on the Arkansas line and parked it on the west side. Then we rowed a boat across the river—this was before the Norfolk Dam—and caught the school bus on the other side, which took us to the school. It was pretty rough on our parents in the winter because we rowed across the river no matter the hour of day or the kind of weather, and there were a few times when it got pretty hairy making the crossing.

"Well, Pearl Harbor was on a Sunday, and sometime Monday afternoon at school somebody said something about Pearl Harbor being bombed: 'Let me see, where is that? Is that where they dive for pearls?' We had no idea at all. And we didn't have any idea how important it was to us.

"It is kind of strange, though, that we didn't know about it Sunday, because my father always read the papers and listened to the battery-powered radio for the news and 'Fibber McGee and Molly' and 'Amos 'n Andy.' "

The boy would soon be drafted, then rejected as a 4-F, and at eighteen was an inspector for bombers before they were flown overseas.

History for most Americans had been a sluggish stream that suddenly, without warning, dropped into a canyon filled with cataracts. That is what happened to Almira Bondelid, a schoolteacher in South Dakota, a young, redheaded woman who was secretly married to a marine. She had married him on a trip with her grandmother to see him in San Diego, but only her grandmother knew because she would lose her job if she admitted she was married.

* * *

"They wouldn't let a woman work if her husband had a job, which was fair because it spread the paychecks around more. But my husband's Marine Corps pay wasn't enough for us to live on. So I got married, then went back home to live with my grandmother, as I had since I was a little girl. Both of my parents had died within a week of each other during the great flu epidemic right after World War I. I had no brothers or sisters, but grew up with four cousins nearby.

"I taught everything: first and second grade, music, glee club, chorus, girls' sextet—you name it. And I was happy to have the job. My husband and I had gone together only a short time, but I had a great respect for him before we fell in love. It was so nice to have someone to go with that was smarter than I was so I wouldn't have to play dumb; women weren't supposed to be bright then.

"I was visiting relatives in North Dakota the Sunday of Pearl Harbor. The whole family was there and it wasn't until night when someone turned on the radio for some show that we all listened to. Then we heard about the attack. One of my cousins' husband was on the *Oklahoma* and we heard that a bomb dropped right down the stack. He was a machinist down in the engine room and he was killed.

"The next morning my husband called from South Carolina. Come immediately, he said, and that was what I did. I called the school principal to say I'd quit, then caught a train and headed south.

"The trains weren't crowded yet, but it was a very slow trip because we stopped at every bridge in case someone had put a bomb under them. The train crews would climb down, crawl under the bridge and poke around, then we'd start up and go to the next bridge. That happened at every single bridge from South Dakota to Minneapolis and Chicago. I finally got to Parris Island, South Carolina, and my husband met me at the depot in a big car. I asked him who it belonged to, since we couldn't afford a car, and he said it was mine. I was going to drive it to San Diego, leaving the next day. It belonged to an attorney from Chicago who had been drafted into the Marine Corps and somebody had to drive it to San Diego for him, and I was the one.

"I said I didn't know a thing about driving because I had only driven a little bit on the farm. 'Oh, you'll do fine,' my husband said. 'You'll be all right.'

"We spent the night in a hotel, and the next morning I saw him off at the crack of dawn at the depot. I was crying, it was raining and cold and terribly dismal. Parris Island is a wretched place. He left on the troop train and I got back in the car and cried a while longer. We had been married six months and had spent only two weeks together and he was going off to war and I was alone with someone else's Packard to drive all the way across the country.

"It was time to leave and I was feeling very alone. I backed the car out and ran right into a huge pile of poles. A black man was standing on the loading dock, leaning against the wall, and he never changed his expression, never looked around, didn't laugh or anything.

"I started out again and drove very slowly, very carefully, until about four that afternoon. I was bushed and stopped for the night and wasn't even through Alabama yet. I spent the next night in east Texas after having a terrible scare in Mississippi. I topped a hill and right in front of me was a Negro on a bicycle. And I was so glad to get out of Louisiana, because if I piled up anywhere, I wanted it to be on dry land and not in a swamp.

"Every time I stopped for gas they'd check the oil and put in a quart. Finally a man in a gas station in west Texas told me what they had been doing to me and showed me how to watch them to be sure they pushed the dipstick all the way down.

"It took me two days to get across Texas, and by that

time I was getting more confident and drove faster across the desert. I put only one little nick on a bumper, but was very glad to turn the car over to its owner in San Diego.

"All the way across the country I dropped postcards to my grandmother in the Charles Lindbergh fashion. I always said 'we' had driven so far each day so she wouldn't know I was alone and be worried about me."

New words almost immediately entered our vocabularies: block warden, blackout, dimout, air raid, Aircraft Warning System. We studied aircraft-identification silhouettes; stored helmets, sandbags, flashlights, buckets, and hoses in our homes; and bought opaque blackout curtains. When the first blackouts were announced, it was a popular pastime for people to climb the highest hill or tallest building to watch the lights go out. Said Charles Harrington, who was a college student only a few weeks away from the Air Corps and pilot training:

"I'd call the first test blackout in our city a modified success. I was standing with a group on a hill overlooking town and it was kind of spooky to watch the city slowly darken until it disappeared. There was no festive mood in our group; just a hushed feeling, as though we were witnessing something that might change our lives. We didn't really understand it, but we felt very vulnerable.

After the city became dark, it suddenly became apparent that the city fathers and military planners had overlooked one important detail. We saw flashes of light—*plink, plink*—all over the city, like flashbulbs going off at random. They'd forgotten about the electric trolleys, and every time a trolley hit a junction, there was a flash. Back to the planning sessions."

A woman who had just started working on a newspaper— and one of the first to insist on covering real, live news rather than society events—was sent with a photographer to the top of the city's tallest building. The photographer was told to take a series of photographs showing the darkening of the city lights, and she was supposed to write a mood piece about the event.

"We got on the roof and the photographer set up his Speed Graphic and we were ready. Suddenly I saw a movement in a hotel window across the street, and what a sight to behold. There was a young woman, nude, with long black hair, doing her exercises. Down she would go to touch her toes, her long hair flying and bazooms bouncing up and down. The photographer and I stood staring, mouths open, because in those days you simply did not see naked people on every street corner. Then she must have seen us out of the corner of her eye because she went down to touch her toes, and stayed there. She began creeping away from the window, her fanny bouncing, bump, bump, away from the window. Down went the shade and the show was over."

Blackouts meant something different to a teen-age girl living inland where the drills weren't held so often and the fear of invasion was not so severe.

"When the first one was announced, my girl friend and I thought we were going to have lots of fun. We invited our boy friends over so we could sit in the dark and kiss and giggle. But we hadn't taken my mother into consideration. During the blackout we sat on the couch, as planned, but my mother sat in the middle. There we sat during the whole thing and nobody said a word because mother was watching, seeing to it that all the vestal virgins were protected."

The blackouts and other civil-defense measures sometimes brought out the worst in people. The block wardens were often men who had never been exposed to authority before, and authority for the meek can be a dangerous thing. There were many incidents of block wardens threatening to shoot out lights, even though they were authorized to carry nothing more lethal than a flashlight.

In Seattle, a heavily military town at that time, blackouts were not unusual, but one was used as an excuse for a minor riot. Charles Harrington was downtown watching the event.

"There were invariably some lights left on in stores or alleys, mostly store doorways. On that night a band of young men and women was roaming around town, having an impromptu party, feeling their oats. At first they started out innocently unscrewing bulbs outside the stores, but it gradually progressed toward chucking rocks or sticks at them. Then the guys started tipping over garbage cans, saying they were looking for something to throw at lights they couldn't reach. If they found a light on in a store, they broke the plate-glass window first, then the light.

"They moved on down the street, smashing windows at random. Then they smashed the glass and light in an outdoor clock. This went on for perhaps an hour, then kids started peeling off to go home or find something else to do. The police never showed up and there wasn't a word about it in the papers the next day. A wire service heard about it and put a story on the national wire, then the local papers had to report it. Some accounts said the leader was the young wife of a serviceman, but I doubt it. I think it was just a spontaneous thing that lasted a while, then dissipated."

And so it went the first few days of war. It was a totally new experience, a new atmosphere in the country, and this excitement and sudden surge of patriotism swept the country. The week following Pearl Harbor a woman drove from

Chicago to Texas with another soldier's wife to visit their husbands for the last time before they were shipped overseas.

"We drove down through the Midwest, and you'll remember that in those days there were no freeways or even bypasses around towns. The highway went right through the middle of every town along the way and you couldn't make any time at all.

"We left home on Monday, December 8, and in every town we went through we saw these lines of young boys waiting in front of the courthouse or recruiting offices to join up and fight. It was very moving, very reassuring to know we were unified."

A high-school girl has a similar memory of the week war began:

"I was working as a part-time bookkeeper for a dry cleaner in my little town in Illinois. I went to work that morning as usual, a few minutes before eight, and would leave about an hour later for school. When I walked downtown I saw this long line of boys at the army recruiter's office, boys I had known all my life and a lot of others obviously from the country and maybe other towns. They were lined up down the street past the dime store. There must have been thirty of them.

"I stopped to talk to one I knew and he said he had been there since about six that morning and some were already there ahead of him.

"You know how boys are at that age. Put more than two together and you have a lot of noise, wrestling, and general messing around. There was nothing like that in this group. They were serious, and if they did laugh, it was quietly. They seemed to suddenly feel very grown up.

"It was very moving for me. I couldn't help it—I started crying and ran across the street so I wouldn't have to walk past the rest of them. All day long the boys gathered there, and high school was very quiet and lonely from then on."

For most of us, the week following Pearl Harbor was solemn. We read the newspapers and listened to the radio and knew our lives had taken a sharp turn. Radio announcers, particularly H. V. Kaltenborn, were given the duty of filling a lot of air time with little information to give. With the skill of a baseball announcer during an endless pitchers' duel, Kaltenborn and the others could only repeat what we had heard before: Our Pacific fleet was virtually wiped out; the casualties would run into the thousands; we had almost as an afterthought declared war on Germany; there were unconfirmed reports that Japanese paratroopers were landing in downtown Honolulu, that Japanese submarines were off the California coast attacking ships.

The depression that had haunted the country for a decade ended overnight. On the previous Friday there were virtually no jobs anywhere. On Monday there was talk of jobs opening up, and by midweek there were pleas for defense-plant workers, no experience necessary. The Depression suddenly was a memory. The wartime boom was here.

The sudden turn of events was difficult to assess. Families that had been struggling for balanced meals suddenly found themselves able to earn a lot of money. But there was a catch: Their sons had to go overseas to fight and probably be killed. Women suddenly had the freedom of mobility they had only dreamed of before, but all the young men would be gone and they doubted their sudden freedom would be permanent.

Still, the war was a welcome relief. The country at least had a direction now, a common goal, and there were jobs for those who wanted them, tickets from the poverty of city slums and rural rock farms to the big money of defense plants where overtime and double time and promotions were assured. For many young men, the war was the ultimate football game, and many parents would be publicly shamed if their sons were unable or unwilling to fight.

We were off to fight a war, a good war, a war we could understand. There has never been another war like it, and it is no wonder those who survived it, and those who capitalized on it, unblushingly refer to it as the last of the good wars.

Of all the sad words of tongue or pen,
The saddest are these: There are no men.

Leather Nectarines
Don't be a spare, be a SPAR.
Back the attack, be a WAAC! For America is calling.
We're the Janes who make the planes.

We called her Crisco; she was for bakin' and makin'.

LETTERS TO BUREAUCRATS

Navy Relief
New York City

Gentlemen:

I got your letter asking is my baby a boy or a girl. Of course. What else could it be?

Divorce Bureau
Los Angeles

I can't imagine why my husband should ask for a divorce. He was home on leave last weekend and everything was OK—in fact, we had Martial Relations.

Excerpts from Letters to Office of Family Allowance

Both sides of my parents is poor and I can't expect nothing from them as my mother is in bed with the same doctor and won't change.

I have already wrote the President and if I don't hear from you, I will write Uncle Sam and tell him about you both.

Sir: I am forwarding my marriage certificate and two children. One is a mistake as you can see.

I am annoyed to find out that you brand my children illiterate. Oh, the shame of it all. It is a dirty lie, as I married his father a week before he was born.

In accordance with your instructions, I gave birth to twins in the enclosed envelope.

I have no children as my husband was a truck driver and worked day and night when he wasn't sleeping.

Mrs. Brown has no clothing and has been visited by the clergy.

I am glad to say that my husband who was reported missing is now dead.

Unless I get my husband relief soon I will be forced to lead an immoral life.

My husband had his project cut off two weeks ago and I haven't had my relief since.

Song Titles

"Don't Steal the Sweetheart of a Soldier"
"The Bigger the Army and Navy Is, the Better the Loving
    Will Be"
"If He Can Fight Like He Can Love"
"I'll Never Smile Again"
"I'll Be Seeing You"
"Sentimental Journey"
"I'm Doin' It for Defense"
"You Can't Say No to a Soldier"
"Right in the Fuhrer's Face!"

2

Women Alone

V-Mail

MY DEAREST DARLING HUSBAND:

This is a very important letter as I want to explain why my letters may fall off for a while. The postal regulations just out say that after January 15, 1943, no packages may be sent overseas to you all *unless* the sender can show a written request from the serviceman approved by his commanding officer, so I am going to concentrate on finishing the two pair of socks that are ⅓ finished and am sending anything else I can think of—*and* if you want anything you must write me specifically so and get Ted to approve it. The ships are overloaded with mail, they say. I can't tell you how crushed I am, but I can't do anything about it and I would recommend you send a request to me *and* one to your Dad for a pistol as we can send it if either of us can find it. And if you think of anything else you want and plan to write me for it, be sure and get Ted's approval. No doubt these orders will come out to you—I'll check here with all available sources.

Aunt Jane writes that your mother enjoyed her orchid—I didn't hear from her. I'm sorry about this brief note, but I have tons of homework.

Loads of love,

MORE THAN 12 MILLION MEN were serving in the armed forces at the peak of the war, leaving behind as many mothers and fathers, and almost as many wives or fiancées. The absence of an entire generation of men between the ages of seventeen and thirty leaves a lonely void in a nation, and a common refrain among the young women was that they got sick and tired of talking only to other women, kids, and old men. Within a year after Pearl Harbor we became a nation of lonely people frightened for the safety of our young, and bored with life without them.

Because there were few men, women had more personal freedom than in any other period in our history. It was patriotic for women to work in defense plants, and girls were able to leave home with a minimum of complaints by their parents. In some cases, parents who had expected their daughters to marry local boys and live almost within sight of them the rest of their lives now found their daughters traipsing all over the country following their husbands or boy friends from base to base, then living on whichever coast their men would return to after the war.

Single girls discovered it was possible to go to nightclubs with other girls without feeling sinful. They could go to parties without being talked about. They could date several men and not be considered "fast" or "loose women." They could earn their own living and not be dependent on men for their financial well-being. Because jobs were so available, they could also live wherever they chose. They reported only to their own consciences and were as free as they cared to be.

It was quite another matter for mothers and wives. While the mail service operated surprisingly well in both theaters of war, often weeks or months went by without letters from the men. It was a common experience for a woman to receive a letter from a soldier assuring her he was in good health, then notice the weeks-old postmark and wonder if he had been killed after the letter was mailed. Another common experience was receiving a telegram that a boy had been killed, then letters from him over a period of weeks, assuring her he was fine.

It wasn't unusual for a serviceman to be gone more than two years without a visit home. It was a rare woman who didn't worry that she was changing, that he was changing, and would they still love each other after the war, or would they be two strangers? Had they married too soon or too young? Should they have married someone else? Should they have waited until the war was over? Would her husband be nice to the child that would be walking and talking when he returned as a total stranger? Would the child accept its father, and would the father be hurt if the child didn't?

It is little wonder that so many wartime marriages ended in divorce. The wonder is that so many marriages survived the war.

While many single women left home to work in defense plants or gravitated to the major cities where "things were happening," many young wives stayed in the hometown, near their parents and friends, and their husbands' parents. They were usually watched with the same intensity the FBI watched suspected subversives. They were watched for the slightest sign of restlessness, for the first hint of a romance with a 4-F or an older man, or a friend back home on furlough. If they became pregnant, the neighbor women made a mental note on the calendar to see if the baby would arrive nine months after the husband's last visit. Pity the poor woman who had a premature delivery.

The women left behind have been the butt of jokes for decades, usually unfairly. They became Rosie the Riveters. They were rumored to be so sexually starved that they were hauling the most pathetic 4-Fs off the street and into their bedrooms. If they weren't man-hungry after a year or two, there must be something wrong with them. High-school boys, too timid to make moves against them, were certain they could "make time" with them if the right circumstances occurred. Those circumstances almost never appeared, but the boys talked about it constantly.

The image of healthy young women alone suffered from the pool-hall philosophy among men. Rumor had it that the women married seventeen or more servicemen at a time so they would receive the $10,000 insurance for each one killed; that women smoked, cussed, wore overalls and coveralls to the movies, drank bourbon from the bottle, and developed lesbian tendencies; and that the easiest women to pick up were those who had a child: "Give 'em a kid and they're pushovers."

The truth was far less spectacular than the schoolboys, old men, and gossiping neighbors believed. The vast majority of these women saved their money. They volunteered for the Red Cross and rolled bandages and packed boxes of food and gifts for prisoners of war. They donated blood. They filled the roles of both mother and father for their children. They visited their in-laws. They prayed, they worried, they waited. Mostly they waited.

Some called themselves camp followers—but would attack anyone else who called them that seriously. One woman, who admitted she was terribly spoiled, was a collector of antiques. At least she claimed the junk she bought was antiques; her husband felt differently. She recalls now:

"It *was* junk. I think women gain a sense of security from ownership that a lot of men don't understand. For me, it was imperative that I own those little bits of junk, and the pieces of furniture I bought from other women. By the time my husband was transferred to Fort Dix, we had a big truck full of my junk. Before we got everything unpacked from that move, he was sent to Fort Benning. Back into the truck the junk went.

"He went ahead of me to Fort Benning, and when I arrived he had rented us a tiny apartment. I ranted and raved that we had no place for my things. He was up to here in my 'things' and told me very bluntly that I should send the precious things home to Pennsylvania, and maybe I should go with them.

"I didn't like it, but he stood his ground and I shipped the stuff home. When he went overseas, I returned home and had a glorious garage sale. What didn't sell went to the Salvation Army. I guess I grew up a little.

"Now, of course, that stuff would be worth its weight in gold and I tease my husband—still the same one, by the way— that he made me throw away a fortune. He just grunts."

Becoming independent after having been brought up in a society that insisted women at least pretend to be clinging vines, many women found the transition to independence difficult. All their lives they'd had fathers, brothers, uncles, cousins, and boy friends to help them solve life's little problems. The war forced them to think for themselves and take responsibility for themselves. Traveling alone for the first time, Mrs. Joe Walker remembers that her first transcontinental car trip was a series of disasters.

"My sister and I were hauling three puppies with us. Please don't ask me why, because it sounds so silly today. We were driving from the Southwest to Washington, D.C., and got as far as Springfield, Missouri, when all five tires completely wore out. It was an impossible mess and we didn't know what to do. Finally, we found a Ford agency that put the car in dead storage for us. Then we went to see a veterinarian, who made us a crate for the puppies, and we caught a train home.

"But the car was still halfway across the country. A soldier we knew was going on leave to Nowata, Oklahoma, and he offered to drive the car back for us. I went down to the ration board and got permission to buy four new tires. The man at the ration board listened to my story and asked how in the world I had managed to wear out five tires between El Paso and Springfield. I told him I'd never thought of it, but just knew it had happened. He believed me and approved the new tires."

She and her sister lived on a small farm on the edge of Washington, D.C., and while her sister worked for the government, she stayed home and took care of the house and the chickens they raised. But everything that could break down did. Once, when she came out of a store, she found every drop of motor oil from the car in a puddle on the ground. Another time the edge of a hurricane went through Washington and blew down a huge old oak tree, which she decided to saw up for firewood.

"Whenever one of those disasters hit, I'd first sit down and cry, then wipe my eyes and get to work. But it was standard to first sit down and cry."

Obviously women who moved to large cities could find

more freedom there. Those who chose to remain in their small towns were subjected to the old restrictions, which people tried to cling to for security against the changing times. A schoolteacher, now retired, had this to say:

"Looking back on the war years, and the Depression years before that, it is just sinful the way we women were treated. I worked as a substitute teacher for years in this little backwater town that only today is just a little better than it was then. You know how little towns like this are: there are people in them who have never been outside the county, and it is a small county. Naturally these little men serve on the school board. You bet.

"Back then they had a neat trick of hiring girls from outside at very low salaries. It seemed we had more girls from the Dakotas than any other place. They just seemed naturally to head for one of the coasts.

"These girls were always single—it was virtually a sin to get married and teach school. When one of the girls did get married, the principal of the school told us specifically we were not to give her a shower. Which we did, of course, without telling anyone. It was like she had committed an unspeakable crime.

"We old-timers had a lot of fun telling the new girls the ground rules for teaching in the district. For instance, they couldn't go to a dance in the clubs downtown. They couldn't even leave town for the weekend without permission from the principal. I'm serious. And if you were interviewing for a job, you stood a better chance of getting it if you wore a red dress.

"Maybe I shouldn't be so hard on the principal, but he was surely of the old school. The school board liked his policies, though; that's obvious, or he wouldn't have stayed so long. He kept expenses down for them by hiring the best teachers he could from the Dakotas, kept them for two years, then encouraged them to move on so he wouldn't have to raise their pay. He'd barter around other districts and hire somebody who was cheaper. Finally we caught on to him, but found there wasn't much we could do about it.

"I think the thing that burned me up more than anything else was that attitude—nobody would come right out and say it, understand—that women, married women, weren't as efficient as men.

"The whole town was really strict about teachers then, and whatever one of us did that somebody didn't like would get right back to the school board as fast as they could pick up the phone.

"We couldn't even wear anklets. It wasn't considered decent. We had to paint our legs if we didn't have hose. Oh, those gents were hidebound. I lived there thirty years before they started treating me like a permanent resident. I always felt like I had some of my belongings still packed away downstairs in cardboard boxes."

Life became very hectic for the young women who went to the major cities—New York, Washington, Chicago, Saint Louis, San Francisco. As one woman put it, "I felt as though my metabolism had taken a sudden spurt. I began running around, going without sleep, dancing most of the night and working all day. It was as though I'd suddenly acquired the metabolism of a bird or a squirrel. I'll swear my heartbeat doubled so I could keep up with the pace."

Another girl, who grew up in Chicago and came of age just after Pearl Harbor, said:

"Chicago was just humming, no matter where I went. The bars were jammed, and unless you were an absolute dog, you could pick up anyone you wanted to. Most of the parties I went to were in someone's house, but sometimes a bunch of guys would chip in and rent a hotel suite. But that happened mostly with guys from out of town.

"Chicago was the center of the country then. You couldn't go from the East Coast to the West Coast, or hardly anywhere else, without going through Chicago. So there were servicemen of all varieties roaming the streets all the time. There was never, never a shortage of young, healthy bucks.

"We never thought of getting tired. Two, three hours of sleep was normal. I was working for a family friend, and I'd go down to the office every morning half dead, but with a smile on my face, and report in for work. There was another girl there who was having a ball too, and we took turns going into the back room and taking a nap on the floor behind a desk.

"Let me be frank: When you got down to sex in those days, it was something you spent a little time thinking about and looking forward to; it wasn't something you did when you were fourteen. I think our attitudes were different and you enjoyed sex more when you got around to it because of the anticipation.

"We weren't as casual about sex as people are now. You held your breath and prayed. It was tough when you didn't want to get pregnant, even in a respectable marriage. It was no joke to try to do everything right and still put your heart into the whole thing. There wasn't anything foolproof except abstinence, and who needed that? I'd already tried that and didn't think much of it."

San Francisco has always had the reputation of being the most desirable city from which to be sent off to war. The Golden Gate Bridge, the Top o' the Mark, and the willing girls ("Hell, they came here expecting to lose their virginity, so why not lend them a helping hand?" asked a veteran of the San Francisco scene) all gave the city an aura it still has of romance without the fussy moral restrictions of New England and the Midwest.

A young woman who had first worked for the OPA (Office

of Price Administration) quit her job and moved to San Francisco to work for the Russian War Relief on the publicity staff.

"The job was very efficient, very posh. The very top people in San Francisco were on my committees, people like the president of the San Francisco newspapers, Isaac Stern's father, and on and on.

"I was very naïve politically and we were collecting goods in kind when I went to work for them, such as English language books, prosthetic devices, and the like. But later we began collecting cash, which was when I bowed out. As long as it was supplies, we could be reasonably certain it was going to Russia. But we could not be at all certain it went there when we got down to cash.

"We had mysterious things happening, such as the new consul general who arrived, and departed very suddenly and we never heard from him again. We asked the Russians what happened to him and they wouldn't answer.

"The whole thing was very uncomfortable. They wouldn't even let us into the embassy, and we were working on their behalf. I don't think it was that way with other agencies, such as the French Relief or the Yugoslav Relief; they were much more cooperative and grateful.

"But the job led to one of the most memorable nights of my entire life. Paul Robeson was doing a series of concerts in San Francisco and he was very pro-Russia. He came to do a concert for the Russian War Relief in some Baptist Church in the Filmore district. I went out to interview him, but I was so frightened because it was a black area that I took a friend's brother along for protection.

"I have never seen such an emotional response to an individual. The hall was overflowing and they were almost hanging from the windowsills. They had to set up a microphone and speaker to pipe him into the basement. The auditorium was just bulging.

"Robeson stood on that stage with no accompaniment whatsoever, just a bare stage, and he did nothing but stand there and sing. You could just feel the vibrations in that hall. Then they started throwing paper money, and it came down like snow. It came down from the balconies and some of it landed on him. My conscience wouldn't let me stay around when the cash started flying like that.

"The Russians got very picky about which books went over there. This and the disappearing consuls and never letting us in the embassy really got to me. I had to quit."

Some women refused to live the safe, conventional lives expected of them, and one such woman was the girl who left home after her sister used her money to take baton-twirling lessons. She lived in a rooming house where she met a man we'll call Jim and shortly thereafter began living with him.

"He and his roommate were working for a produce company, and even though I was three years older, we singled each other out. I went to bed with him on September 13, 1938. Who doesn't remember when they were deflowered? We moved into an apartment and put both our names beside the doorbell. It wasn't as bad as it sounds, because nobody made me feel ashamed or any particular thing like that.

"The funny thing is the only people who ever drew lines or looked down their long, slanty noses were my own family. It kills me, just kills me. I'm the oldest, and one of my sisters, whom I've never liked—she was pretty and I was not—would not set foot in my apartment because I was 'living in sin.' But then she got bored with her husband, and their little group from their little high school began switching partners. And I thought: Gee, I'm only with one and they're sampling everybody, so what the hell is that? We're all prudish in our own way. Another funny thing about her: Her husband told me years later that he had never seen her nude, and they were married at eighteen. My sister the swinger. She dressed and undressed inside her nightgown.

"While Jim and I were living together, we had many discussions about the coming war. I think I'm basically a pacifist, until somebody irks me and I deck 'em. But Jim and two of his friends swore they wouldn't go. Jim said he would hide out and the others said they would, too. When the moment of truth came, one became a conscientious objector and went to the same camp in Oregon where the actor Lew Ayres was sent. The other marched off to war without complaint. Jim wasn't having any of that.

"I knew, of course, he was making preparations, but he wouldn't tell me anything specific. He said that if I didn't know, I couldn't be tricked into telling anything. When he left for good, I did not know he was leaving. I did not know. I kissed him normally and he was on his way. He told me his adventures years later.

"He had packed some supplies in cans and took them into the mountains, where he spent the month of January 1942. That is rugged country at any time of the year, but he knew of an old cabin and he was good at living off the land.

"The isolation finally got to him and he went down the other side of the mountains, crossed some bad rivers, and went to California, where he met a waitress. They moved in together, then he talked her into moving to Tempe, Arizona.

"Finally he decided to communicate with me and the damned fool started the letter with 'Dear Wife.' The girl found it and threatened to turn him in. So he pacified her in and out of bed for hours and hours and then rammed his thingie down her throat. When she left for work in the lettuce shed on the night shift, he ordered a cab to the airport, turned around there, and took a bus out of town. God only knows where-all he went, but he was rid of the girl. He traveled all over the West, went down into Mexico a few times, but generally lived like any guy on the run.

"I was pregnant when he left—I'd already had two abortions but wanted to keep this one. It is an obsession all women seem to have. I wanted a child. I started labor at one o'clock and my father-in-law came to help and was so scared he forgot my suitcase. I should have dropped the kid in the yard; it would have saved everyone a lot of trouble.

"When we got into the car finally, he drove slow so I wouldn't jolt the unknown out into the known. And I had to heave. I didn't want to make a mess in the car, so I stepped out to heave, then we went on to the hospital. That man was so scared that when I went in, he naturally vanished.

"I was put in a room and I had to go to the toilet. So I got out of bed and went to the toilet. The sisters came and said, 'She's gone! Where is she?' I heard them yelling up and down the hall and I told them I was in the toilet. One came in and slapped me in the face. 'You want to embarrass us by having your baby in the toilet?' I told her I just wanted to go. She said it was their job to take care of that and I said they weren't there when I had to go, and so much for hindsight.

"I moved into a houseboat when it was obvious Jim wasn't coming home for a while. In those days houseboats weren't hooked to the sewer system, which didn't make them very desirable real-estate investments. Anyway, one day somebody knocked on the door, and there stood Jim. I almost fell into Turd Bay.

"Jim turned himself in to his own uncle, a federal marshal. They looked through the papers and told him to go home because they didn't have anything on him. But before he could get out of the building, somebody found the warrant for his arrest. He was tried and sentenced to six months, then reduced to four. They even had a prison break while he was in, but he sat it out, playing cards.

"Then he was taken by the nape of the neck and inducted and spent fourteen months in the United States Army. And he loved it. He absolutely loved it. It was the best thing that ever happened to him. He had a ball.

"Don't get the idea I was staying home all the time Jim was gone. Nothing was too good for the GIs. I was alone and I was attracted to quite a few people. I do drink beer and I've been to a few places I hate to admit.

"I think I would have been healthier-minded if I had done what I wanted to instead of wanting the men's good opinion of me, which, when I look back, was as phony an attitude as you can find. They had wives at home. They didn't want to see their wives at the jumping-off places because they figured they'd never come home again and that would be the end of screwing and all the rest of it.

"I even leaped off a bus one time and ran back to a man who wanted me to go to bed with him. I was terribly excited and attracted to him, but unfortunately he disappeared in the crowd. I had to catch another bus and went home alone. So much for belated action. With fishermen, they only remember the one that got away. Those who didn't get away, you say, 'Jesus Christ, I wonder what his name was,' or 'Gee, I'd forgotten all about that one.' "

More traditional was Florence Rudell Marx, whose brothers and all their friends went into the service. There was nothing left for her at home, so she went to Chicago and lived with a married sister whose husband was a traveling salesman for an auto-parts supplier, even though precious few auto parts were available. He traveled primarily to keep his sales territory open for the day when automobiles would be manufactured again.

Her sister didn't intend to work, but one morning they saw a plea in the classified section for employees at the Bit O'

Honey and Beechnut Candy Bar Company. On the spur of the moment, both went downtown to apply, and both were hired immediately. But when her sister's husband returned, "he hit the ceiling. That's it. No more. He told me I was going downtown to get a decent job and that my sister was going to stay home where she belonged, and no arguments. Do as I say!"

Her sister stayed home and she went to work at the Continental Trust and Savings Bank of Illinois, at that time the largest single unit of banking under one roof, with 5000 employees on ten floors.

"I'd never seen so many people in my life! I felt like I was working in a city within a city. I operated an IBM machine and there were 500 machines on the fifth floor and 500 people operating them.

"Once a week we all stayed after work and went down in the basement to the Red Cross station and rolled bandages. It was a pleasant way to get acquainted with people, and after I met some nice girls, a bunch of us would go out to see Hildegarde or Harry James, people like that. Most of the people in nightclubs seemed to be women. I'd never been in a nightclub before and of course we all drank Cokes. We never spent more than three dollars, and I know the club owners hated to see us coming. We never tipped anybody, because we were too stupid.

"My sister and her husband adopted a baby from an orphanage in Wisconsin after waiting seven years for one because they wanted a half-German and half-Italian since those were their nationalities. When they got their little girl, it was with the stipulation that they live in Wisconsin, so I was left in Chicago without a place to live. I could have gone back home, but didn't want that, so I finally found a place out in Oak Park, a bedroom/sitting room with kitchen privileges for $20 a month. Imagine! And I was making $115 a month.

"They had a colored lady who kept the rooms clean, a really sweet person, and the first colored person I'd ever met.

"All of us wrote letters during the war years; there really wasn't much else to do. Every night I made it a point to write several letters to boys from home, and one afternoon I was sitting in my room when the maid came in and asked what I was doing. I told her and asked if she had children. She said she had two sons in the service. I said I supposed she wrote them often. She said she didn't know how to write!

"So once a week she came in, sat down, and told me what to say, and I wrote her letters for her. When the boys wrote her, I read the letters for her and she would always embrace me. I never saw anyone who appreciated anything so much. But you know, it was so little for me to do.

"Before my sister and her husband moved, we spent that Christmas period sending boxes to boys we knew. The post office had a certain size box they made us use to send things overseas. My sister and I got twenty-five of them and baked cookies and made candy until we swore we would never bake another Christmas cookie.

"We put the cake and cookies in, some writing paper, shaving gear, and a toothbrush and toothpaste, maybe a couple of washcloths because the army never seemed to give them out. And we always tried to get a little gift—a jackknife or something like that. We sent books to those we knew were readers. But we never spent more than $2 a box. You couldn't put a lot in those boxes, but you could put something of home. The cookies and cake and candy might be all squashed up when they got it, but it was something of home."

Constance Stirrup Lackey, who lived near Fort Ontario in New York, was dating a soldier from New York City. She worked in a shoe store on the main street and one morning she heard soldiers marching down the street and stepped outside to watch.

"There went my boy friend marching past. They never told them they were being shipped out or anything, and there went the boy I was in love with, heading overseas with a marching band leading them off to war.

"Tears were running down my cheeks and not a soul teased me. Nobody thought it was funny at all. It had already happened to too many people.

"He was sent to Italy where the fighting was very intense for a long time, and he wrote me whenever he could. Then, in one of those V-mail letters, he told me he cried many nights during the heavy fighting. In my sheltered life with my stereotyped notions of what being a man constituted, the thought of him crying turned my stomach. I was convinced I had loved a coward. I never wrote him again.

"Poor fellow. He didn't have any family to write to, and I was so stupid. Many times I have thought of how callous my act was and I would love to know if he survived the war, and if he is happy today. I hope so."

Because so many of her relatives were in the service, Florence Rudell Marx went home every weekend she could get a seat on the train, just to help give her mother some comfort. One Easter weekend she was there when the telegram arrived.

"I was doing the dishes with my mother when the doorbell rang. She went to the door and came into the pantry with the telegram. She wouldn't read it and handed it to me to read. I refused. My dad walked in and he read it. One of my brothers was missing. He was a bombardier in a B-25 and went down in a raid on the oil fields in Turkey.

"His wife and her two small children were there and she went to pieces. My mother looked at her and told her he would come home. 'I know he will. I know he will come home.' And she wouldn't shed a tear.

"Later we received a letter from the War Department saying they hadn't found a body and there was a good possibility he and the others had been interned in Turkey, which is what happened. His plane had caught fire and it went down. He was badly burned, but the English found him and treated him in a hospital before shipping him back to the States. We were told when he arrived in a hospital in Florida and they said he would be coming home before long, but they didn't know exactly when.

"I was at work and someone at the reception desk said I had a visitor and told me to come right up. I didn't know who to expect, but thought it must be somebody from high school. I went upstairs and there my brother was. I just couldn't believe it. We kissed and embraced, kissed and embraced. Then I realized everybody in the office was crying. Everybody."

Life for most married women was painful and uncertain. Those who had to leave home to find jobs usually headed for one of the coasts where they expected to meet their returning husbands. Although there was an abundance of jobs, most had lived such sheltered, narrow lives that having to be independent was as much a shock as the fact of war itself. Finding places to live was much harder than finding work, Almira Bondelid recalls:

"Just before my husband was shipped overseas, he found us a place through a want ad. It was in a bad part of San Diego—down in the tenderloin district—but we needed a place immediately so we could be together as much as possible.

"Then he left for overseas. They wouldn't let us get close

to the ships and we had to say goodbye through a fence. It was just awful. Things looked so black.

"I decided to stay in San Diego and went to work in a dime store. That was a terrible place to work, and as soon as I could I got a job at Convair, found another place to live, and brought my grandmother out to live with me. I worked in the tool department as a draftsman, and by the time I left there two years later I was designing long drill jigs for parts of the wing and hull of B-24s. I also did some similar work on PBYs.

"Women couldn't work overtime beyond six days a week. The only other day I had off in two years was Christmas Day. The pay was better than anything else in town, but naturally women weren't paid as well as men. Other than that, I really liked the work. I took a course that lasted three months in drafting for aircraft, and they took two of us women and put us in tool design.

"You should have seen the looks on men's faces when they saw Jackie and me walk in there. 'The women are taking over,' they said. We were teased a lot, and some asked us for dates or propositioned us. The whole bit. But generally I've found engineers are great to work with. They have rather logical minds and think of every situation in a problem. I've read that statistically engineers have a good marriage record.

"Sometimes a group of us women would come out of Convair and we'd see army trucks or navy trucks full of guys in their combat gear going down to the ships, those big gray ships, and the guys would whistle at us and we'd wave at them. But we knew where they were going and we practically cried for them.

"When we were first married, early in the war before we learned exactly what war was all about, I told my friends they should get married too, how wonderful it was. But after the war progressed and my husband was gone overseas, I stopped offering advice of any kind. I felt that maybe the girls could take the fear and the waiting, and maybe they couldn't. There were a lot of hasty marriages and a lot of 'Dear John' letters. In a lot of cases the 'Dear Johns' were blessings.

"There were some really sad love affairs during that period. One girl I knew, a really fine girl, was going to marry a boy against her parents' wishes. Suddenly he disappeared and a few weeks later she got a letter from him saying he was shipped out the exact day they were supposed to be married.

"She got a typing job for the navy and about a month later married a marine. I wondered about poor George, her first love, but didn't say anything. Then she got a bunch of letters back with the news that poor George had been killed. She felt awful, but her parents were relieved because they preferred a marine who was a stranger over George.

"Her marine husband was sent overseas and she was totally faithful to him. Then he was shipped back to the States. She never saw him again. He wrote her that he had fallen in love with another girl. They were divorced, and a few years later she remarried."

When the war started, few women had careers, other than the traditional ones of teaching, nursing, and working in offices as secretaries and file clerks. As noted elsewhere, government and industry discouraged both husband and wife working during the Depression so that the meager job market could be spread around to as many families as possible.

One exception was a young woman who had a flair for writing and editing. After attending one of the prestigious women's colleges in the East, Charlotte Paul moved to Chicago, where several magazines were published, married a newspaper editor who wasn't drafted, and settled down to write stories, rewrite other people's work, and try to carve a career for herself as a writer who also happened to be a mother.

* * *

"We started our married life in a little apartment on Chicago's South Side with my husband working nights to my days. We had a little one-room apartment that you'd call an economy or a studio, with a tiny kitchen behind these two little doors, and to get the Murphy bed down we had to move the furniture twice a day, although we didn't have that much really.

"One Sunday just after the war started and before gas rationing began, we decided to take a ride out in the country, out toward the Fox River Valley, which is on the way to Dubuque. We had a Sunday paper and decided that instead of just taking a ride, we would look at something. I guess my eye fell on the farm listings and I suggested that. We had *never* discussed this before and I had no idea he would be interested in a farm, because he was reared on a ranch in the West and didn't like it a bit.

"So we went to the first thing that was listed, thirty miles out of Chicago. When we went into the farmhouse owned by a Swedish couple, she had just finished baking some bread, and the tomatoes were ripening on the windowsill, and she had a crock of dill pickles she was working on, and a cat was sleeping in the sun. The whole nostalgia thing came welling up and we bought the place an hour later.

"I had some money in the bank I'd inherited from my grandmother, who had died at a very convenient time for this sort of thing, and the five-acre farm cost $6000. It had a little white house, a big barn, a chicken house, a garage, good soil. We spent our honeymoon cleaning the chicken house.

"We had to buy it through a realtor, and on the farm at that time they had a dozen pheasants penned up with wire overhead. I forget what the time gap was between buying it and moving in, but it wasn't very long. When we moved in, the pheasants were gone. It was understood that we had bought everything on the place, pheasants included. But they were gone. We charged down to the realtor, who also lived on a farm, and asked what about this.

" 'Well—uh—we didn't mean the pheasants.'

"My husband argued with him very logically, and finally the realtor said he was sorry there had been a misunderstanding but that was that. Apparently the seller had promised him the pheasants if he made the sale.

"We were kind of stymied, but my husband looked across the realtor's farm and saw goats all over the place—he raised them. My husband saw a baby goat and made a spur-of-the-moment decision.

" 'Okay, if I can't have the pheasants, I'll take that baby goat.'

"The man gave it to us, but then said, 'You've got to remember, she has to be fed on the bottle. You're taking her away from her mother and she can only drink goat's milk.'

"We swallowed this, hook, line, and sinker, and he sold us goat milk at 45¢ a quart in 1942 until finally I met a farmer's wife who set me straight. But can you imagine the money we paid him for that milk? At least a dollar a day. A dollar a day to keep the goat we had taken as sort of a spite thing because he took the pheasants.

"Well, the farmer's wife down the road asked why we were feeding that kid goat's milk when we could buy milk from her—cow's milk—at 60¢ a gallon. I said cow's milk would make the kid sick, and the farmer's wife said, 'When were *you* born?'

"So we switched over to that. I got a letter from her just today, strangely enough. We've kept in touch all these years.

"Well, a little later she came over again and asked how we were doing with the goat and why were we still buying milk for her. I said she had to have the milk because she couldn't eat greens. The woman looked out the window and said, 'What is she doing to your grapevines right now?'

"That darned goat had already stripped the whole thing—all the leaves, all the new shoots were gone.

"But the goat became my pet. She sat in my lap while I typed and she smelled like sweet hay, just like fresh hay with the sun on it, and she'd sit with her head on my arm while I'd do my writing. Her name was Saddle and she was just darling.

"And we had geese, twenty-five or thirty of them. The problem with them was that they liked to make friends. They're very friendly. Very. And in the summer—there was no such thing as air conditioning then—when all the windows were open, they'd come under the window where they heard our voices and they'd all honk and yell at us.

"And another thing about them: Instead of metal, the car licenses were made of a soybean thing which had oil in it—a kind of plastic—and the geese ate our license plates. It was terrible! We had to get new licenses. How do you explain something like that? The geese ate them. We'd go outside and there would be ten of them chewing away.

"Then we obtained a maid, a live-in maid, which was fantastic. The only reason we were able to do it, especially considering it was wartime and there were much better jobs available, was that she was having legal difficulties in Chicago with a former husband who didn't think they were divorced. She wanted to get away from him where he couldn't find her. She liked to work in the garden and she was a big help there.

"Then my mother came up from Texas. She was an artist who ended up working as a Girl Scout field executive, and when she arrived she said, 'Oh, honey, I have something for you.'

" 'What?' I asked.

" 'I thought a little horned toad would be such a cute little fellow and I offered a Girl Scout troop ten cents to find me a horned toad to bring you. It cost me five dollars and seventy cents. There are fifty-seven horned toads in the car.'

"Which we released in the garden. That was all right—

they look like little dragons and are awfully cute. But that ended my maid's help in the garden. She went out and picked up a cucumber vine and three little dragons looked at her. She let out a yelp and that was the end of that.

"Our garden was huge. One of the ways to take care of our need for food was to have a very large garden, which was a mistake because neither of us had ever gardened before. I don't think a kitchen garden was at all in the realm of experience for my husband, but he was enthusiastic about it and we had a garden that every year got larger than the year before. We always had this thing that if one will do, ten will be better. We were completely temperamentally attuned to this philosophy.

"When we bought the farm—it actually was a little thing in amongst farms that were 100 or more acres—nine leghorn hens and one rooster came with it. And out of those nine hens, to our amazement, we got seven or eight eggs a day. So we got out pencil and paper and figured: 'Let's see how . . . if we get eight eggs and if we have fifty chickens . . . and a hundred chickens . . .'

"Of course this ultimately turned into a disaster because when we had parlayed this up to about 500 chickens, we had a lovely rampant case of coccidiosis. They dropped like flies and we were back to almost a dozen chickens by the time we were through taking out the carcasses.

"So then we started raising rabbits. Of course. We had enough eggs from the remaining chickens for our own use, and when my husband got about four dozen eggs together, he would haul them into the office in shopping bags—eggs in one bag, rabbits in the other, and so much for dignity in the office. His coworkers would complain if he didn't bring enough to sell meat and eggs to everyone.

"I believe people had locker space then more than now because we didn't have the home freezers then. It was a different kind of thing, a great big warehouse and a sort of bin for your stuff. The stuff in the locker wasn't counted on your ration tickets. When we bought a hog from a neighbor and had it cut up and wrapped, we didn't need stamps because that kind of arrangement didn't show on the rationing system at all. So there was a little bit of cheating involved there.

"As for me and my friends, we would hear that such-and-such a store would have some meat on Friday morning, and I remember lining up at six o'clock outside a store that opened at eight, and having that line go almost two blocks. And all I could get was a pound of hamburger. And you waited patiently in line for a couple of hours. If you didn't get there at six o'clock, it was gone by the time your turn came. As we stood outside waiting, rumors would float around about the A&P having some meat, too, and they were almost always false rumors because people were trying to keep the lines down and spread people to other stores.

"But I remember taking the Chicago Northwestern into town and seeing every little strip of ground in garden. The railroad gave up all their right-of-way lands for people to raise food. It was a pretty sight. We could see them from the train and some would be no bigger than a coffee table. Any little strip had something growing on it. You'd see people from all over town and they'd be business executives and everything else, trying to extend the food supply. It was very patriotic to do this because then you wouldn't have to use your blue stamps, which were for vegetables.

"This reminds me of a friend who was a very high-paid doctor. He started tomato plants on his windowsill in the dining room of his Grosse Point home. The plants looked a little bit sick to him, so he figured that what they needed was a shot of vitamin B-something, and he took about $50 worth of this stuff and used his hypodermic needle to give the plants a shot every week. Well, the tomatoes were as big as your head, and they cost only ten bucks apiece. He should have given himself the shots and forgotten the tomatoes.

"We could have made some money selling rabbits to a lab, but we realized that we could make more selling them for meat. We had some really beautiful ones, and went into the rabbit business like we did gardens and chickens. But we had many moments of indecision. Do you put the doe in the buck's hutch, or the buck in the doe's hutch? If you leave them together for any length of time, that guy will kill himself. He's there to satisfy this kid and he will until he drops dead. In order to save your buck, you have to impose limits on him, sort of like some guys in college—but not too long *after* college.

"When our baby was born, I always had these writing and editing assignments to do, so when I went to the hospital I packed not a lovely bed jacket but the manuscript I was working on for *Coronet*. When I came out of surgery—it was a cesarean section—the first person I called was the editor of *Coronet* to find out what to do about the manuscript, and the second person was my mother, to tell her I had a baby. Oh, yes, I was a real pro.

"The hospitals were terribly understaffed on nurses. There seemed to be plenty of doctors, although I knew lots who were taken into the service. But the nurses disappeared, and those who stayed were probably a little older and a little cranky because they had more duties than before. A lot of them were really pretty tough people.

"When my first was born by cesarean, I was a little bit weaker and couldn't stand up and fight like I would have if it had been a normal birth. The other mothers were eating chocolates in twenty-four hours and calling up their friends. For me, twenty-four hours later I was still in morphine up to my eyebrows and was for a couple more days.

"But then the nurse came around, and after saying 'How are *we* today?' she said *we* have to fill out this form about your name and occupation and so forth. And when she came to occupation, she said, 'Housewife.'

" 'What did you say?' I asked.

" 'I asked your occupation and it is housewife.'

" 'No it isn't,' I told her. 'I'm a writer.'

" 'Well, you're a housewife because that's what you really do.'

" 'No it isn't. What I really do is write.'

" 'We can't put that down,' she said.

" 'Why can't *we?*'

" 'Where do you write?'

" 'At home.'

" 'See? You're a housewife.'

"You'd think that with her occupation she wouldn't have felt that way about women, and all over the bed were the manuscripts I was working on. I was heavily bandaged across the middle, which made a very good spot for my note pads. But wouldn't you have thought that woman would have seen something a little different about the way I was going about things?

"So you have your babies during the war and you can't buy diapers or hardly anything you need. All the cotton was going for bandages (and government surplus later on, of course). But fortunately I had an uncle who was a national sales manager for Bauer & Black, which owned Curity products. In wartime you just can't have a better uncle than that. I think I had twelve dozen diapers when most women felt they were lucky if they had a dozen or two. They would cut up any kind of material they could find and use it. You just couldn't find any of these Kotex-type things they use for diapers now.

"We had this old-fashioned washing machine and plenty of diapers, but we had no diaper service as we know it today. I was working all the time at home before the maid came and had these diapers to contend with. Luck struck again. After the uncle produced the diapers, it turned out that the owner of the little laundry and dry-cleaning establishment in town had something like seven grandchildren. Because of this, he had been doing diapers for quite a while. Nobody else would wash them. Since we were pretty good customers, he volunteered and told me to bring the diapers in and he'd throw them in with his grandchildren's. That was one of the nicest things that happened during the war."

The newspapers soon were printing lists of those killed or wounded in action; and for the first time in their lives, young people were as anxious to read the obituary columns as their parents and grandparents. Some cities and small towns put up great plaques to which nameplates of the war dead were added as the telegrams, letters from commanding officers, chaplains, and fellow warriors began arriving.

Virtually nobody in the country remained untouched. If it wasn't a son, husband, brother, father, or other relative, it was a boy who had grown up down the street whose name was added to this running obituary. Before the war was over, everybody in the nation knew someone who had died.

Here a mother, a sister, and a friend tell their reactions to those inevitable deaths:

"I didn't want my son to go in the service until his injured foot was healed, but he was anxious to get in and it was difficult to keep young men out of the service then. It was one of the few things my husband and I disagreed on. My husband signed the papers and I refused to.

"My son's foot had been crushed while working on a dock and he was on crutches for eight or nine months, and was still limping when they accepted him. He was in pain but wouldn't admit it. He was in training for such a short time that I believe to this day he wasn't properly trained before being sent into action. We hadn't heard from him in two or three days, which was unusual, and then we got a letter saying he was being shipped out and that he had not been allowed to write or call. That was the last I heard from him.

"He was shot down in Sicily. We got a few things back. Nobody knows how it is until it happens to them. I had a letter from somebody later on saying he could fly circles around anybody but he was in the wrong place at the wrong time. Carrying that feeling of resentment all these years isn't easy. I just know he was taken in when he wasn't really in shape to go and he had such inadequate training."

"I was in school and had a younger brother in the service. While we weren't particularly close, we kept in touch. He was a tail gunner on a bomber and one night I received a phone call from him and he said he was in Gander and that I wouldn't be hearing from him for a while. That was the last time I ever heard from him. It was just a little over a week later that he was killed over Hungary on some big Italian push where a lot of people were killed. Since that time there have been revelations that those planes were not fit to fly. The men had complained about them. But the men were expendable."

"Three of my friends were killed in the war. I had been writing all three of them, and eventually I got letters from their parents that they were dead.

"One in particular I remember was a kind of shy, sensitive kid when the war started, but he became very gung-ho and joined the navy. He told us several times that if he was going to die, he wanted it to be at sea. Of course that is where he died. I've always felt the boy had his death wish with him.

"I had been dating a Jewish boy before he went off to

war, a nice kid and the only son of a couple who owned a clothing store. He was killed at the Anzio beachhead in Italy. It almost killed his father. He just folded up his shop and left. It was as if his life ended, too. That store he was running was for his son, and there was no question about it—that would be his son's life as it had been his life. I think a lot of people who lost a son felt their lives had ended, too.

"I really don't know what happened to the other boy. I never dated him; he was just a friend, somebody to write to. A lot of boys we wrote to were just school friends. That kept a lot of us going, I think. Our letters gave us something else to do. You just got tired of women. I know I did. Letters and the guys coming through, that saved us from going crazy. The sad part of it is that we didn't have pictures taken with more of the guys we knew."

Most women who left home to take advantage of the jobs that were suddenly available after a decade of the Depression took the more menial defense-work jobs on assembly lines. A few, however, had already started training in fields that were traditionally women's jobs, such as nursing. While many defense-plant workers were paid well for doing very little, the medical profession was operating on shortages of drugs, equipment, doctors, and nurses: A student nurse at the time recalls:

"We were very short of fellows at the university and we had a little Jewish fellow working with us and he was a hunchback. Yeah. Things got so bad that even he looked good! My grandmother used to bake these big, old-fashioned fried cakes and she would send them to me in the big four-buckle Arctic boot boxes. This would arrive at the nurses' residence and I'd be lucky to get any of them if I wasn't there when they arrived. This poor little Jewish fellow really enjoyed them until he found out that grandma was making them out of pork fat. I can still see that look on his face when he found out.

"I remember dancing to an old record called 'Shine.' We had that in the recreation room and I'll swear that drove us crazy. We did all kinds of things, like Rockette lines, but it was strictly us girls because there wasn't anyone else.

"One of the first girls to get married had to do so secretly or she'd be thrown out of school. So the word went out that she was pregnant. The school couldn't prove she was married, but they were going to prove she was pregnant. They wanted a urine test for everyone on the whole floor in the dormitory. We all knew what they were up to, so we put ginger ale in all the bottles and sent them off. We got reprimanded, but so what? They left her alone.

"They were using us as beasts of burden. They didn't have any nurses' aides. They could go to work in a defense plant, and we didn't have any janitorial service for the same reason. What few janitors we did have had a physical disability that kept them out of the plants. But they could both make money, a lot more money, in the defense plants and at the same time feel they were contributing.

"The hospital at that time had 450 beds and I remember the first IV I ever started. This is a true story now. I was a sophomore, which meant I had been there less than a full year. I was on night duty on the surgical floor. I called downstairs and asked for someone to come up and start an IV. They had one RN in the whole hospital on that tour. She said, 'It's about time you did that damned thing yourself,' and hung up.

"At this stage I had never had any instruction on putting one in, but my mother was an anesthetist and I had listened. So I went down to the room, a four-bed room, and the ceiling light was out and there was no light on the end of the woman's bed. She held the flashlight, and that's how we got it started.

And she lived. I don't think any patient was watched better than we watched her.

"We had eighty-seven beds on that floor and there were two of us, and do you know, we each had a pair of shoe roller skates and that's how we got where we were going on night duty. I guess those roller skates are still there. Toward the end of the war we were skating in the dorm, looking for a little excitement. The dorm was kind of half-octagon-shaped and we were roller skating on the third floor for fun and went around a corner and there was the housemother. She confiscated the skates. Nobody knew we were using them on duty, because there was no one to watch us.

"The doctors that were left were all older because the younger ones had gone to the front, which left some with an awful lot of experience. Like the man who taught me obstetrics. He had fifty years' experience. Can you imagine what he gave us? It was just fantastic, and of course he expected results.

"He would come in and actually sleep with his head on the foot of the bed. Imagine today if a woman was in labor and her doctor slept with his head on the foot of her bed. If anything went wrong he was right there. I actually saw him perform things that today they would say is lethal. One of the things was what they called the Barnes bag. It was inserted into the uterus and then he would inject just so much air into it to cause irritation that would cause the woman to go into labor and deliver them without a cesarean section. So I wouldn't give up watching him and the other things he taught me for anything in this world.

"The surgeons were the same. They would be operating and they would close the peritoneum, then turn it over to the nurses to complete. There was nobody else to do it because they had to go on to the next case. We knew the patient was fine and the students could close the skin themselves. Of course the patient didn't know this was being done, but it didn't matter. They had so many cases that this was the only way they could get them all done.

Another student nurse remembers:

"I was in nursing school in Buffalo all during the war—I didn't meet my husband until it was nearly over, and we were married in the summer of 1945.

"The effect the war had on me is that we were terribly overworked. Most nurses who were able to found it more profitable to join the service, and the students were left behind to carry a tremendous load. We were forced to perform far beyond the level we should have, or that anyone should have expected of us. However, we did it. We had to.

"We had training, of course, but we had to work nights much more than we would have as normal students. We would be on night shift maybe three weeks and have to go to class during the day, then go back to bed, get up and go to class, then go back to bed. Then we'd work all night. This was a terrible kind of life. And instead of being on nights like three weeks, we might be on nights for three months. We had only one day off a week. We would work from 7:00 A.M. to 11:00 P.M. and then from 7:00 P.M. to 11:00 A.M., which are the heaviest times. Between times they'd have housewives come in during the day just to take care of things We all worked far harder than we should have.

"Then during a full year of 1944–45 we had a terrible epidemic of polio. Terrible. Hundreds of people were affected and we turned the nurses' gymnasium into a unit and had people in respirators there. The senior-class students were really the brains and the brawn of that unit. There simply weren't any graduate nurses; it was probably a supervisor and a technician in charge, but the students worked around the clock some days. It was a terrible, terrible epidemic.

"We had Kenny Packs—Sister Kenny Packs for the patients. She was an Australian nurse who developed a method of hot packs which had some paliative effect on muscles that were affected by polio. But you had to stand with one person and put the hot packs on, and this went on and on and there was no end to it. This was the only kind of treatment we knew of. We did have iron lungs for those whose respiratory system was affected. All I remember is that it was hard, hard work.

"All nursing was just drudgery because we didn't have any of the paramedic support we have today. We washed the floors, we cleaned the furniture, we took care of the patients. We did everything. There was nothing or nobody to support us. We just did it until we were done.

"When I completed my training and went on to get a degree, I was down to ninety pounds and exhausted, so the doctor said I couldn't start school again and that I'd better go home and rest. And that's when I met my husband.

"I never had any boy friends in the service—I mostly went out with doctors. Most of the girls in Buffalo smoked and drank when they went out on dates. So I tried to smoke and didn't like it and I couldn't afford it. Once or twice I went on dates to nightclubs and that turned me off entirely. I didn't know how to act, what to wear. I didn't know how to behave and that was the end of that."

As the war progressed, hospital ships delivered more and more wounded to the coasts, where hospital trains distributed the patients around the country. Unlike the Korean and Vietnam wars where the civilian population tried to put the wars out of sight, including ignoring the wounded, the World War II casualties were treated more like heroes. Families often had the ambulatory wounded over for meals every weekend of the year. The wounded were not shunted aside and forgotten.

Of course this generosity by civilians had inherent dangers:

"There was a hospital right outside Chicago where they brought the wounded, and we were encouraged to invite the boys in for dinner. One Sunday a group of us gals decided to call the hospital and have them send some of the boys over. We cooked a big dinner and got everything spruced up for them.

"It was terrible, just terrible. They sent us some psychos. They acted very peculiar and a soldier goosed one of the girls. We got rid of them as fast as we could, and then raised hell with the hospital for sending some guys who could be dangerous. We never volunteered again."

Rosie the Riveter was one of America's favorite wartime characters and it became a catchword for any woman working in a defense plant. Its implication depended upon who was using it and how the word was used. But some women just weren't capable of becoming a Rosie:

"I went from high school into the Rhode Island School of Design, which was sponsored by the government, and learned to run all sorts of things such as milling machines, lathes, drill presses, surface grinders, and so forth. Then we could either get a job through the school or go to the factories and put our name in. We'd get called by everyone. Jobs were so easy to find that we could be picky.

"My first job was as an operator of a turret lathe and I was a little scrawny teen-ager at that time. It took my whole weight just to open the chuck. No kidding, I had to brace my feet on the front of the lathe just to open the chuck. It definitely was not woman's work, so I quit after three days.

"Then I went to work at the Liberty Tool and Lathe

where they were making bullet dyes. I operated drills and reamers to bring the metal up to the shape of the bullet. But after a while they put me in the office, where I stayed all during the war. I was sort of glad to get into the office, though, because I rode the bus to work with a bunch of the Rosie the Riveter types, and, boy, were they a rough crew. Really tough customers."

Not all work was so hard in the factories. In fact, some women, like Rosair Earley, discovered that so-called man's work was pretty easy:

"I worked a short time in the shipyard as a coppersmith. In those days they gave us about ten days of training, put us to work, and for the next two or three months gave me more training about twice a week.

"It wasn't heavy work at all, and that is where I found out a little about men's work. I thought men did a lot of heavy work, but I found that they have a pretty soft deal. That was rough on a lot of men after the shipyard work because we found out that they didn't have to work so hard after all. Nowadays, of course, nobody works very hard anyway.

"But we worked six days a week and got time and a half for Saturday. They treated us pretty well. In fact, there was too much help. People were falling all over each other. So far as I was able to make out, it was the same in all shipyards. I don't think it was that way in some of the aircraft plants; they worked harder. We certainly didn't work hard, though.

"I think most people tried to do a good job, though. The help did what they were told, and if there was any bungling, it was done by the brass because they had some of those DPs (displaced persons). I remember one fellow, a little Polish fellow. Oh, he was a stuffed shirt. He thought he was so important. He stood about five feet two or three and he was one of these Napoleon types. He was a navy inspector who worked directly for the navy. He was an abominable little beast. Everyone hated him. And so one day they had a bigger ship on the dock out there. He didn't see who did it, but somebody gave him a shove from behind and he went into the drink. He couldn't swim, so they had to fish him out. Anyway, they took him away from our yard.

"I don't know if he really qualified for the job or not. He certainly didn't act like he was qualified for anything. With the navy it depends on who you are. Some of the Poles that came over were the moneyed people, but most of the inspectors were the finest type of people in uniform. But he wasn't a uniformed guy.

"I left the shipyard when there wasn't enough work to do and so many of us were falling over each other. It was definitely tapering off. Right after I left they began letting a lot of women go because thirty-five percent of the help was women.

"We had some unfortunate experiences later in the war with some DPs, particularly one from Yugoslavia and another from Hungary. They were perfectly capable of the work, but they had very, very poor attitudes. They fled their countries when Hitler started his conquests across Europe, and a lot of them ended up in this country. We hired several of them. We found homes for them and tried to make good, productive citizens out of them. But all they did was pick at everything. They were not happy with anything they were given. They wouldn't cooperate. They were very hard to work with.

"You'd have thought they would have been just the opposite, considering that it was their country we were trying to save. But they were very arrogant. Everything was beneath them over here. They claimed they had so much over there. Maybe they just liked to say that because there was no way to check their stories.

"It made us often wonder if we were doing the right thing by getting involved in their war. They were the only people with that attitude."

This feeling about refugees was common during the period, though one suspects that the majority were not so arrogant or ungrateful. However, it is an attitude that developed after a few such incidents and became the accepted view of those we were helping in Europe.

Women with jobs that involved daily contact with people were in a position to see whether the threat of invasion brought all people closer together, or only some. Rosair Earley had a wealth of experience with the wives of servicemen and with the small-town girls away from home the first time:

"I had a little lunch counter on the edge of an exclusive neighborhood and a small army post. When the war started, they increased the number of troops to install some antiaircraft batteries, but it was always a small base. A lot of servicemen's wives came around, so hard-up they would come in and beg for work, just for the meals. I used to feed a bunch of them because they were having such a hard time making ends meet. They'd rent a room near the base from those people out in that exclusive neighborhood, cold basement rooms for $30 a month. The fellows would get a little extra if they lived off the base, but it still wasn't enough to live on.

"We had such a tiny place that I didn't really need any help, but they'd come in and beg to help in exchange for a lunch and I had more help than I knew what to do with. There'd be a dozen of them working for lunch sometimes!

"They got so they knew each other, and the group kept getting bigger and bigger. I let them use the restaurant as sort of a home base. They were a nice group, just hard-up and young and away from home for the first time.

"I didn't make much profit that winter. One of them was a pilot's wife and he was pretty well heeled, but his wife ran around with the others. They were awfully good to each other. They shared. If one had more than the others, they'd help each other. It was sort of a carry-over from the Depression, I guess."

Later in the war she was able to buy a larger restaurant closer to the center of town, where new problems occurred:

"I had a hell of a time with waitresses. They were patriotic, you know, and had to entertain the soldiers. And sometimes on Monday morning you'd have them all in the jail. They'd entertain the troops on the weekend and get caught in a hotel and into the hoosegow they'd go for ten days. They'd put them in and keep them ten days for observation in case of disease, then turn them loose. No charges.

"Most of the girls were only eighteen or nineteen years old and they'd come over from the small towns in the mountain states, and most of them were farm or ranch kids, really decent kids, but they were just in over their heads. They didn't know what they were doing. They'd never been away from a farm or small town before, you know, and they ran in groups like they all do.

"You had to employ them in restaurants, though, because they worked for less than any other help. The good help was working in defense plants. You couldn't get union help because you could call the union hall until you were black in the face. They just didn't have anyone.

"Most of the girls were transients, but some stayed a while. If they stayed more than a month I was supposed to send them down to join the union, which I did, and they paid dues. But so many of them either didn't stay long or you didn't want to keep them that long. Some of them were pretty slippery with money, too.

"We had one that got messed up. I kept her on as long as I could. She got pregnant. She was one of these gullible kids and had been playing around. She didn't have her health card, so I kept after her, yapping about getting it, when it finally dawned on me she was pregnant and couldn't get one. So I kept her on a long time—five or six months—and some of the customers were pretty grouchy about it. But I got sort of a kick out of her. I asked her just who is this father anyway? He's got to do something about it. Have you been to the doctor? and that sort of thing. I went right after her. And do you know what her response was?

" 'Why, I wouldn't do anything like that,' she said, and here she was seven months pregnant.

" 'I know you wouldn't do anything like that,' I told her, 'but I do know you're going to have a baby and you'd better get to a doctor and find out what's what.' The doctors would fix things up so that the babies could be adopted out.

"I had a few pious old ladies who thought it was dreadful keeping her around. She was the only one to get pregnant. But she was a good kid. I paid her room rent—she didn't have any money—until she had her baby, and then she came back to work for me. It was adopted out and she never saw it. When I asked her who the father was, she said, 'I really don't know,' in a pitiful voice.

"I had no particular problem getting food, but of course we were on the point system and had to do a lot of arithmetic to make it come out right. You had to serve so many meals and plan accordingly because that was the way rationing was based. So every cup of coffee we counted as a meal or we wouldn't have had any meat. It was just one of those things you learned to live with.

"We had one case where two guys used to come in every Friday and we could have bought a load of rustled beef from them that they got every week, a whole truckload, and they were selling it at half-price. Some guy got shot by a rancher while he was skinning an animal out in the field and that scared some of the rustlers out. But these fellows came in every Friday for lunch and they seemed to be nice fellows. But, God, I wanted no part of that because we could get by without it. They showed me the inside of their truck and I saw at least a dozen animals in it, and once a week they'd make the rounds of all the restaurants."

When the war began, thousands of young couples were faced with immediate decisions: get married or remain single and hope their love would survive the war. Before the war began, they were faced with the difficulties of getting a job while the Depression was keeping the country operating at a snail's pace. Now their lives had suddenly speeded up and there was no time for pondering the future.

Although the divorce rate took a frightening jump shortly after the war ended, a surprising number of the hurry-up marriages are still intact four decades later. Julie Stewart was a college student when the war began:

"We were supposed to be married in the college chapel at Principia College, a very midwestern college of 1942. But at the last minute, literally, the Marine Corps told him they couldn't let him fly to Saint Louis because if he got hurt they had spent too much money on him. So my mother and I bundled up my wedding dress and went by train to Quantico, Virginia.

"The wedding service was planned and four of the fellows who weren't drunk came and the Methodist chaplain was there. A warrant officer stood with us, mostly because he had found Al wandering around like a little lost sheep who didn't know where to turn or what was going on. Al told him he needed licenses and all the other stuff, so the warrant officer tucked Al under his wing and hauled us around all day.

"There was a line to get married and we were about

fourth in line. I don't actually remember that much about the wedding, but I do remember the minister had to play the piano for his own service because there wasn't anyone else there.

"My poor mother was sick about the whole thing, of course. I was in a blur and Al was in his blues and on the twentieth of June it was like 102 degrees.

"We survived the wedding and got on a train to go into Washington, D.C., which is about forty-five minutes away. We were on the train for an hour and a half, no air conditioning. I had on a going-away dress and a white panama hat and white gloves, and the sweat was just pouring. Al was miserable in his winter blues and I thought he was going to drop in his tracks. There was no place to sit; mother and I sat in a seat, and Al sat on the arm.

"The train just sat there on a siding. We got off once to see what was holding us up, and as far as we could see there were trains, a solid line going into Washington for a weekend liberty.

"While we were off looking at the lineup, the train gave a lurch and these obliging marines picked me up under the arms, slapped me back into the train, and I ripped the whole sleeve off my going-away dress. I didn't want my mother to know, so I sat the rest of the way stiff-armed.

"In my own typical 1940s mentality I didn't know what in the world to do with mother that night. She was going somewhere else to visit friends. She had worked it all out and was very kind about it, but we were getting closer and closer to the last bus of the night and I didn't know what I was going to do with her if she missed it. I'm sure Al didn't either. It was pretty traumatic, except that it was so hot that for Al it was just one more thing in a bad day.

"We finally did get into Washington, mother caught the bus, and we did spend one night in a hotel, the Hamilton, which was a kind of fleabag, but we didn't know it.

"That's all we had, the overnight liberty for our honeymoon.

"When we came back the next day, Al had found this one room for me out at Triangle, Virginia, which is five or six miles from Quantico. Of course he delayed going back until the last minute, and went out to catch a cab. There wasn't any. So he started to jog. Then he ran a little ways, and finally wound up running the whole way in his blues. When he got there, his company was lined up waiting for him, and he really had a rough time for a while. They said he was the only person they knew who could run that far the day after his wedding, and any man who could do that would end up commandant of the Marine Corps. We've had to live that down for a number of years.

"After Al left, I went back to the college, but they wouldn't admit married women, even though I had just completed my third year there. So my mother was stuck with a married daughter who couldn't go to school and who would be underfoot for who knows how long. She went through a lot at that time.

"At one point I had a baby, my sister had twins, and we were all at home with her at the same time. She had a zoo on her hands. Three babies at once.

"I don't think she ever got it in her head to say, 'Go! Go your own way and let me have my life.' Parents do that now, you know. But I'm sure there were times when mother would have given her eyeteeth to be rid of us, even though it never entered her head that she could tell us that. By the same token, it never occurred to us that we shouldn't unload ourselves on her."

The family unit was generally much tighter in the 1940s than in following decades, and parents and grandparents thought nothing of taking in the young people during the war. On the other hand, the number of nursing homes was much lower in those years, too. Families were expected to stick together. Three generations under one roof wasn't unusual then.

"Besides family members helping each other out, everyone was willing to help servicemen.

"I went out to Washington University in Saint Louis to work in the ordnance industry. I thought I was the white hope of the industry, but I'm not really mathematically inclined, and took all those tests, and at the end of it they just put me at a desk shuffling papers. I never amounted to a hill of beans in the ordnance industry.

"Everybody was working six days a week, and I was living at home and going out to help the Red Cross on Sundays. They had what they call a 'gedunk' out at Lambert Field, a way station where the boys could stay when they came through there on military flights. We fed them.

"Now this is typical of the time: Here I am, a twenty-one-year-old girl driving Red Cross vehicles at midnight on Sunday nights, a car full of servicemen. I'd park the Red Cross car in what is now a terrible part of Saint Louis and then walk across Forest Park to my own car. I wouldn't walk through Forest Park today, and my kids can't. And I never thought a thing about it. Not a thing.

"If I saw any marine—my husband was one—it never occurred to me that they might not be absolutely pure gold through to the core. They could have anything in the house and I lugged them home all the time and fed them, and nobody gave it a whole lot of thought. It was just right. One of the saddest things for our generation is watching that point of view deteriorate, and I feel very badly about it."

Some women managed to think of life as a series of small adventures and stored them away to tell their husbands when they returned.

* * *

Betty Bowen: "My husband wasn't in the service, but he was involved with the navy in some super-secret stuff that kept him away for long periods of time. We went more than two years once without seeing each other. I was working full-time because I had to do something, and he wasn't making all that much money. Since I lived on the Coast, friends of his were always dropping by and I found out a lot about his activities from them.

"Once, a dear old friend was in town for a short time while waiting for another ship—his had been knocked out from under him—and I was showing him around, catching up on family news and so forth. One day I went with him to his hotel room while he had to make some calls, and I sat by a window looking out and thinking of nothing in particular, not even really seeing what I was looking at.

"What I was looking at was a sailor and two women in a hotel across the street in a room on the same level as us. The sailor and one girl were in the bed nude, and for some reason it didn't even register with me. It really didn't. I was just looking and not thinking about them at all, hard as that is to believe. People always have to tell me things.

"So there I was watching this scene, and pretty soon the second girl began taking off her clothes, and at that moment my friend got off the phone, looked out the window, and almost tore the shade off the window pulling it down over my innocent eyes. Only then did the whole thing register.

"That was the day we had a false alarm about V-J Day and the whole town was wild. As we drove down the street and stopped at a light, a sailor came up to the car and said, 'Lieutenant, do you mind if I kiss your girl?'

" 'Of course I mind,' he snapped, shocked, and drove off.

"How did he know whether *I* minded getting kissed?"

* * *

Mrs. John Keller recalls: "Like a ninny I started a victory garden when I certainly had better things to do. I enjoyed flower gardening and that sort of thing, but had never taken it quite so seriously. We lived on a small farm where the loam was about five feet deep, just fantastic soil that was too good to waste. I had a little spring where I grew watercress, and I was raising a crop of artichokes.

"I didn't know I was bloodthirsty until the gophers came. Damned gophers! I sat in the dining room one morning looking out the window and the artichokes were about the size to start picking them. While I was looking out, zip!—one disappeared, the whole thing just vanished. Then another—zip! zip!

"I had no idea I was so bloodthirsty. I put on a pair of shipyard boots I had acquired, went out to the garden and kicked one gopher to death."

"Since my husband was gone so much, he decided that I should learn to shoot in case I had to protect my family. I had shot once or twice in my life, never very successfully, and didn't care for it. But I was willing and wanted to learn to shoot a shotgun on the grounds that with my poor eyesight I'd be more liable to hit something. He insisted a rifle was better. Anyway, I never did learn. I decided to trust my knives and one of those wooden hammers an orthopedic surgeon uses to break bones. A friend had given us one that was imperfect, so I spent the remainder of the war with a long Filipino knife and the hammer by my bed.

"After we moved into a big old house, my husband was in Washington and I was alone with the children. We'd closed off the upstairs because I'd grown tired of carrying logs up to the fireplaces since the children weren't big enough for heavy chores. I was sound asleep—I've always slept raw, and back then I had long blond hair. I had my hammer and knife beside the bed. I was awakened by the outside door opening, and there was a man in the hallway. I didn't yell, because I didn't want to wake the children and have all that confusion. I climbed out of bed and threw on a long Japanese black and silver dressing gown I had. I couldn't find the sash, so I didn't bother with it and started out after him with the knife and hammer.

"It was pitch-dark. He didn't know the house, but I did and I knew where he was by the creaks in the floor. When I had him spotted, I pursued him, long blond hair flying, practically naked, robe flowing back, and not making a sound because I was barefoot. His eyes were accustomed to the dark and he saw me coming and stumbled around until he found a door and escaped.

"The next day I went down to the meat market and the butcher said he'd been hearing about a haunted house up on the hill with a witch who had long, long hair and carried a knife and pursued people. I found out that the guy had been drunk, stumbled into my house without knowing what he was doing, and told about this witch coming after him. The butcher complimented me because he knew exactly who the witch was, and said he doubted I'd be bothered again."

"The war didn't change us," one woman insisted. "It only gave us the opportunity to do things we couldn't do before." The constraints of society before the war made it difficult for a woman to do as she chose. The war brought opportunity and freedom that did not exist before. In that sense, the war years weren't that much different from the liberating 1960s.

"No, I never did run around on my husband. For some reason it just never occurred to me. I guess it was mainly because I had a baby to take care of, and I was brought up to believe that mothers were just that and not some siren making the rounds.

"I don't think we cheated on each other as much in those

days as people do now. I really don't. Sex wasn't that much out
in the open then. Or if they did cheat, nobody knew about it.
It just wasn't talked about. Now they brag about those things:
Young kids shacking up in the woods, and the expressions
they use are something else—'balling' and all that stuff. We
didn't have the Pill, for one thing, and then the morals were
a little better. I mean I wouldn't dare do anything like that.''

"Chicago was humming no matter where you went. The
bars were jammed, the hotels were jammed, and unless you
were an absolute dog, you could pick anyone you wanted to.
Most of the parties I went to were in someone's house, but
sometimes a bunch of guys would chip in and rent a hotel
suite, but that happened mostly with guys from out of town.

"My first real acquaintance with Italian people was a
guy I dated a number of times. He invited me out to a party
on the near North Side somewhere on Division Street, a tall,
three-story apartment house with the party on the top floor.

"We were having a ball and the food was delicious. But
every few minutes the doorbell would ring and somebody
would go to the door and yell down the stairwell: 'Go away.
They're not here anymore.' I kept thinking, Gee, this is
strange—don't people let their friends know when they
move?

"Finally my date pulled me to the side and said, 'I've
gotta tell you. They'll get mad at me if they find out, but this
place used to be a whorehouse.' ''

"I think the two months I spent in San Francisco waiting for my husband to return were the two swingingest two
months of my life. I'm not going to go into the lurid details—
if you talk about it, it takes the edge off, you know. Everybody
was either coming or going in San Francisco, so they were
spending their money and raising all kinds of hell. That was
the bunch to be with, I'll tell you. Never a dull moment.

"What's the saying? You can't go back again. Isn't it the truth? In fact, I had so much fun in San Francisco that I don't even want to go back there. Can you understand that? It will ruin my memories.

"Understand, I was married at that time, but my husband and I said that whatever we do while we're apart is our own business, and it has had no effect on our relationship during thirty-three years of marriage and a fine family. It works real well. The kids today were a little slow starting some things they try to take credit for; I read somewhere that only about one percent of the population has this kind of arrangement. I didn't realize I was such a rare duck."

"My father owned a tailor shop in a port town and I worked there after school and on Saturdays. I was a cute blond high-school girl and that didn't hurt his business either, I suppose. The Filipinos in town working in the shipyard liked blond white girls, too, and sometimes we'd have to shoo them away.

"These guys would come into the shop to buy campaign ribbons or to get a new set of blues, and they'd always try to talk to me. Some of them had trophies from the war, and one of their favorites was pictures they'd taken off dead Japanese. They were usually girlie pictures, and the girlies were usually white, too. Most were bare from the waist up, and I'd always catch them sizing me up that way, too. Normal. Routine navy stuff.

"So they'd come in to buy a ribbon—usually the Good Conduct and the Pacific Theater. Then they'd argue with me about where they were supposed to be sewn on, just to make conversation, and I'd always win because we had this big chart right behind the cash register they could see while they were arguing with me. And I remember what we charged: 35¢ a ribbon, and that included sewing it on."

* * *

"I lived in a port town where they had a big yard to repair as well as build ships, and just before the war they brought in this English battleship, *Warsprite*, for repairs. That was when everybody in town got the permanent impression of 'Those goddamned limeys.'

"We were used to servicemen, especially navy guys. But not these birds. They'd come into stores and snap their fingers—do this, do that—and the only part of their uniforms that was clean was those white things on their sleeves and shoulders; that was the only part of them that was in the least bit clean. Their teeth were filthy. They were just unclean people.

"The workmen could work only about a half-hour down belowdecks on the ship because there was so much stench from urine and stuff. They took the mess tables topside and scrubbed them—the workers refused to eat on them. No sooner did they lay the clean tables down on the weather deck to dry than these limeys would walk right across them. What the heck did they care?

"They weren't very well received by the townspeople at all. I'd never have anything to do with them. They were there about three months and left a few illegitimate children behind. But that's true of any port. What I still can't understand is how any local girl could stand to let those guys get near enough to make a baby with those green, scummy teeth and dirty bodies. Ugh!"

During the war it became fashionable to hate the Red Cross, and it became the source of horror stories, the butt of jokes, and a convenient agency to blame for a variety of injustices. Soldiers came home insisting that when the Red Cross set up canteens overseas and in depots across America, they charged for coffee and doughnuts. Right next to the Red Cross stations, the stories went, stood a Salvation Army canteen where those same things were free.

There was an element of truth in the latter charge. In 1942, the British high command complained to American military leaders that their men were forced to pay for snacks and coffee in canteens, and that it was only fair that American soldiers be required to pay in their canteens. The Red Cross, which relied, and still relies, on contributions instead of government funds, was "requested" by Secretary of War Henry L. Stimson to charge American soldiers. The Red Cross objected strenuously, but lost the argument.

Since the Red Cross was involved in so many mercy functions as well—informing families that their men were injured or killed, etc.—it was only natural that such a powerful organization drew criticism, if not resentment. It was also natural that those seeking power over others would enjoy working for such an organization.

The following quotes are from two women who were in contact with the Red Cross. The first is Charlotte Paul:

"A friend and I volunteered to roll bandages for the Red Cross and went down two or three times a week to the office, where they brought out gauze and we were to pull thread. A woman who sews would know what this is all about. You pull a thread when you want to cut material straight; the thread you pull out gives you your line for cutting. So we pulled a thread, measured the gauze, pulled another thread, and measured again, and so on. And we cut it by hand.

"My friend's husband was a doctor and she watched this operation awhile with ten or twelve women doing this slow, painstaking work, then went to the director and said, 'Look, down at the hospital they've got a cutting machine. Give it all to me and I'll get the whole thing done in twenty minutes.'

" 'Oh no,' the director said, 'we can't do that. We have to pull threads.'

"In spite of that, we stayed with it, until we were told that at this particular point we would have to buy Red Cross uniforms and head gear if we were going to continue our volunteer work. They said it would cost only thirty or forty dollars and we could go down to this particular department store and buy them.

" 'Wait a minute,' I told the woman. 'What's this for?'

" 'Oh, it is very necessary,' she said. 'We don't want any hair dropped into the bandages.'

" 'Okay,' I said, 'I'll come with a dish towel and I will wrap it around my head and that will take care of that.'

" 'Oh no,' she said, 'we can't have that. You have to have the official uniform.'

"Simultaneously my friend and I put down our scissors, turned to her and one of us said, 'Lady, when you need bandages, you let us know,' and we walked out the door.

"That's, frankly, a lot of my opinion of the Red Cross. It had apparently developed such a social aspect, such a rotogravure attitude toward itself, that its purpose was forgotten sometimes."

"I'd been a secretary before my marriage but hadn't worked for three or four years until the war broke out. My husband was overseas and I was going nuts living with my mother. The kids were old enough for me to leave during the day, so I went down and volunteered for the Red Cross.

"Well! They said they appreciated all my secretarial experience but I would have to take six weeks' training in office procedure. Just for a volunteer job. Imagine! So I said the heck with you, you don't need help very bad. I'll go somewhere else where they do need help. I went over to the USO Travelers Aid and went in as a volunteer. It wasn't two weeks until I was on the payroll.

"The part I worked in was helping the people the government had recruited from all over the country—hillbillies mostly—to come and work in defense plants. The USO would

advance them the first month's rent and some food money
and help them get settled.

Not everyone felt so strongly about the Red Cross, and,
indeed, it performed functions that were humane, such as
work on behalf of the Allied prisoners of war.

"Saint Louis had a prisoner of war packaging center,
which was really kind of interesting. It was in an old shoe
factory, way, way down in south Saint Louis in an ungodly
neck of the woods. My father and mother and I went down to
help a few times one summer.

"When we went in, we had to strip down to our under-
wear and put on a Red Cross smock and stand in an assembly
line and pack little brown packages that looked about like a
three-pound candy box. They had absolutely specified con-
tents: such things as a chocolate bar that was so condensed it
was terrible—we broke one open once to try it, and it was so
strong it was horrible. Then there were C-rations, instant
coffee, and a few other items like that. I suppose thirty people
were there at a time and we worked three-hour shifts because
it was so hot in there we were baked at the end of a shift.

"The Red Cross was very cautious about everything, and
the volunteers could wear only wedding bands, no other
jewelry, because if something—contraband—showed up in any
of those boxes, the Japanese or Germans could refuse the
whole shipment.

"I never heard of any Japanese prisoners getting the boxes
we packed, but we had boys who had been German prisoners
come down in the evenings to cheer us on. They had been
pretty badly shot up, which is why they were chosen to come
down, I suppose. They told us they had gotten their packages, and it helped us bear up under the Saint Louis summer
heat."

* * *

For some the Red Cross provided unforgettable experiences and a unique education.

"Our receptionist was a little gal from Des Moines who had never been out of her hometown before. She was a very prim and proper little thing, a pretty little girl, newly married, just a babe in the woods. She just didn't know how to handle these people. They frightened her. Of course some would frighten anyone.

"One morning a big fellow came in and he was just soused. He could barely speak English because, like so many of them, he was a hillbilly from down south. He was drunk—oh, he was drunk! He had on a pair of bib overalls that were filthy and didn't fit well. He was asking her if he could go to the bathroom and he was so drunk that even had he spoken normally I don't think she could have understood him. He was just absolutely incoherent.

"She came running back to me and said she was frightened, and told me to come out quick. Just as we walked out front, he lost control and he zigzagged out the door leaving a puddle of urine behind him. His overalls were soaked.

"I couldn't help it, I started laughing, but we wanted him to get out the door because he might pass out inside the office. He made it out and slumped down beside the building. We were all in stitches. Here's that tiny little girl with the great big eyes and she pointed at the puddles and the zigzag trail and said, 'Look what he did!' It broke up the office for a week."

Another form of officialdom universally hated was the censors who read all personal letters between servicemen and wives and blotted out words, phrases, sentences, paragraphs that they deemed dangerous to the Allies' security. This rankled both husbands and wives; the privacy of mail was something all Americans took for granted.

Thus it was easy for everyone to rationalize the harmlessness of creating their own codes. It was inconceivable that the Axis nations would take the time to break a code developed between husband and wife, and it was equally inconceivable that they *could* break such codes, because, unlike professional codes, these matrimonial codes couldn't possibly mean anything except to the people who used them.

When a husband mentioned that he had just talked to Sam and he said he wasn't feeling well, who could ever guess that it meant the ship had just been in a major battle? If a husband sent his wife flowers by telegram, who could suspect it meant the battalion had just arrived in San Francisco? In Leon Uris's first novel, *Battle Cry*, one soldier wrote his wife that he couldn't tell her where he was, but suddenly he felt lots of "new zeal and energy." In a code, a nearby town, such as Springfield, could mean Manila. The possibilities were endless, and wives and husbands used them all.

Back home, life went on in the new concept of normalcy. The women complained, "but all we had was boredom and loneliness. We weren't getting shot at. My husband's ship was hit by a torpedo and they were loaded with tons of ammunition. The torpedo was a dud—thank God for the code we had—but when I deciphered it and figured out what had happened, I was more frightened than he was. At least he told me that."

"I don't remember much of our code," one woman said, "but there was one key word I'll never forget: 'Jeb Stuart' was our word to let me know my husband was going into battle, and I saved one letter that had this in it:

" 'Things are keeping me very busy and Jeb says he's gonna stop writing his wife for a while so if I don't write and Jeb doesn't write either, you'll understand. I'm sure Jeb's wife will understand his stopping all together for a while. When I see Jeb I'll remember him to you.' "

For many, the war was like having a loved one suffering

from a lingering illness. Your own life must go on, and for the young that means social activities. Those who cared soon learned to put aside the fears, and the feelings of guilt for having a good time, and get on with their own lives. The threat of death, and the fear of death for loved ones, can act as a stimulant:

"There wasn't much entertainment. For heaven's sake, the lights went out at ten o'clock! But when the first fellows started coming home and coming over to the dorm, they must have thought we were nuts because we were all just hanging out the window looking, staring at them. Unless you've gone through it you don't realize. We had no young men around because we were too far inland for the navy bases on the Great Lakes and all we had were reserve people—young kids and old men. I looked up the picture of my graduating class a little while ago and there were seventy-six of us who graduated from high school that year, and there were only three boys. They had extensions to stay home and help with the crops. One of those was later killed in the service."

And there were always slight deviations from what others considered the norm:

"Some of the girls at school got a little squirrelly about the man shortage. You bet. It especially bothered girls who had sexual experiences before. It was the first time I was aware that some girls could act like boys. I'm sure there must have been some in the little community where I grew up, but I was very protected and didn't know it. I don't think I was aware of lesbianism at the time it was happening as I was when thinking back on it. We had girls who were very chummy, would sleep together even though we had individual rooms.
"As you look back on it, you bet."

* * *

Mrs. S. D. Wattles recalls: "I don't know all the details—except of course that it didn't work as planned—but when the army talked about putting an air base near the Reno-Sparks area, the local police had to agree to shut down the prostitution. And that was silly of course.

"You see, I'd grown up in the area and my mother didn't think a thing about my walking down Second Street past the bullpen with all the girls around there. I don't think it ever entered her mind that my seeing them would make me want to become one. So I'd walk past there on the way home from school and the girls would be going on their four-to-eight shift and it was all very blasé to me. I had my life and they had theirs, see. There was just nothing to it.

"It was the same with gambling. There were people who worked for a living and there were people who gambled. So none of this bothered me. In fact, I didn't even know about white slavery and all that until I started reading books. Darned books!

"When they closed down prostitution, you know what happened. They just spread it all over the area. They had guest homes where the divorcées could come and live for their six weeks, and a lot of prostitution was in these guest homes throughout the area. What they accomplished by closing it down was to lose control of it.

"I was in college by that time and living on Greek Row on Sierra Street. The first house was Gamma Phi, then the Tri Delt—I was a Tri Delt—and the Kappa Alpha Pheta, and the Pi Phis. Those were the four houses on Greek Row so far as sororities go.

"Now I have to admit I'm second party to this story, but apparently here's what happened. Some Air Corps guys came to town looking for whores and saw some girls going into the houses on Greek Row and they surmised that this was what they were looking for. So two or three of them came to our house and asked one of the girls if they could see the madam.

These were freshmen girls, and one of them said, 'Oh, you must mean the housemother.' And the guys said yes, figuring maybe out here they call it something different.

"At this point, remember, the air base could call down and say we need a hundred girls for a dance because we're having a big social out here, and they'd send busloads of girls out to dance. Everything was all very patriotic then.

"Anyway, after a bit the housemother came out and she was the sweetest grandmotherly type you'd ever meet, gray hair and very proper. She asked what they would like, and the boys said they would like some girls. And she asked how many they had in mind. And the conversation went on and on— How many can we have? . . . Did you have a certain kind in mind? . . . It was wild. I don't remember the exact terminology but the boys were thinking which rooms do we go to and how much.

"The story goes that at the point money was mentioned, the housemother said there'd be no charge—you know, anything for the boys. About this time some seniors came in, and after they'd listened for a while they knew what was going on. Rather than embarrass the housemother and the boys, one of them said, 'Fellas, you've got the wrong house. The one you want is two doors up.'

"So they sent them to the Pi Phi house, whom we didn't like. And our story is that we never saw the boys come out.

"I know the incident happened, but it is one of those stories that gets better the more times it is told."

While the home-front years were noted for national solidarity, that doesn't mean that each citizen felt love for his or her fellow man.

"People were so rude! The people who worked in railroad stations, the ticket agents, anyone you'd ask for information was just terrible! They all knew that they wouldn't be fired no matter what they did. Their favorite saying was 'Don't you know there's a war on?' Everybody got sick of hearing that.

"I think that's where the terrible service on trains and other public places began. It wasn't only them. It was waitresses, store clerks, the government offices, the little tin gods who ran the ration boards.

"One time my husband took a leave and we went up into Canada. The Canadians treated us extremely nice everywhere we went. They were so friendly and helpful, and went out of their way to make us comfortable. The hotel people couldn't do enough for us, it seemed.

"But then we had to come home, and I've never been treated worse than the Customs people treated us. Never. I can't remember exactly what they said to us—I've tried to blot it out of my memory—but I remember they were very insulting and were very suspicious and kept us waiting like criminals over in the corner.

"And remember, my husband had been overseas and almost died, and he had never committed a crime in his life. But I guess that's the home front for you."

Everyone traveled—to jobs, home on weekends and holidays, to see servicemen, to accompany bodies home. Nearly everyone traveled on the modern equivalent of "standby" because the government established a priority system. Those low in the pecking order took their chances. But everyone traveled.

"I spent a lot of time traveling back and forth across the West in those horrible trains. Everybody was miserable, of course, so we just tried to make the best of it. Everything was blacked out at night then, and on one trip a guy in uniform was sitting next to me and started getting fresh. I pushed his hand off. He put it back. All right. I lit a cigarette and jammed it into his hand. He jerked his hand back, wiped off the sparks, and kept it up. This was too much, so finally, at the top of my voice, I hollered at him: 'If you dare touch me again I'll hit you on the head' or something. I just screamed it. Everybody woke up and he walked away. I could never understand how I could put out a cigarette on his hand without *him* doing the screaming. Guess he was serious.

"But my last trip back to the Coast was the strangest, I guess. We had saved our money and bought a 1940 Studebaker for $400 and we drove it home. With us was this poor, crazy bird. Some guy had got drunk one night and bought this poor old canary bird. The other drunks were trying to feed it all kinds of crap, and my husband felt sorry for it and took it away from them. He didn't want it and I didn't especially either, but until it died we took our bird with us everyplace we went.

"In spite of everything we went through, I still married the wrong guy, and was married to him twenty-six years. I guess it was the time. I was a pretty girl—a goddamned prick tease, if you want to know the truth—but all the other girls were getting married, so I did, too. I couldn't wait for a guy I knew who was over in Pearl Harbor. Not me. I had to marry the wrong guy."

"I lived in one room above a drugstore and had never been away from home in my life, and there I was in a primarily colored district. That wasn't much of a problem to me because my background in segregation was so strong that it never really entered my head that the whites' and blacks' paths would ever cross. It really didn't.

"But I was scared away from home. He would be home every Saturday night, and most of Sunday I spent crying because I was sure I was pregnant. Everybody did. Then we went to Washington, then Parris Island. We were sent first class on the train, but when we got aboard there was no such thing as first class. It was all coach, but so crowded that they put us in a baggage car. And we sat on a coffin because there was no other place to sit. I was scared stiff, and that's no pun."

"We had planned our wedding for June 7, 1942, which was Pearl Harbor Avenger Day, when all the fellows were going to avenge Pearl Harbor. It was a big deal in our navy town. We got the licenses and then they shipped him out, to boot camp in San Diego. I was mad and I was crying, and on June 7, our wedding day supposedly, I was was listening to Kate Smith sing 'God Bless America' on loudspeakers. For years I couldn't stand her or that song because she and everybody else were having so much fun and I was so miserable.
"I drove down to San Diego with his parents, and when we got there we couldn't find him. White hats everywhere. When we found him, four days later we got married and four more days and he was shipped to Chicago.
"The wedding was kind of interesting. He had an uncle down there and we used his house for the wedding. We brought in a Methodist minister, and a little girl next door played the 'Wedding March' on the piano. We opened all the doors and windows so we could hear the music."

"Probably the most difficult thing for my family—other than the waiting and the fear—was going from Tennessee to San Diego for our daughter's wedding. It had been originally planned for home, but at the last minute his ship had been put on alert and he couldn't leave. So we decided to take a chance and go out there for the wedding, not knowing if he would be there or somewhere in the Pacific when we arrived.
"My poor husband had it the roughest. He was looking after four women—me, both our daughters, and his mother— and fourteen pieces of luggage. He really had his hands full.
"We were able to spend only one night in San Diego for the quick wedding, then return home, so it was a very tiring trip. The saddest part of the trip, though, was when we were

sidetracked time after time for troop and hospital trains. Troop trains were going to the Coast, and hospital trains were bringing the wounded back. That really broke my heart. There were so many of them. We counted eighteen troop trains in one night, and I don't know how many hospital trains we saw on the whole trip.

"It was a solemn experience—car after car of men in uniform."

"Traveling on the trains was an experience, and each trip was different. The worst trip I made was the time I couldn't find any guys to flirt with. The best was when I met this dreamy air force lieutenant with his fancy uniform and wings. So I've always figured that I could tell who was on the train when a woman, in later years, talked about how miserable or how great train trips were then.

"I had a job with the USO that required quite a bit of travel, and since my job wasn't priority, they usually sent me on a train. Which is just as well; flying wasn't all that great in those years: freeze half to death, get your teeth rattled, and then scare you half out of your wits when you hit a storm. Lots of fun.

"One time and one time only I went across Texas on a train. When we crossed the border from Oklahoma, they stopped the train. Conductors and brakemen went through, car by car, shooing all the Negroes into one car. When we left Texas, somewhere around El Paso, the Negroes started slowly wandering around the train again.

"I didn't care much for Negroes, myself, but I cared a lot less for Texans after that."

Julie Stewart remembers: "I can honestly say that while I was traveling I was never fearful. I was consistently treated nicely. I can't do that now. Here I am up in a ski resort and it is full of transients. Bums. During the war when people were alone and those of us at home had many, many potential romances if we were halfway decent-looking and everybody treated each other as if there was no tomorrow—somehow you could brush those off with great ease. It is because they were just not as crummy in attitude as people are now. I never pick up a hitchhiker anymore. I never passed anyone during the war and I hitchhiked myself, all over the place with babies. There was no marine base near any town, and if you got out on the road, that was the way you got from place to place. Nobody had a car. Where would we get one?

"But now I am so scared and I am so sorry.

"The kids say people could never have been that simon-pure, nor could they have been that black and white. It didn't seem to me I had much problem making a direct choice between right and wrong then like we do now. Now I am expected as an adult to be super-flexible because all the things I see now, all the things we've gone through—the SDS, the Vietnam War, drugs, abortion—and we're expected to keep the lines of communication open. I try to be flexible because I want to keep the lines open, but there are times when I want to give them a swift kick. I wouldn't be at all surprised if my mother felt the same way about me, but when she laid down the rules, nobody fudged.

"I find it very difficult to say this is a flat right and this is a flat wrong. But during the war it was so easy."

"I worked as a waitress in the hotels and clubs and places like that. Most of our customers were officers at first, but when the boys started coming back we saw more and more enlisted men because now they had plenty of money to spend. They'd order a quart of milk along with their meal, then another quart, and sometimes two or three heads of lettuce. They were *so* hungry for that sort of thing.

"Our house was a kind of depot for all the relatives going through to and from the war. I went over to the courthouse many times with couples to get married, and when the boys came home we got in on all the homecomings. I'm from a big family, so we had a lot of that kind of excitement.

"Once a cousin was at the house, back from the war, and his mother and sister took off shopping and left him alone with me. He was a kind of quiet kid and he had been through all those battles in North Africa and Italy. He was just a kid. He sat there and got to talking with me and I lost track of time just listening to that kid. He wouldn't talk about it to anyone else afterward. I was the lucky one. I got the whole story."

"The whole period was a kind of sad existence for women. All the guys we grew up with were gone, and our brothers were gone, and we got so tired of having nobody to talk to but other women.

"Other women had it much rougher, of course: I lived in Chicago; and if you lived there, everyone going across country had to come through. All railroads seemed to go through Chicago.

"When one of the guys from my hometown would come through, I'd ask him if I could bring my friends, and we'd go to a nightclub. There's this one little guy sitting in the middle of a bunch of girls. We'd always go dutch-treat and never would expect him to treat us; in fact, it usually was the other way around. It was just the idea of having a man around for a change, a man to talk to. My friends would keep asking when the next one was coming through.

"A lot of the girls I grew up with went into the service, too, and I'd thought seriously of this, but my parents wouldn't allow it. My father felt that his sons in the service were enough. But I got to see them as they came through Chicago, and I always envied them."

*   *   *

Almira Bondelid summed up the whole waiting process:

"While he was gone there was just that kind of hurt, an ache inside that must be there when someone in the family dies. I always had the hope he would be back, and I could be laughing and talking to friends, and the ache would be right there. All the women I knew experienced pretty much the same thing. It must have been like that for parents, too. I know it was rough on my father-in-law. All during the war while my husband was overseas, my father-in-law took piano lessons just to keep his mind occupied. The day my husband came home for good, he stopped the piano lessons."

Sign over a Los Angeles toilet:
Notice to Okies: This ain't no spring so don't drink the
water.

Okies' reply:
The miners came in '49,
The whores in '51.
And when they fucked each other,
They begot the Native Son.

Be polite to our waitresses. They are harder to get than
customers.

WANTED—Registered druggist; young or old, deaf or
dumb. Must have license and walk without crutches.
Apply Cloverleaf Drug Store.

3

Men at Home

THE MEN LEFT AT HOME were either too old, too young, too ill, too important to the war effort, had too many children, or were simply lucky. In the case of those declared 4-F by military doctors, it helped if their disability was obvious, because patriotism has tunnel vision: If you looked young and healthy, you should have been fighting. It has never occurred to civilized man to send the physical and mental deficients off to be killed—that would be unfair; only the healthy should be sacrificed. Philosophers find an incongruity in this attitude that governments do not.

It was the only time in the nation's history when there was absolutely no excuse, other than illness, for being unemployed. There were jobs available for everyone, more jobs than could be filled, and in a male-dominated society men had the first choice of jobs. Some men were able to work at manual-labor jobs and save enough money to enter the peacetime economy with their own businesses. But, like the women at home, there was a price to pay in worry and fear for relatives and friends off fighting the war that had brought this sudden prosperity.

Most of the men who stayed home remember several unpleasant incidents arising from their civilian status, but with the passage of time and the revolution in our attitude toward war, most now consider themselves lucky. As one 4-F said, a lot of country boys like him were used only as cannon fodder anyway.

Defense plants were scattered all over the country—in big cities, in tiny backwater towns, almost anyplace served by a railroad or highway. But not all people learned good work habits during the period; the factories were so desperate for employees that they had to be tolerant when workers wandered in and out almost at will.

"My father owned a steel-fabricating firm in Chicago, and shortly after the war started he won a contract to build what we called 'kitchen cabinets' for tanks. It was a small assembly that went into the turret where the driver sat, and held a variety of equipment—maps, binoculars, and a whole bunch of instruments. Several hundred pieces were welded together and bolted and it had to slip into a very small place. It was a difficult thing to turn out within the tolerances required. We also built what they called 'track shoes,' the links that go in the tank track itself to link them together when one broke.

"You kind of grabbed people to work as they walked by. It was always a problem, and when you got someone, you'd go to a lot of trouble keeping them. One particular guy we had I'll never forget. He was black—we had a number working for us—and had a shiny gold tooth and was a typical Bojangles type, except that he was short and on the plumpish side. Everybody loved him. But every time he got paid, he'd be gone up to four or five days, then come back with his tail tucked between his legs. He'd say, 'Well, boss, I did it again.' He had bill collectors all over the place because he was driving a Cadillac and wearing a diamond ring. You couldn't help but like him in spite of the fact you wanted to tell him, 'Look, you silly goose, get yourself together.' I think he and a lot of other

people made money for the first time in their lives and didn't
know how to handle it."

Bruce Vance recalls: "During the summer of 1942 I
worked in the shipyards and my function was working on a
thing called hot slabs. That was where the ribs for ships were
bent. We would push big channel irons down into the furnace
and it would take about forty-five minutes to an hour to heat
them enough, then work like hell to bend them before they
cooled. It took about ten of us to make a crew, and half of us
would be working like hell with a jackhammer bending those
things and the others would watch until someone's clothes
caught on fire from the radiant heat. Well, I'm only exagger-
ating a little. But we'd take turns and sometimes the clothes
would start smoking or burning, and we'd trade off while the
other guys cooled off.

"I suggested once that we could almost double production by heating another rib while we were shaping one, rather
than waiting around and wasting furnace time. But one of
the union guys told me in no uncertain terms to shut up. And
I did.

"Everybody down there had a sense of humor. Yeah. One
of their favorite stunts was based on our desire to get out of
there at quitting time as fast as possible. We would have
everything lined up so we could make a run for it—lunch
buckets and vacuum bottles. So some bird would sneak in
with a welding torch and spot-weld our lunch buckets to the
bench. Very funny. You'd go running through there, grab
your bucket and bottle, and if you didn't tear your arm out of
the socket, you walked off with only the top of your lunch
bucket and bottle. Very, very funny."

Agricultural deferments were one of the most common
methods of keeping young men at home, but one which many

farmers and ranchers refused to consider. However, the production of food was essential and these deferments were one of the most difficult to abuse. It was, for example, difficult for those receiving the deferments to cheat on them and move to town for more money. In some farming communities, German and Italian prisoners of war were used to work the land, and in a few areas Japanese-Americans who had been relocated away from the West Coast were used.

A young man near San Antonio, Texas, who was given an agricultural deferment, recalls that he didn't have an easy life during the war years. B. J. Claussen tells the following story:

"I told the draft board that if they'd leave me on the ranch I'd work seven days a week because somebody had to take care of the stock. And I did. I broke horses—I broke 116 in my lifetime—fixed windmills, rounded up sheep, built fence, drenched sheep. Stuff like that. I worked on our ranch six days a week and on Sundays helped out the neighbors because labor was so short.

"My own brother—he's dead now—was overseas for forty months. It was a long time and he was shell-shocked. But he made it pretty good. I left the ranch in '47 because he run me off. I left the ranch after thirty-seven years and I was flat broke and my brother denied he ever told me to stay on the place. But that's okay.

"I done my part. I was never examined for the service, see. I wasn't even married either. A lot of them would say, 'How old are you?' and I'd tell them, 'Uncle Sam knows how old I am.' That was enough for them.

"I worked seven days a week and didn't go very often to town. Breaking horses and working seven days a week, brother, you need your sleep. But when I went to town, that's when I'd help the soldiers. We had a lot of soldiers here in San Antone because Fort Sam Houston and Kelly Field was right here. Randall Field, too. I helped more soldiers back to camp and to the bus station than the good Lord allows. Because I wasn't in the service, they always said a soldier would knock me over the head and I was a darn fool for helping them. But I told them, 'Well, I've got to take up for the soldiers, poor boys.' And sometimes I would just get them on the bus within a minute or two before the last one pulled out. And sometimes they'd have a date with girls who would say, 'Well, you're just ten minutes from the bus station,' and they'd be more like ten miles. These were local girls from San Antone, see, but they didn't give a hoot for the poor soldiers, and I took up for them.

"The girls always got mad when the MPs took the boys away from them, see, and they always told them, 'You damned MPs. You're not good enough to be a soldier so they made an MP out of you.' Boy, the MPs sure didn't like that, but they had to take it. 'You weren't good enough to make a soldier so now you want to tell the soldiers what to do.' Whoeee!

"Like I say, you couldn't do more than help the poor boys.

"I never had any help on the ranch. I was the Lone Ranger 'cause I'd round up our cattle by myself. I had a cousin across the road about two miles away, and they didn't call him on account his father was in bad health, too. We helped each other when we could, and I helped all over.

"We wasn't running many cattle then because my dad lost quite a bit of land during the Depression. About 150 cows was all we had then. Prices? Lord, Lord, they was awful cheap. We were horse-poor during the Depression. Yes, sir. We sold forty horses and colts for $10 apiece, and thirty-nine bred brood mares for $7.50 apiece. That was money, wasn't it? My dad sold all his steer calves for $12.50 apiece. Boy, that was money, wasn't it?

"My old man wouldn't take tickets [ration stamps] to the grocery store for something to eat. He'd rather of died. He just didn't believe in it. We could kill our own beef on the ranch, see. We killed sheep and goats to eat. But like I say, dad wouldn't have taken any tickets from Uncle Sam to get something to eat at the grocery store for any money. It was America, and if I gotta go to the grocery store to get something to eat, they can have them dagbummed tickets. So I had to buy all our eats. He wouldn't buy a nickel's worth. No, sir.

"And we had a neighbor that I heard a little later was the same way. He just lived about a mile from the store, but he wouldn't have bought food with some ration tickets for no money. Well, his wife went to the store. He wouldn't go, and dad wouldn't go either. Oh, no. And then when all of us were raising several hundred head of hogs during the war, dad he raised hell because he couldn't buy no bacon. He wouldn't kill a hog and butcher it himself for no money, and he raised several hundred head a year.

"I couldn't figure that out, but, brother, he was a pig-headed German. And that's the honest truth. One of my cousins came to him and said, 'John, dadgum it, if you haven't got no bacon, why don't you feed a hog and I'll butcher it and I'll furnish the beef and we'll split everything half and half?' He wouldn't do that neither. Some folks, like Art Linkletter says, 'People are funny.'

"Yes, sir. I broke horses. I broke my ankle two times when old Number 99 jumped a split second too quick and I looked up and he was coming straight on top of me. I tried to whirl around and he took my boot back down and laid the tip of my boot on my leg.

"My dad, like I say, he was so contrary that he said, 'You're not hurt, and I rode that bronc out in the pasture and rounded up sheep on him and come back and I told my dad I couldn't ride him anymore. And he says, 'Ride the gentle one,' and I told him, 'You gotta saddle him because, man, my ankle hurts.' Brother, I rode the gentle one in the pasture, but I didn't meet my dad where I was supposed to meet him, see.

I hollered that I couldn't stay in the saddle no more. It was bright sunshine, but the sun was going black on me.

"He heard me holler and he said, 'Why in the devil don't you come up where you're supposed to meet me?' And I tell him I can't ride, except I'll ride where you can get me with the car. He said, 'What should I do with the sheep? I found some.' I told him I didn't give a whoop about the sheep no more, I wanted to get to a doctor. Brother, I was in pain.

"That happened at nine o'clock, and at three o'clock that afternoon I finally came to a doctor. I was on crutches six weeks, but the doctor said to stay off it for six more weeks. They put it in a cast. I came home to the ranch that night after they took X rays and they put my ankle in a cast on the kitchen table. Oh, I had quite a bit of fun.

"It was just dad, mother, and I on the ranch. I took care of them. My mother was in bed for two months and I even cooked for her. I cooked and took care of her and broke horses and everything else. Like I say, you don't get much chance to tomcat about.

"I helped dad and helped the neighbors. Windmill work was the most important part, putting new washers on them and such. We pulled pipes and pulled the rods. I had to go as high as twenty miles away from home to help fix windmills. There was hardly no help here, see? I just had to help them, that's all.

"We had a round pen on our ranch, see, and they always brought horses over and I broke them. I got five whole dollars for it. How long does it take to break them? Brother, that's the sixty-four-dollar question. One horse it took me two Sunday afternoons and he balked under the saddle. And my own horse that became one of the best baby horses in the country took me over a year and a half to break him. Yes, sir. A year and a half to the day. He shattered my jaw and I had to eat soup for six weeks. And, boy, I got mad at him and cut a green limb off the size of a baseball bat and knocked him over the head as hard as I could hit. And he dropped on all fours.

"I had a helper on the ranch and he shook my hand and said, 'You finally done what you should have done a year and a half ago. Killed the damned fool.' I said, 'Well, it looks like we gotta drag him away,' and we didn't know what to do. He still had the saddle on him and he just laid there dead, what I mean, dead. He didn't move. He didn't breathe. He was just out.

"My friend was looking away, and all at once I saw the horse raise his tail about an inch. I told my friend, 'Gee whiz, I don't believe the damn fool is dead yet.' He says, 'What do you mean? He's been laying there about five minutes.' But it wasn't long before he raised his tail again, and all at once he got up and, brother, he was a different horse. He was just as gentle as a dog. Boy, I was sure happy 'bout that, I tell you.

"That broke him right there. He became one of the best baby horses in the country. Like I say, a sixteen-month-old baby rode him all by himself. I took eighteen preschool children riding, and if it wouldn't have been for that horse, I couldn't have done it. That was after I left the ranch and became a dude wrangler.

"We raised horses and I broke quite a few. There was Morgan, and the last stallion we had was a paint Arabian. One horse went backwards with me in the round pen, and we had twelve boards and I could get off a horse regardless how he went—backwards, forwards, or pitching. This one went backwards and I got out of the saddle or it would have been a post he would have hit going backwards. It would have been all she wrote because I broke out a one-by-twelve with my shoulders and the saddle broke out the second lowest one and my head was against the top ones and the horse was leaning against me, then fell over inside the pen. If it had been a post, I would have been killed right there. It's no easy chair all the time on a ranch. No, sir.

"But I always took up for the soldiers where I could. The soldiers I dealt with were all strangers, see, because whenever I met soldiers was at night, see. I never did see a fight. Once I was in the Majestic Building. In the rest room all these soldiers were sitting on the commode. . . . They puked all over the place and they were what you call *out*. O-U-T. I bet the MPs had them a time of it. I pitied the poor bellhops who had to clean up that mess. It was the most discouraging sight I ever seen in my life. Not one of them, but three of them on commodes. Whew! Stink!

"Well, sir, the ranch is gone now. At one time it was over 7000 acres, but during the war it was down to around 3000. Most of it is in San Antone city limits now. Dad sold it for $35 an acre, and now they're selling lots of it for I don't know how many hundred dollars each.

"I was a wrangler for over twelve years and then a stagecoach driver, and one finally got me. That's why I'm crippled now. He got away with a stagecoach just by a split second and I had fallen between the wheels. Boy, that was as close to death as I've ever been, but the good Lord didn't want me yet. But as the Mexican says, tomorrow is another day."

Governmental waste, bureaucratic cupidity and stupidity, small-time bribery, and basic dishonesty were discovered one by one when a businessman joined the war effort.

"When the war broke out I was up near the top age of draft-eligible people—getting close to forty—and I had never been an outdoor person or an athlete or anything like that. I was scared to death—I thought I was wide open for the draft. About that time I was walking down the street and a bunch of young soldiers were walking ahead of me and talking about the goddamn hardships and everything. . . . Gosh, I couldn't picture myself in that. But I was really eligible, single and in a nonessential industry—publishing. I was one worried guy.

"Then I remembered that an old friend had just been appointed a big shot on the War Labor Board in the Chicago region. He had been an outstanding guy all through high school and college, an excellent speaker, and the Chamber of Commerce had used him as a speaker for a lot of projects. So I sat down and wrote him, explaining my situation, and asked if he had a job for me on the War Labor Board. He wrote right back and said he'd be delighted and offered me a job. I took it, and wrote him asking for something to show my draft board to get them off my back. He sent a wire telling me to report on a certain date for an important job with the WLB. You can imagine my relief at getting that wire, but a couple of days later I got another wire from him saying to forget about that date; it was just to show the draft board. Relax. Take my time. Tell them whatever I wanted to. I damned near died at that one. It made me a slacker for sure, which I knew was true but didn't care to admit so brazenly.

"He and his partner had been in business in Chicago and they wrote and asked me to make my headquarters with them. They had rented an old forty-four-room mansion on the South Side and they used about two-thirds of it for their business and the other wing was their private quarters, and would I like to live with them there? They had a cook, a chauffeur, an Oriental room (whatever that was), a dining room, a bar, and I would have a private room furnished with lovely antique furniture, a private bath, and so forth.

"I couldn't see how I could afford such grandeur on my salary, but I assumed he knew what the hell he was talking about, so it sounded just fine. A couple of days later I got another letter that was almost a duplicate inventory of the first, but a few additional rooms had sprouted and a few more luxuries—a combination chauffeur and houseman and so forth. What the hell? I took the job and went back.

"I disliked leaving the Coast, because I had already accomplished about what I wanted—a nice beach home, a nice home in the city, a new Buick, and so forth. I hated like hell to give it up, but there was no way to get out of it at that time—so, Chicago, here I come.

"I had never been there before. I took a cab out to this address and I thought the cabdriver looked at me rather peculiarly. I thought, well, God, it must be because this is such an aristocratic address that he doesn't expect a yokel to be welcome there. We started out, and as we went the district got worse and worse and worse, and when we got to the bottom we stopped and I was home. It was in an old, old aristocratic part of south Chicago of lovely homes that had degenerated into just nothing. It was as dangerous as all hell. My God, people were getting shot all around there.

"But it was a beautiful old place. It was built by a very, very wealthy man and it was U-shaped. He had two daughters who had both married, so he built this and sort of cut it in half so each daughter would have half of this mansion. It cost something like a quarter of a million dollars, and in the old days that really built a house. It was an absolute mansion, but long past its prime. The living room was gorgeous, but there was a stain on the ceiling about the size of a nine-by-twelve rug. The shower wouldn't drain in my bathroom—it was just horrid.

"After a few months I finally decided I just couldn't stand it there anymore. We did have a couple of people working there he'd mentioned—the driver, and a housekeeper who was—oh, God, she was a horrible person. The kitchen and our little dining room were in the basement. I'd go down there for breakfast and my eyes would be just about level with the snow outside, which was always a dirty gray. One day I put a piece of bread in the toaster and it started to squeak and the housekeeper said, 'Turn that thing upside down, will you? There's probably a mouse in it.'

"Another time I was at the table—there was a little lavatory off the breakfast room. A colored guy came in, a very rough-looking guy, and took a loud leak. Didn't close the door. Then he turned around and left. I never saw him again. I finally decided I couldn't stomach that anymore, and moved into the Chicago Athletic Club.

"There were about thirteen employees with the War Labor Board when I joined it. Money was not particularly important to me since I had some income from my business back on the Coast, so I accepted the first job that was offered me, thinking that civil service was, well, just a set thing, that there was no bargaining in it, that everybody got the same deal. I've forgotten what my salary was—about $2500, I think.

"We started with thirteen employees, and within three months that had grown to over 300. And as it grew, we needed more supervisors. I was put in charge of public relations, which was fine. I had a secretary and an assistant. Everything was going fine and I was not dissatisfied until I discovered that my assistant was making $500 more a year than I was. He was familiar with civil service and how the regulations work. It didn't disturb me particularly at the time because I knew then that I was going to be made assistant chairman, which was the best job in the whole outfit with a nice increase in salary.

So I took the new job, and was fairly happy until I discovered that my new assistant was getting $1500 more a year than I was. I was dumb enough to really think that the war was a serious thing and that people were willing to sacrifice something. I caught on not at all. The people in the War Labor Board were making far more money than they had ever made in their lives, and they were going to protect their jobs no matter what. One way to protect them was to do nothing, to make no waves. Don't say yes, don't say no on anything; just stall.

"If they could, the staff would go through the file and pick out the little cases, ones that didn't mean anything. At one time we got so choked up with applications that something had to be done. They had a big meeting of the top people in the agency and they decided the cure was to return every application that was in the file, saying that it was returned due to incomplete information. That helped the war a hell of a lot.

"We were supposed to pass on wage increases for factories and so forth, to judge if the increases were just and within guidelines. These were the little factories and so forth, not the big ones. Those were handled by the Treasury Department.

"I was really a green pea, so damned naïve that it's really hard to believe now. But those wage increases were extremely important to anyone really trying to follow the rules. I had quite a bit of authority and I was amazed at how popular I got. People would bring in all kinds of things. They'd come in to talk to me and then leave without the package they'd brought in. I'd go chasing down the halls after them and tell them they'd left it, and they'd say, 'I didn't leave any package!' Sometimes it would be a couple quarts of valuable scotch. My God, I was just showered with things like that.

"There was a big-shot attorney who was a real nice Joe and we used to go to lunch together. One day we were coming back from lunch and it was colder than all hell. The heaviest coat I owned was the one I had brought from the Coast. I hated Chicago so much that I was not going to buy another overcoat, because I didn't want to be that comfortable. We passed the finest clothing store in the city and he said, 'Come on in here.' I asked him what the hell for, and he said he was going to buy me an overcoat. I said, 'You sure as hell aren't going to buy me an overcoat,' backing up like an offended old maid.

"But, God, I just had that stuff all over the place. At Christmastime so much of the stuff arrived that I contacted somebody in the Police Department and asked what the hell I should do with it—boxes of apples, subscriptions to magazines, cases of liquor, and so forth—and I was really frightened. They said don't do anything; don't take any money but the rest of it is just part of the system in Chicago. So I accepted the stuff and gave it away at Christmas parties and so forth. But, oh, God, I've never had so much stuff thrown at me in my life.

"Pretty soon they had us all make up an outline of our responsibilities with the WLB to get the salaries in line. I wrote up mine honestly and without knowing anything about civil service. The smart guys wrote theirs up and they puffed themselves up as big as possible so that a guy who was several notches down from me ended up elevated three higher notches and recommended I be dropped a couple or three notches. And here I was the assistant chairman. That was so ridiculous that they had to send someone in who knew a little about what was going on, and it came back with me getting upped several notches.

"The applications were very interesting sometimes. Of course in some cases the increase they asked for was very, very necessary to keep people working. In other cases, the managers would do anything to avoid raising the salaries. I remember one time getting an application asking for increases, declaring they were absolutely essential to the war effort. Then the letter had apparently been taken out of the typewriter while this guy made some duplicates to put on the bulletin board showing his employees what a fine generous guy he was. Then he'd added a p.s. that said something like, 'I hope you will find it impossible to comply with this request.' If there was ever one you wanted to turn down, it was that one.

"The last day I was there, as a matter of fact, there was only one application approved all day, and that was from the Chicago Printed Twine Company. They made little twine that they used to tie candy boxes which said 'Martha Washington' on top. With the whole world in chaos, that one had a good letter from a congressman or governor asking that it be approved. Those were always the ones that got what they asked for. It was really disheartening.

"The WLB was just a beautiful thing for so many of these guys. They were canvassing the colleges and we had a great many college professors who just didn't have the slightest idea of what the hell was going on or how to figure the salaries and wages. It really became a mess, with cases backed up months and months.

"One night I was leaving the office and outside at the reception desk were two men sitting, just sitting there. They were nice-looking guys in their thirties or early forties. They were there the next day, the next night when I went home, and the following day again. I think it was four nights before I finally stopped and asked what their problem was. They said they couldn't get anyone to talk to them and they were just going to sit there until somebody did see them. I told them to come in and see me the next morning. They were there. They were representatives of the Brown & Bigelow Company in Saint Paul. They were trying to get some wage increases approved and nobody would see them.

"The wage increases they proposed were clearly acceptable, no doubt about it whatsoever, but it was just the reluctance of anybody to stick his neck out. They preferred to just deny everything. So I approved their applications. They went back to Saint Paul, and within a few days Saint Paul began to descend on me. It turned out these two guys had gone to a Chamber of Commerce luncheon and announced that if anyone had any trouble at the WLB, see me. They really fixed me up.

"Then Brown & Bigelow decided they'd like me to come and work for them. By that time I was pretty damned disgusted with the WLB because it seemed to me we were more of a hindrance than anything else. If an application came in and there was a letter with it from a congressman or a governor, someone like that, the application was clearly approvable right off the bat, and they would come in and go out of the office like a shot.

"Shortly before I left, the chairman came to my desk one day and had a whole stack of applications from the big shots, like Sears Roebuck, and a few others. He dropped the stack of applications and said, 'Here, approve these and get them out.' I picked them up and went back into his office and threw them on his desk and told him that if he had agreed to approve them, go ahead and approve them himself.

"And incidentally, he and his partner had a publishing business in Chicago called something like Research Associates. They put out aptitude tests for schools and businesses. When these big shots would come in to get acquainted with him—and he was a very, very impressive guy, loads of personality and so forth—he would get to talking to them and then mention the tests that he and his partner published. The people would be very, very interested—"Why, that's the very sort of thing we need in our factory"—and some very nice orders would flow in. And their requests for salary increases would move through our office with the greatest of ease, always with someone else's name on them, of course.

"It didn't make things any better between us when I decided to move out of that barn we had been living in. I finally got into the Chicago Athletic Club, and the last day I was there, my old friend called me into his bedroom. It was a beautiful big room, private bath and everything, furniture that years ago had been gorgeous, a fancy four-poster bed with only three posts remaining. He looked around and said, 'Jesus, aren't we a couple of lucky guys?'

"And there I was. I felt so damned disloyal because it meant a lot to me staying out of the draft, but to stay there . . . no thanks. He was never really friendly to me after that.

"I never went without a thing during the war. Nothing. I never started a meal at the Athletic Club without the waiter bringing two pats of butter. As fast as I would eat them, more would arrive. I could have steak anytime I wanted it. Anybody with the dough could get anything they wanted. Every time I went home to visit my family, I'd load up on candy and butter and scotch and all the luxuries the poor could not get. It was a very, very nice war for the people with money.

"The poor weren't the only ones who got hurt, either. I was coming down the elevator in the club and the operator was a black guy, a real nice guy who had been badly shot up in the war. He had to get around with a cane. Two guys were on the elevator, and one told the other that as soon as the war was over he was going to get rid of every one of those goddamned niggers; he was going to kick them out of his place; they'd been forced on him by labor shortages and so forth. And right there in front of Johnny, the operator, a veteran, as if he didn't exist. God, I felt embarrassed, and reached over and tapped him on the shoulder, gave it a little squeeze. I didn't know what else to do.

"Well, the War Labor Board and everything else in Chicago finally got to me and I told my old friend I was leaving. He raised hell, raised the ante, and offered me a suite of offices, assistants, and a big jump in pay. I couldn't go for it. Brown & Bigelow had put the pressure on me to work for them, and I finally agreed to go up and meet the president, Mr. Ward. When I went into his office, he asked the guy I was with if I was going to join them. He said he didn't know. Mr. Ward shouted, 'What the hell is the matter with you? Up your offer a thousand dollars!' My God, that wasn't the reason I was holding back. I was frightened about accepting the job because the money was so damned big that I thought they must think I had something I just didn't have. But I went with them, and moved up from Chicago.

"When I first got there, I would meet people and they'd ask what I did and so forth, and I had a cousin who was socially prominent and entertained a lot. I'd tell them I was with Brown & Bigelow and they'd all kind of look at me peculiarly. It wasn't for a long time that I found out the company had a hobby of rehabilitating ex-cons. God, practically everybody around me was an ex-con. It sounds like a comedy; the whole thing was unbelievable. They put me beside the company's secretary and told me to watch what he did because on January 1 they were going to fire him for me to take over.

"I was getting so much money I just couldn't believe it. I think it was $7000. That was a pot of money.

"I went to dinner one night with some of the other executives at the country club and all I heard that night was how grand Mr. Ward was. He was some kind of god to them, and I got a little sick of it. When we left we walked out to the cars and it was a beautiful night with a big, beautiful moon, and they were still talking about Mr. Ward when someone mentioned the moon. I said, 'Don't tell me that Mr. Ward put that up there.' They just didn't get it, or, if they did, they pretended otherwise. It was funny only to me.

"On my first trip for the company, to Chicago to talk to the Treasury Department, I was gone a few days, and when I came back Mr. Ward met me in the corridor and asked me if I brought home the bacon. I told him I had, and we went into the treasurer's office and Mr. Ward told him to raise my salary a thousand dollars a year. I started to argue with him that all I'd done was earn my present salary, but the raise stuck.

"He had a neat little trick he pulled several times. They'd send someone to Chicago to put in an application for, say, twelve carloads of paper to put out these girlie calendars as essential to the war effort. They knew damned well they'd be turned down, so they'd take the guy to lunch, get acquainted with him, and then say something like, 'Say, you know, you're the kind of guy we'd like to have working for us.' Then they'd ask him if he'd be interested in a job that paid eleven or twelve thousand a year. Well, you're damned right he'd be interested. So he would always accept the job and would always approve the application for the ten or twelve carloads of paper.

"At one time I think we had about a dozen of these guys there, and one of my responsibilities was to give them something to do, which was pretty tough. I remember one of them I put in charge of train tickets for people going to Chicago and so forth. Just pure sham.

"There got to be a lot of that kind of nonsense, and a lot of backstabbing, so I took a job with the Fred Harvey Company, the restaurant chain, who had been after me for a long time. It was an old-time outfit and the original Fred Harvey sounded just like a saint. When I went in to see Mr. Harvey the first time, he told me his office was open eight hours a day and that anyone who wanted to see him could just walk in, whether they were a busboy, a janitor, a waitress, or a vice-president. He was honest about it, but not very smart about it. Nobody got in to see him. Absolutely nobody. If anyone came in with a gripe, they'd be headed off by an underling. So he sat in his little ivory tower just thinking everything was great, completely out of touch with the firm."

Not all get-rich-quick schemes worked as planned. Ken Cloutier recalls:

"My father was in the blind-pig business during the Depression—he ran a speakeasy—and one night the police came around to our door. He told my mother to run down and bury all the whiskey in the coal bin, then he got me and started pinching the hell out of me and I was screaming, of course. He went to the door with me screaming and ranting and raving, and told the police not to bother his baby. So I came by my training in the booze business the right way. Real on-the-street training.

"Detroit was a pretty tough town then because it was so near Windsor, Canada, and during Prohibition days they ran that whiskey across the Detroit River like crazy. So when I came home from the army with a punctured eardrum just before the end of May in 1945, I bought this little bar with several other gentlemen.

"There was a severe shortage of beer back then in the Midwest, so everybody in the bar business opened certain hours and closed all day Sunday, because in those days you couldn't sell liquor on Sunday, only beer.

"A contact contacted me and said I could buy this black-market Mexican beer. And it was green as hell. We had to absolutely freeze it, not chill it, and when we'd spring the cap it would go absolutely wild. We used the kitchen to open the beer, where none of our customers would see how wild it was.

"Of course we knew all the kids in town, and the first place they headed was to our bar. We were it. We were young GIs home trying to make a buck.

"I started opening the bar on Sunday afternoons and did real well for about a month. I got 75¢ a bottle on Sunday afternoons, which in those days was a lot because good local beer was a quarter, import 30¢, but 75¢ for this famous Mexican import. It was nothing but nice raw beer, and selling as fast as we could open it.

"Then one Sunday afternoon a young kid walked in with her aunt, and I was working the door. We had the twenty-one-year-old law and I said the girl didn't look old enough. But her aunt pulled out some papers that said she was twenty-one, so I said go right in. Pretty soon the aunt left—we handled about 300 people every Sunday—and the girl got picked up by a man and she was found later downtown in a city park, thrown out of a car and drunk. She turned herself in to the police saying she had been assaulted, and told them where she'd been drinking. I got a citation and a thirty-day suspension of my license, even though I had checked the ages.

"So I've got all the money in the world invested in this wild beer in my basement, and I'm a young man with all the answers, all the angles, and I'm really going to turn the world over. So summer is coming on and we're closed down and painting the place, and this wild beer starts getting hot. One afternoon while we're painting, the beer starts to go like popcorn. *Pow! Pow!* There's glass flying all over the basement and we're afraid to go down there.

"Then the cases get wet and they start falling over. So instead of buying my new Cadillac, I have to sell my old Ford to get the doors open, to get back in business and pay off my investment.

"As I sat there listening to it explode, my eyes would just well up. One time a big pile fell down and I thought the whole damned building was falling down. I called the high school, where I had one favorite teacher—you know, the one old guy all the kids looked up to—and told him I had a problem. He agreed, and said he had only one recommendation: 'You've got to stay away from that room until it gets cold and it rains.' Then I started hoping for cold weather and a rain. In August.

"I guess I was able to salvage about seventy percent of it, but while we were closed the beer shortage ended and people could get their traditional local beer again and they didn't want a thing to do with this Mexican beer, so I was selling it at a dime a bottle.

"In about 120 days we had to sell out. The beer put me in such a hole there was no way out. There was just no way we could get our breath. When we opened, there was an hour's wait outside our door. Now there was no one waiting. Friendship can get only so deep. It has its limits.

"It was heartbreakingly funny as I got older, but not when we stood there with paintbrushes in our hands staring silently at each other while the beer exploded beneath our feet."

*   *   *

It was very easy to rationalize bending some rules, because waste has been an integral part of American history. Take gasoline, for example:

"I was a certified ski instructor and was with the National Ski Patrol, so the army hired me to certify skiers and mountaineers for the mountain troops that were trained in Leadville, Colorado. They gave me a 'C' card for an unlimited amount of gasoline to go skiing on the weekends, but I had to use my 'A' card for three gallons a week during the rest of the time. In other words I was getting unlimited gasoline to go play, but limited gasoline to work, which was just the opposite of everyone else. But because I was doing government work, I just didn't dare monkey around with the gasoline, although I knew lots of people who were. I just couldn't do it.

"But you'd better believe I had a long waiting list of people to ride up to the mountains with me every weekend. One of the guys who went with me owned a small butcher shop and had a contract to supply a hotel, and he seemed to be able to get unlimited quantities of meat. So every month I turned my meat stamps over to him and was able to get meat anytime I wanted it. You had to work the angles—good old American ingenuity I guess—and it didn't hurt anything.

"My brother was a navy pilot and he told about how the squadron mechanic devised a way to cool Australian beer with the evaporation of gasoline. He would go through maybe fifty gallons to cool down ten bottles of beer and nobody thought anything of it. I didn't feel quite so bad about my deals after I heard that.

"But my main job was to observe the guys and recommend who would be best for the mountain corps. I remember one was a middleweight boxer, a good athlete. He'd had no skiing or mountaineering background, but I certified him so he wouldn't go into the mule troops as a packer.

"After putting all the guys through the skiing and mountaineering program, and with several ending up as mule packers, I took a lot of needling in later years for the soft job I got in the service. I went into the Marine Corps, partly because I didn't dare show up in the mountains with the guys I'd trained. But I got the softest job imaginable. I saw no action at all and wound up in an administrative unit. We could go into any unit that had lost its records and interview them and set up new records.

"One more hassle I had on rationing before I joined the marines: A friend had a combination wood-and-coal cookstove and I went out once to get some Presto logs for it. The gal selling them made me fill out a form for their use, and then said I couldn't buy any because they were only for heating stoves, not cookstoves. So I had to explain they were used for heating *and* cooking, and I had to fill out another form saying they were for heating only. Isn't that something?"

The postwar construction boom with its Levittowns was yet to come, but the Forest Service was deeply involved in the war effort because many planes still used wooden spars and ribs. Keeping the wood coming to sawmills and plywood factories was a major problem since logging didn't pay nearly as well as other war-effort work.

Nevan McCullough relates the following: "We had a lot of temporary, transient labor in the woods. We generally had older guys from the local area, but there were a lot of transients rolling through. We got a slug of winos and had the usual problems with them. You were pretty near the bottom of the barrel for help, and at the same time we had this accelerated cut for the war effort. We really scratched for help.

"One thing against us was the age limit of eighteen. You couldn't hire them any younger, and all the others were in the service. We did end up with a few guys released from the military for various reasons, psychological and otherwise.

"I had one draft dodger. He was a psycho and I had a real problem with him. He was on a lookout with his wife, and one night a lightning storm came up and was hitting near him. Then it cleared up and the stars were shining again, and he called down and said the Japs were coming in on him. He hung up the phone and took off like a March Hare, heading out into the brush.

"I called another guy down the line and told him get out and put a halter on this guy and tie him to a tree. But this psycho kept going and nobody could stop him. We didn't hear anything else about him, so we had to pack up his wife and their stuff and ship her back down to California. She was at the lookout two or three days alone, but she was a little bit on the dingbat side herself. It turned out the guy was AWOL, and they finally caught up with him somewhere in California.

"When we first started on this big cutting program, all our scaling of logs was done in sixteen-foot lengths and we had what we called a 'caliper scaling.' After they felled them in the woods, one of the guys had to gallop over logs with these big calipers and measure them at sixteen-foot intervals. Eventually we worked out some deals where the logs were designated and went to the mill, then were scaled there as they hit the saw. This solved some of the problems, but in one case I hired a guy to scale and took him out on the job, and when I got back to town, who should I meet but this bird walking down the street. He'd beat me back to town. That was typical.

"One season we got a bunch of migrant Mexicans who had gone over into the Willamette Valley to pick peas. The harvest kind of fell apart at the seams, so they shipped them over to our side of the hill to work on brush piling and fire-fighting, or other kinds of simple jobs. They were native mountain guys, not city guys, and they had an ex-marine as a cook. We also had an interpreter. We tried to set the tables up American family-style, but these guys would grab onto a dish of jam and try to eat it all without passing it around. They liked chicken with a lot of chile and salt. They got to wrangling among themselves and we had a knifing in one of the tents one night. When payday came, some of them turned up missing and were picked up as far away as Medford.

"They went around barefooted, actually on firefighting duty. The skin on their soles was damn near as tough as leather. Some of them bought shoes, and when they came back, they had them all cut up and made into sandals. They worked there about two months, then were taken back to another harvest.

"We were cutting a lot of timber in southern Oregon for the war effort, most of it going into box shook for ammunition cases. We were sawing anything that was easy to get to, a lot of high-grade pine went into those boxes. We were more concerned about keeping the mills running at capacity at that time than anything else. Right after World War I the Indian Service down there made a lot of big sales that run for twenty-year periods or more, and they put in mills in the Klamath Basin to cut more than a billion board feet a year. They had just about cut out when war broke out, and the War Production Board set a quota system to keep the mill going at capacity.

"I was district ranger for everything on the east side of the divide, and we cut pretty heavy, about five times the allowable cut a year. We were running around like chickens with their heads off trying to keep the timber rolling in and trying to do a reasonable job of timber management at the same time.

"The loggers down there were what we called pine men; they'd been cutting yellow pine for years, but it was pretty well gone by the time the war was ending. The only thing left was some stands of pine and Shasta fir, some sugar pine and lodgepole pine. When the War Production Board would make these allocations to the loggers, they knew where the really good pine stands were, and if they didn't get one, they'd really cry.

"At one of the meetings we had with loggers, one of the guys ended up with a bad package, not much pine, and somebody said we were going to leave some stands of pine for posterity. He kept trying to talk the WPB guy into a better deal, and finally beat his fist on the table and said: 'Gentleman, I want you to know posterity is here.'

"He got his package.

"One plant had a sizable mill on Klamath Lake and a good allotment of timber. There was quite a bit of lodgepole pine in it, some yellow pine, and some Shasta fir. This was quite close to the end of the war and he had been maneuvering around for more yellow pine that we were trying to save. But we kept him halfway under control so that when the war ended he had about seven million feet of lodgepole and scrub-fir crap left.

"The day peace was declared, some square-headed Swede threw a wrench down in one wheel of the mill and busted it all to hell. That ended the mill, and seven million feet of lodgepole ended up in Uncle Sam's reservoir, and that was that—the end of the war effort."

As one young woman said, "You wouldn't be caught dead with a 4-F-er; they were really looked down on." But as the war progressed, the presence of more and more young men became accepted as normal. Many had been wounded and discharged, then left the hospitals for defense work. The resentments against the physically unfit gradually diminished, but the young men themselves never knew when the next insult, or hard glare, was going to be aimed at them. Ilda Weatherford remembers:

* * *

"My brother was in his early twenties, six-foot-two, rosy-cheeked, bright-eyed, and a 4-F. And he was bitter that his only brother and sister were in the navy and all his buddies called up with their unit of the National Guard.

"One day in 1944 he was having lunch at the soda fountain of the corner drugstore when a pouter-pigeon-type matron was bewailing the fate of her dear boy in the service of his country. Soon she was making very audible remarks about the slackers who stayed home reaping the high salaries of the defense industries.

"As soon as he finished eating, my brother got up, tapped the woman on the shoulder, and in an oily polite voice said: 'Madam, the only reason I'm neither with your son, one of my best friends, or reaping a high salary is that my heart is in only slightly better condition than your manners.'

"Then he smiled, tipped his hat, paid his tab, and left the red-faced woman to face the snickers of the other customers.

"He was always proud that his sister (me) served as a Civilian Air Force repair electrician and that both our younger brother and I joined the navy together. He carried pictures of us in uniform in his wallet until he died of his heart condition in 1970."

The schoolboy from the Ozarks, quoted in chapter 1, was also ultimately designated 4-F. He recalls:

"I was sick when I got my draft notice, but they let me stay a while longer before hauling me off for a physical. But when that notice came, the war was all of a sudden very real. My father was an army veteran from World War I and he at first wanted me to go into the army, but with the war really here, he changed his mind and tried to get me interested in the navy. I guess he wanted me to have a bed to sleep in. But prior to that, he had tried to get me to ask for an agricultural deferment—you know, anything to keep his kid from getting shot.

"As the time drew closer for me to leave, I took off and visited one sister in Saint Louis, then the other up in Minnesota. I'll tell you, it was just like you were getting ready to go somewhere and never come back. Really. That's the way I felt.

"So I went back home and early one morning I went up to Gainesville and caught the bus with another bunch of draftees. You have to live through something like that to understand it. I don't believe there's any way to describe the feeling I had when I boarded the bus to go to war. None of us were intelligent enough or well enough informed to know there were still people against the war or that they might have good reason to be. It was the flag stuff. You'd see it and just tremble with emotion, and when I heard the Air Corps song: 'Off you go into the wild blue yonder . . .' and that sort of stuff, boy, I could just visualize myself flying, you know? For me, not knowing what it all entailed, I thought I could walk up to one of those planes and just take off.

"So I went through the line a Fort Leavenworth, Kansas. I knew I had a bad back but I didn't even give it a thought. The only thing I did know was definitely wrong with me was my eyes. But I have this big nose and when I took the eye exam I knew the examiner couldn't see across my nose. My left eye is bad and he was standing on my right, so I just kept both eyes open through the exam and he wrote down '20/20' and I thought I was in. I'm gonna fly!

"When I got through with the exams, they called me back and said my X ray didn't look too good. My back. So they kept me up there two or three days and sent me to various places for another round of examinations, and finally gave me a little slip of paper that said: 'Severe asymmetry of articular frocus five and six tuber.'

"That's what some character typed up. That's exactly

what it said. I don't know how many doctors have looked at that slip of paper and said: 'Well, let's see. Yeah, that must be the fifth or sixth lumbar. Severe asymmetry. That means crooked.'

"So they sent me home and that was it. I never heard from them again. Not one time did they call me back.

"It didn't bother me too much. It was kind of like your mother-in-law driving a car over a bluff; you have mixed emotions. I was a dumb kid, but I didn't want to get shot at, either. I felt kind of let down, but I didn't let it worry me too much. As I look back, I think any man who missed out on the service missed a lot, because there are certain things in the service that is good for boys. But on the other hand, there were a lot of guys who went in then and were really used for cannon fodder, and I think a lot of them were big country kids like me. There's always that to think about, too.

"But when I got back I thought it was pretty dumb in a way because I was generally pretty healthy, but there was a kid from Bakersfield I went to high school with who had some kind of fainting spells and looked like he wasn't too healthy. He'd keel over once in a while at school in a dead faint. And they took him in the navy. I thought, 'Golly, I *must* be in bad shape.'

"There were two times in my life I really disturbed my mother. One was when I was a little fellow and she caught me trying to drown a cat. The other was when I came back from Fort Leavenworth with a towel that said 'The Hell with Hitler.' So twice I really shook her up. '*What happened to my little boy?*'

"Another thing. I got home on a Sunday while the rest of the family was at church, about a quarter of a mile away, and my two younger brothers ran on ahead and found me at home. I'd just laid down to take a nap and they asked me why I was home and not off fighting Hitler or Tojo. I told them I was 'lacking in the head,' and they ran back as fast as they could to meet the parents and told them what I said. They probably believed it.

"So then I went to Saint Louis and worked in a dee-fense plant. Remember? That's exactly what we called them: dee-fense plants.

"It was a big joke, in a way, probably the biggest joke of the whole period for me. I was just a kid, eighteen or nine-teen, when I started work there and the government selected a bunch of us and sent us to an intensive ninety-day training course in Stillwater, Oklahoma, and taught us how to inspect every part of an airplane. Every part. Actually, they just gave us a quick overview of the whole works—the electronics and the engine and the whole works. Then they sent me to Gar-land, Texas, to inspect airplane parts they were sending over-seas for our boys to use to fight the war. And I wasn't even twenty years old! Isn't that something? We did the best we could. We looked at them and turned some down that didn't meet specifications, and, you know, that was the only job I've ever had that I felt was absolutely necessary. The only one. The rest have been simply to earn a living. But then I really felt necessary and essential.

"The pay was really something. A joke. Remember, I was civil service and we didn't get the overtime pay. I got a hun-dred and forty bucks a month. While I was in school they paid us an extra per diem of about ninety bucks a month, but when they sent us out to work for a hundred and forty bucks, boy, it was rough. I would have been much better off not being in civil service, no question about it. So when they tried to transfer me, I just quit and went to work on an assembly line helping Rosie the Riveter and made a lot more money, plus overtime. The works.

"Later on I quit the defense work and bought a truck and started hauling—wheat, barley, corn . . . anything. Then I got educated on how patriotic people really were, and after a fashion joined them. I went into a garage once to buy some truck tires and the salesman called back to the owner: 'Bob, he wants to buy a couple of eight-and-a-quarter-twenties.' And Bob said, 'With or without a permit?' and I said, 'With.' 'We ain't got them,' he said. He just wanted to sell the hot ones. Those were the days.

"You've heard the joke about hoarding, I suppose? The fellow who crawled out of bed to get a tire he had hidden under it and he knocked over a can of gasoline and spilled it on a sack of flour? Well, there was a lot of truth in that.

"I remember hauling a load of barley from Kansas and I'd bought five gallons of lard to take home and hid it under the load. And another time I found some chocolate chips up in Illinois and hid them under a load of corn.

"Of course there was nothing illegal about that. That's why I hid it.

"In self-defense, though, I guess that attitude was part of our country upbringing, to have little respect for authority. My father's cousins were the guys who captured themselves a game warden once and tied him way up in a tree and left him there overnight. Just for the fun of it. Bureaucrats didn't do too well down there.

"Looking back on the whole period, I guess being a 4-F was pretty hard on guys like me. Those of us who had an inferiority complex already just looked for anything to feel inferior about. It was *so* uncomfortable. I was just a big lumbering kid and I didn't limp when I walked and I had all my faculties—supposedly—and I could sense people saying, 'Look at that guy. Why isn't he in the war?' I don't remember if it was ever mentioned—I doubt it—but I always felt like someone was saying it. 'Back trouble? Ha!' Those were the patriotic days. But after I got married I had other things to think about and it didn't bother me so much. But it was always there in the back of my mind."

*   *   *

Those like Martin Hagen who remained in defense plants during the war had a hard lesson to learn when victory finally came.

"I wanted to go into the service and tried to go, but had a perforated eardrum. They took me into one of those big hotels in New York and checked me out. A friend and I were all set to get petty-officer ratings and serve on PT boats. They'd gone all over us and given us an OK. We were just starting to walk out the door when the doctor called us back because he'd forgotten to check our ears.

"I tried to get in some other services, but none would have me. I'm not resentful, understand, but late in the war when they were beginning to take older men with families, here I was a healthy-looking fellow and some of the people they were taking were really in tough shape.

"At the plant I had maybe ninety girls and twenty men working for me, and the men were older and the women younger. The first thing the girls wanted to know was why I wasn't in the service. But Frank Sinatra had the same problem I did, and that is what I told them.

"I was a foreman in an ammo factory owned by Frenchmen who had fled France and come to Long Island to run munitions plants and, at the same time, start getting ready for peacetime business. They were testing a three-wheeled car when the war ended. It was kind of strange working there, because every time we won a battle in North Africa, out would come the champagne for everybody.

"Generally, I would say that it was 'business as usual' during the war for most of us who stayed home. Everybody was out to make as much money as they could, and a lot of people wouldn't have minded if the war had kept going another five or ten years.

"It wasn't unusual for prostitutes to get jobs at the plants—for on-the-job earnings, you might say. They'd work in corners, the lunchroom, rest rooms, and after work. It might be two or three months before they were caught.

"The day after V-J Day the company locked the gates. I reported to work and the people were standing outside. Grumman Aircraft sent out telegrams to everyone telling them they had no jobs. Snap. Just like that. I was lucky because I was a supervisor and still had a job, but there were suddenly thousands out of work and a lot of them had tools still in their lockers inside the plants."

Others, like Frank Denta, saw many injustices around them, not only in the factories but in the neighborhoods where the workers lived and shopped.

"I lived in what was then a small town on Long Island and operated a nursery my father and mother had started just after they came over here from Europe in 1901. My father and I raised a lot of vegetable plants for the victory gardens, and there was a lot of sham in that. A lot of people out here on Long Island had relatives in Brooklyn or New York, and they got extra gas to come out here on Saturdays and Sundays to work their victory gardens. Most of these gardens were no bigger than a bathroom. It was clever, but *I* didn't think it was clever at all.

"It was tough then for us businessmen because we were rationed, too, and in the flower business you have many, many customers in the outlying areas, anywhere up to twenty-five miles distant. So the florists got together and we agreed to take turns delivering flowers on trains to other areas so we could conserve gas. Otherwise we wouldn't have made it.

"There were several antiaircraft batteries around Long Island to protect the aircraft plants and other defense plants. Most of the wives of the guys were young country kids and it was just shameful the way people took advantage of them. That still bothers me. Two of these girls rented a room in

Farmingdale—I won't tell you the nationality of the person who rented the rooms, but they charged them enough. When their husbands got forty-eight-hour leaves, the landlady charged the girls extra for their husbands to sleep with them. They charged a full week's rent for those forty-eight hours.

"These girls went to work for me in the greenhouse and I heard about it and went straight up. We had a big house and only one child then, so I told them that they were going to stay with us from then on, and we weren't going to charge them any rent. And do you know, today we still get Christmas cards from them, thirty-five years later. They were real nice ladies.

"They were good workers, too. When it got too hot in the greenhouse I would tell them to get out because we'd pay them the full eight hours when it got that hot. But this one told me that her father and mother told her that if she was going to get paid, she should do her work. And she wouldn't leave.

"We had more women working for us than men because the men would stay only until they got a job at Republic Aircraft. We couldn't afford to pay them defense wages, of course. After the war ended and the plants closed down, some of the guys came over asking for a job and I wouldn't hire them. They'd ask why not and I'd tell them they had that 'Republic gait,' which would not do in the flower business. There were a lot of goldbricks. Oh, God, some of these people would feel proud of how little they did. I know. I worked in defense a while.

"You see, I knew a vice-president of Liberty Aircraft through Rotary Club. One day at our lunch meeting he told me that he would like for me to work for him. 'We need workers so badly at night. We have a day shift to make parts for Grumman and Republic and we just can't turn them out fast enough. Why don't you come out and work?' It was only

five and a half hours a night, but I didn't know. I was working ten- and twelve-hour days already at home.

" 'Well,' he said, 'it will protect you, too, because if you
work for us you won't get drafted.'

"I didn't want to be a shirker, but I had one child and
another one on the way and I didn't want to go into the
service. So I went to work on the speed lathes. I never drank
excessively or smoked and I kept my mind on my work. I must
have been pretty good, because the foreman asked if I could
get some more young men like myself to work nights. I talked
to other Rotarians in Queens Village, and there was another
guy in the same boat as me: married, children, and a business.

"This may sound strange to you but after two weeks the
day lead man hung around and, when we were working, he
asked our lead man if he minded if he spoke to some of his
men. The night lead man said he didn't care, go ahead, and
he came over to see me.

" 'I've been looking over your work,' he said. 'You're turning out more in five and a half hours than our nine people are
doing in the regular eight hours with two hours' overtime. It
makes it look awful bad for our people.'

" 'Any rejects in my work?' I asked.

" 'No,' he said, 'No, no rejects.'

" 'Look,' I told him, heading him off, 'don't talk to me
about slowing down. I know George, the vice-president of this
company, very well. He's a personal friend of mine and he
asked me to work. I work the same here as I work at home. I
don't spend time in the men's room smoking, because I don't
smoke. I tend to business. Why don't you pep up your own
men? Don't tell me to slow down. I'm not made that way.'

"He was a Polish fellow and he got red in the face he
was so angry. A German working next to me slammed his fist
on the table and said, 'Ach! You told him good.' He was so
proud of me.

"I had joined a battalion of the State Guard on Long Island because I figured I'd have to go in sooner or later. I hadn't handled a rifle since I was six years old with my BB gun and I said I'd better learn what army life was like before I got into it. I entered as a private and came out as a platoon sergeant. I also worked in civil defense as sort of an MP, directing traffic and so forth. We were a good unit, closely knit, and I got pretty good insights on what military life was like. But the regular army guys who worked at the antiaircraft batteries told me to stay out as long as I could, that the military was no place for a man with a family because I wouldn't be thinking about what my job was; married men were absolutely no good, they said; get a baseball bat and break your arm or leg.

"Well, I was finally drafted on Friday, April 13, 1945, right after Roosevelt died. And that reminds me: A state trooper I knew told me for sure that Roosevelt had blown off the top of his head, and one of my relatives in the Pacific heard it, too. He said the ship's radio announced that 'Your commander in chief has committed suicide with his own service resolver.' Then about five minutes later they came back on the speaker and said there had been a mistake, forget you heard it, a mistake was made. But why else would they have a closed casket rather than having him lie in state like other presidents? Besides, funeral directors are past masters at making anybody look ten or twenty years younger even if you had a stroke. My mother was paralyzed for six years before she died and the funeral director made her look twenty-five years younger. She looked wonderful. I don't see why they couldn't do that with the president, unless he wasn't all in one piece.

"I'll never forget my examination. I went down to be examined and I had hurt my back and eight or ten different chiropractors and orthopedic physicians had told me they could ease the pain with dope, but what good is that?

"Boy, do they ever ask you some stupid questions! They

asked me what doctors I'd been to and I told them. He looked at me and told me he thought they were all fictitious. So naturally I blew my stack. Then one doctor would write in red pencil that I wasn't fit, and the next would scratch it out and write over it. It was a farce. Finally it ended up with me and a fellow from Amityville, a fellow I'd played ball against in high school. They asked him if he had had any major surgical operations and he told them the technical name of the post-nasal-drip operation he had. The doctor said he had never heard of such an operation in his life. So this guy blows *his* stack. 'Why, you dumb son of a bitch. What the hell have they got you here for if you don't understand the technical names for an operation?'

"I had such a backache while I was there—oh, Lord—that the sweat was just pouring right down off my chin. They had lunch there and I was a devout Catholic and they gave us hot dogs. Only hot dogs. I refused to eat it and they told me I was in the army and to eat it. I told them I was not in the army and I was not going to eat it.

"I guess I was a little headstrong, but finally I was up in front of a doctor and he told me to duck walk. I didn't know what he meant, and he showed me. Gee, I could hardly get down, but I did and walked across the room. I hurt. I really hurt. He tried to brush it off by saying, 'Oh, you'll have backaches once in a while.' But I was in absolute agony and was afraid I couldn't even get home from there.

"I asked him if they had an orthopedic surgeon or somebody who could get my back in shape so I could get home. 'We have no authority at all,' he said. "All we are responsible for is to get you here. Not for getting you home. You'll have to get there the same way you came.'

"I managed to get home and told my wife I was on my way into the service. Then I asked the man in town who was head of the draft board about it and he told me to appeal it. 'They have to listen to the appeal,' he said, 'and they will give you another month.' The upshot of it was that they lowered the top age for drafting and I didn't have to go. I could speak very good German and fairly good French and they would probably have shipped me off to Japan anyway."

Philosophically, the war was difficult for many ministers, especially those who believed that when the Bible said, "Thou shalt not kill," there were no legal loopholes in the command.

"My grandfather and my father had all been ministers, and while I was growing up all my classmates told me I'd be a minister, too. But my attitude was, 'I'll be damned if I will.' You get stereotyped as a minister's child.

"About a year before Pearl Harbor when the war clouds were gathering, I was employed by the John Hancock insurance company and worked in the group department. It looked as if I had a pretty good future, and as I look back on it, there were times when I could have kicked myself for not staying there. I could see my whole future before me; it was a small department and young and has since grown a great deal. So I had to make a choice and I became determined to go into the ministry.

"At the time of Pearl Harbor I was in my second year of divinity school and was a student pastor of a church in Fall River, Mass. I had been very active in the National Student Federation and I was one of the fortunate few to have a job. By 1939 I had a sense of security and the satisfaction of the work, but the evidence was that we were not going to have the peaceful world I had hoped for by doing business as usual. I have to say there was always a question in my mind if I was influenced by the fact that I knew the clergy was exempt from military service. I had the convictions of a conscientious objector, but I hadn't had to test them on my own conscience. I talked it over with the first reserve chaplain in the navy and he said that if God was leading me in this direction, I'd know.

He helped me, and the fact that I've stayed in the ministry the rest of my life has convinced me I had a call. And it can be a rough way of life.

"I have a distinct recollection of being in an elevator on the Thursday or Friday before December 7, 1941, when I met an older minister in the Methodist Building who knew me slightly, and he said, 'Well, have you heard anything from the ultimatum?' and I asked what he meant. He said Roosevelt really gave them—the Japanese—an ultimatum. That sort of thing was obliterated afterward and all we were told was that they had sneaked up on us totally unprovoked and we were into war. But because of my father's influence, I was among those who couldn't buy the propaganda.

"So we were aware of the fact that Roosevelt was taking steps that would lead us to war, and I had never heard of Pearl Harbor, to tell the truth. When it happened, I was driving some of our young people to Woods Hole, Mass., and I didn't have a radio in my car. When we arrived, the people in another car with us told us about it.

"Of course that made a great difference in the lives of people in the churches. The fellows in the seminary were divided between those who were preparing to be chaplains and had come there expecting we were going to go to war and the others who were absolutists, opposed to the war and becoming chaplains.

"I continued as a student pastor on into my senior year, and in December of that year I took a full-time appointment at a regular church in Providence, Rhode Island, because the pastor had gone in as a chaplain. We had a program for girls whose boy friends or husbands were overseas in the service, and we had a number of military installations around the area, so a lot of our programs were designed to provide an opportunity for the servicemen to meet some of the girls and have some sociability.

"Once in a while we'd hear about somebody who had

been lost, and because of the fact that this was the church away from home, we remembered them in our prayers and would write to them and try as much as possible to find out about them. And some would be back after a year or two overseas.

"In my own personal life, I had not yet made up my mind if I was a conscientious objector. I wasn't sure where I stood, and one day I was talking with one of my pastor friends who was an admitted pacifist who has been a pastor in Ohio for a number of years now. He listened to me and handed me an application for the Fellowship of Reconciliation and said, 'You're more of a pacifist than I am.' And I allowed as how he was right.

"I had the beginnings of convictions that war was wrong, but they just hadn't jelled. And at the same time I had the feeling that I might consider going into the chaplaincy. I know a man who changed his feelings and became a chaplain and maintained he was always an absolute pacifist. It would be difficult to reconcile my convictions in that way. I don't see how he can bless war and remain a pacifist. Most chaplains were what you'd call military and pretty supportive of the war system. They'd have to be.

"Those things were very important in my mind, and in 1945 I was offered an opportunity to meet with the staff of one of the largest churches in the country—in Minneapolis— and I went out and preached for them as part of the interviewing process. Apparently everything was satisfactory until I met with the top committee in the church and someone asked why, since there was a need for chaplains, I wasn't one. I had to defend my views, so they sent me a nice letter thanking me, but they didn't want me. The pastor, who later became a bishop, said that if I were married or if I could have found some way of weaseling around that question, I could have had the job.

"One of the active young men in the church at Providence was a CO who was doing his work for an iron company, and he refused to do any drafting on war work. He was offered a promotion in another company and he couldn't do it because his present employer had permitted him to work on civilian projects only. He wrestled a good deal with his conscience before turning down the offer. But they said it didn't matter; they were buying his company anyway. He rose to become a successful engineer.

"As I think about it today, I think I might have jumped into the war had I known about the atrocities. I don't remember too much about the Bataan Death March, but it was the ovens in the German concentration camps that would have sent me into the war had I known about it at the time.

"There's no question in my mind that it is the technology of the modern media that has kept us out of World War III. You can't do anything today that we won't know about within twenty-four hours. I think we've been smarter in the later wars in Korea and Vietnam, and our attitudes have changed about the government statements. For example . . . when Nixon insisted he absolutely would not resign, that was good, we'd say, because that meant he was going to resign.

"Throughout all my preaching, I've found it very important to try and have your people willing to hear what you have to say. I remember that I preached twice in one day in Providence because the senior minister had been transferred. They had me in charge and brought in a guest minister. So for five months I was the intern pastor. On this particular day I had to preach both in the morning and in the evening. The morning sermon was on radio and it expressed my conviction without tackling the subject head-on. The sermon in the evening was on the high cost of hating. And another time I preached on to hate or not to hate. The chairman of the committee on pastor relations came to me in kindness and pointed out that I had preached two pacifist sermons in one day. I didn't argue with him, but actually we could preach on the high cost of hating anytime.

"Throughout the whole period there was a feeling of restraint for me as a young minister because when we'd date girls, there was that fear of firing across the bow of another guy who was overseas. I didn't meet my wife until after the war.

"There are some incidents that stand out and are unrelated to the ministry. I remember being in a restaurant one day with my father and the waitress was distracted and getting orders mixed up. I was really irritated but didn't say anything to her. But when I went to the counter to pay I told the cashier that I felt like leaving a message: 'Here's a tip. Why don't you smile?'

" 'Oh sir,' the cashier said, 'her husband has been missing for five days.'

"And we ministers had the 'C' cards for gasoline, the best one. Obviously we exercised it with caution, and I had very few problems. But one day I went into our church in downtown Providence and, since I was going to be there only a minute, I left the engine running, thinking it would burn less gas running than starting up again. When I came out there were two men standing beside the car and they let me have it.

" 'You ought to be in the army,' one said, 'and I don't mean the army of the Lord.'

"I wasn't aware of a loosening of morals during the war. Of course, I was dealing with these young people who were coming to church. In one case I remarried a couple who had been divorced. They were war workers and working different shifts. As so often happens, they didn't see each other very often, and I don't think either met anyone else. But he had quit his job and was going off to war. Their remarriage was one of the most touching events of the war for me. With tears in their eyes, they were renewing their vows.

"But the class of people we were dealing with were not the kind to go through a moral upheaval. They would seek out a church in which to have some kind of social life and they would not necessarily be the type who would be 'with it,' to use the terms of today. They would be from the Midwest, church-oriented, and from a middle-class kind of family."

If the nurses in hospitals were treated, as one said, "like beasts of burden," the war wasn't much more pleasant for doctors, especially those in small towns who had no hope at all of getting help until the war ended. Compounding this in Dr. Thomas J. Taylor's case was the enormous buildup of a nearby military base, which attracted dependents and girl friends as well as the hundreds of thousands of young men.

"I entered private practice just after the war began, and after I thought I had been cleared by the army. I had an infection in the bone of my left leg as a child and had recurring trouble with it throughout my life. I was told by a number of orthopedic physicians that most likely I would not be eligible for military service, and had received clearance before I entered private practice. But I found out later this was only preliminary. In June 1942, when things were going full blast in the Pacific, Africa, and Europe, the army sent a medical officer around to see me, and he told me that even though I had a verbal clearance, it was essential that I report for a physical examination, particularly in light of the fact I had ROTC in college.

"I reported in on a hot day to Fort Lewis, early in the morning. Of course Fort Lewis then was a madhouse and I wandered from one place to another trying to find out where I reported for my physical. I never did find the place. After a couple of hours I got tired and noticed a line of people ahead, standing and leaning against the wall. They were beneath a canopy, which looked welcome to me, so I just casually leaned against this wall and the line filled up behind me. We shuffled along and I just stayed with it until I found myself inside and heard a gruff voice tell us to take off our clothes. The next one said, 'Pee in this,' and the next one says, 'Bend over,' and pretty soon I was getting the works. After I had been stabbed and stuck and blood taken and a rectal done, I finally got to a doctor. He looked at the letter and I extended to him, looked at me, and said, 'For Christ's sake, what are you doing here, doctor?' and I told him I was there for a physical. 'Don't you know what kind of physical you're getting?' I told him I had no idea, and he said, 'Well, you're going to wind up in the Parachute Corps.'

"He took pity on me and gave me a private and a jeep and sent me off to some far-off corner of the base, and from there on I was given the VIP treatment. I got my physical and came home wiser with a letter of rejection, thanking me for my offer to volunteer for the Medical Corps.

"It wasn't until that November when practically all the doctors eligible for military service were removed. And they left reluctantly—one by one—and believe you me, some of them went with great bitterness. I can't say I blamed them. There wasn't a single one of them happy about it and I think in some ways it was a shame. Some of them had just got started and were heavily in debt. It was a time of crisis for everyone, of course. War always is.

"In any event, we lost about two-thirds of the doctors, and those left were older but active for the most part, and there were those like myself upon whom the bulk of work fell. If you pare a community down from a normal complement of, say, twenty or twenty-five doctors to near ten, you've got a work load. From 1942 until 1945 I really didn't know what it was to sleep a whole night through. Anytime. I saw from forty to sixty cases daily and operated every morning and sometimes during the night. I saw emergency cases anytime, and weekends were spent treating the emergency cases at the local hospital. It was a busy life, and, contrary to what some of my colleagues felt or thought who served, I didn't get wealthy. As I look back on my books, we were only getting a couple of dollars a call, and while that was a whole lot more money in those days than it is now, it wasn't a great big fee. I really was so busy that the necessary financial investments were neglected. But I did get ahead, of course. I couldn't have failed to, because I didn't have anything to begin with.

"The main impact of the war on our area was the large numbers of soldiers coming through Fort Lewis. They must have had well over 100,000 out there at a time, although I doubt if they ever knew exactly how many were there at a time. As the pace of the war grew, so did the intensity of activity on and around the base. The spillover came into the community through these young troops on leave and on weekend passes, wandering about the streets looking for some excitement, some fun.

"When the troops came, right on their trail would come the little war brides, fifteen- and sixteen-year-old kids from every corner of the nation. They'd just be dumped off in our little town, and of course every one of them was pregnant and ready to deliver. They would wind up in the hospital by one conveyance or another, just dumped off there. They'd be in all stages of labor and somebody had to take care of them. All the doctors in practice in the community then had to take their share of them. They had no choice.

"Of course we'd never seen them before. We had no work-up on them. We wouldn't know their pelvic measurements, we wouldn't know one thing about their medical history, and we would be forced to deliver with no knowledge whatsoever from the obstetrical point of view. It's a wonder we got away with it with as little problems as we did. Of course I brag. I never lost a full-term mother or baby, and I didn't intend to.

"During one twenty-four-hour period I delivered five babies from women I'd never seen before. They would be in all stages of complications. It would tax the ingenuity of the best obstetrician and we managed to do it. We had a baptism of fire.

"Early in the game we had to look for ways of getting paid, and that was a laugh because none of them had a dime. Most of them were Georgia crackers and had never seen 5¢ in their whole life. So it turned out to be charity. Shortly afterward the federal government stepped in, and I think we should be damned grateful that they did. This problem exists in all wars, and they set up what came to be known as the EMIT Program, the Emergency Infant and Maternal Care Program. They set a minimum-fee schedule and the doctors and hospitals could be certain of getting something. It wasn't much to begin with. It started out at $15 a delivery and got up to around $25 and then $35. I think finally about 1945 they were paying somewhere around $50 a delivery.

"This took care of the obstetrical problem, but it didn't take care of their living expenses. When it came time for discharge from the hospital, these kids would be thrown out on their own and try to find a room to hang their hat and money to get home or someplace. It really became a severe social problem in the community. I gave a few kids the fare back home, but it had to be few because there were hundreds of them and I didn't want to be broke. So we'd send them to the Red Cross.

"That Red Cross! They would at least help them out. But do you know what they'd do? They would insist on a loan. They wouldn't give them the money. Oh, no. There's no funds available for gifts. So these kids had to sign a loan, and if the Red Cross had any way of contacting the parents, they'd do so.

"The best organization was the Salvation Army. There

were no questions asked. The Salvation Army's ability to provide funds to care for these people was remarkable. They weren't asked to sign a note or asked to borrow money from their parents. The Salvation Army just took care of them and gave them money to get home.

"Maybe now you can understand why I've never given a dime to the Red Cross. Well, I take that back; I did a time or two. But I just don't like them. They are a very, very poor organization. Most of the Red Cross money then and now goes for administration, in *fat* salaries.

"Where in God's name, you're wondering, did these poor kids stay? I asked myself the same question in those days, and every rooming house and second-rate hotel and barn was filled with them. I vividly recall when a second-class rooming house was jammed with war brides and babies and I was called there because of a rather severe flu epidemic. I remember walking through that rooming house and each room had three or four mothers with babies, all of them, and they all had the flu. A bathroom down the hall, no money, desperate. I tried to do right and called the Salvation Army. In that particular case they did a heroic job of cleaning up that mess.

"This was repeated over and over in staging areas throughout the country until finally, late in the war, the message got through to most of these kids and they didn't follow their husbands out. But this was by late 1944 and early 1945, just before the war ended.

"This wasn't limited to young wives and girl friends by any means. It was parents and relatives as well. One episode I recall was about a mother. One night I'd been on a terribly hard day, and about one o'clock in the morning I got a call from the desk clerk of a big hotel saying he needed a doctor to come and see someone because apparently a patient had died in the hotel. I tried to talk him out of it and said I couldn't come. He said somebody had to come, so I went down there and up to the room.

"Here in the room on the bed was a dead woman. There were two other women with her, apparently relatives, both screaming their heads off. They were all elderly, and the dead woman had had a spontaneous rupture of what must have been an aorta aneurysm that ruptured in her trachea and she had coughed the blood out of her mouth, into the bed, and all over the room. It was a horrible death and a horrible sight. It was just like somebody had butchered a pig and spread blood all over. I don't blame these women for being hysterical.

"There wasn't a thing I could do. I couldn't calm them down. I couldn't take the time to sit down and hold their hands, although I wished I could. I just said, 'Ladies, this woman is dead and there isn't a thing I can do,' and I went home to bed.

"I got a terribly nasty letter some weeks later from one of them saying how cruel I was and that they never met such a horrible person in their life and how unfeeling I was. I think probably they were right. I could have tried to comfort them, or give them something, and stay and help get the body out and that sort of business. But, so help me God, I just didn't have the energy. Delivering, three or four cases of surgery, seeing thirty or forty cases, making house calls, two or three hours of sleep a night—what a terrible drain that can be on a person. But to this day I regret not being able to give more in the case of those two surviving ladies.

"I really enjoyed the obstetrics part of my practice. We had a lot of illegitimate babies during that time, and this led to children being adopted out. Mothers didn't want their babies and they weren't keeping them like they are today. It wasn't socially acceptable. There were also a lot of babies abandoned around here and we had to do something about it. We did, and I'll explain that in a moment.

"The most amusing fatherless baby I delivered was from a young gal about sixteen years old who lived in a community nearby. She was a very beautiful young girl. I don't remember her name, but we'll call her Nellie Gray because it reminds me of the tale. Her mother brought her in to me and said she was about four or five months along. Of course in those days it was not considered socially acceptable and they would either take them out of school and bring them home, or send them off to Aunt Mary for an extended visit.

"In this case they just took her out of school and didn't want her delivering in her hometown. So they brought her down to me. She was a lovely child, very innocent and very dominated by her mother. She was going along normally, and about three weeks before term I told her mother to get her down to our town. It was winter and the mother was afraid to drive in snow, so I said, 'Oh, shucks, if you think you'll have snow and get stuck out there, bring her down here and we'll put her up in our house.' Lo and behold, who should show up about three weeks before delivery but mom and Nellie Gray. And I hadn't told my wife about it.

"We had extra rooms upstairs because we had two boys and two bedrooms up there, and here they were. I put them upstairs and tried to smooth things over a little with my wife, and both stayed until delivery. Her mother waited on her hand and foot, demanded this and demanded that from my wife. They'd sit around and stuff themselves with bonbons and food, and my poor wife was just beside herself by the time that girl delivered. Everything went along all right and we adopted the baby out.

"In those days you could do that and the courts and social workers didn't have their fingers in the pie. It was very common. But in 1947, when I was president of the local medical society, the practice came to an end. By this time I had cut down on my obstetrics, but many doctors were still continuing to adopt illegitimate children out. We didn't conduct a baby racket, of course, and all we asked the adopting parents to pay was the hospital expenses and any reasonable fee on our part. All adoptions were handled through local attorneys, and one who worked with a lot of such cases subsequently became head of a state department of children and youth.

"We were contacted by a judge in 1946 or 1947 to the effect that the medical society should be on its guard because the courts were looking with considerable concern over the adoption of babies in the private sector. He gave us a definite cutoff point, after which all adoptions were to be handled through the courts, after first going through the welfare agencies. I suppose this is the only proper way to prevent abuses, because I'm certain that in some locales there must have been people taking advantage of this thing, baby banditry and racketeering and so forth.

"I would say, though, that every other doctor's conscience in our area was as perfectly clear as mine. I have no regrets and would make these adoptions over again. I wouldn't say I had a great number—maybe twenty-five in a period of four or five years. This is probably true of another four or five doctors in town. I don't know for certain, of course, because those records have been destroyed.

"There were other cases from those war years—so many cases—that stand out in my memory, one in particular because it was so funny at the end. A chap had tried to commit suicide and the state patrol called me saying they badly needed a doctor because a boat had been found in the mud outside town and there was a man aboard with the engine still running. I agreed to go and the state patrol picked me up and took me out there.

"It was a beautiful moonlit night about ten o'clock, in the spring, and the tide was out, and down over the hill was a bunch of people running around and out there in the mud was a little launch with the motor going put-put-put. By the time I got there, the would-be rescuers had not been able to reach the boat because the mud was so thick. So they wanted me to go out there, of course. I picked up some boards and made a sort of sled and we slid out there. I was dressed up, had on a good suit, but got out there. The launch had a side curtain and I pulled it aside and looked in. The chap had rigged it up so that the exhaust had been flowing right into the cabin, and here he was, laid out cold. He was one heck of a big man and it took about six guys to get him back ashore. I gave him some oxygen, got him to the hospital, and put him in an oxygen tent. My God, I was just mud from head to foot.

"He stayed unconscious for two days, two days under oxygen. Then he woke up. The nurse called me one morning and said he was awake, so I went in. 'Isn't that wonderful?' I told her.

"When I made my rounds I went into his room and this fellow was lying on the bed. I introduced myself as the doctor who had saved his life. He rose up on one elbow and looked me in the eye and said: 'You son of a bitch!'

"He refused to pay even the cost of cleaning my suit."

Casual or professional friendships made before the war sometimes resulted in difficult decisions when those friends were suddenly considered the enemy and a target for bombing raids or attacks.

"I was a college teacher during the war, a professor of engineering at Tulane involved in several research projects concerning metal fatigue and that sort of thing. All during the late 1930s I had been corresponding with other professors all over the world—England, Poland, Japan, Canada, and so forth. We exchanged papers and correspondence right up to the outbreak of the war. One wall of my office was virtually lined with papers from different countries my foreign colleagues had sent me. I assume theirs was the same.

"Shortly after Pearl Harbor, the FBI and Naval Intelligence came in to see me. They weren't accusing me of anything, understand, but, oh, my, did they have a lot of questions to ask about the Japanese professor. Since I had nothing to hide, and it was a time when the country trusted the FBI without hesitation, I hauled out every scrap of correspondence I had, including carbons of my letters. I watched them haul the papers out, and then back in again after presumably they had copied them.

"When they came back for the third or fourth time, they asked if I had any knowledge of Tokyo itself. I told them I didn't, had never been in Japan, but that I thought somewhere in the stuff from the Japanese professor there might be a map. I started digging around and came up with a paper he had published, and inside it was a note with a map showing the location of the university in Tokyo. He had drawn an arrow to the building he worked in. They took that away, too, and it wasn't much longer before Jimmy Doolittle made his raid on Tokyo.

"Of course I never heard from the professor during the war, and I hoped to after the war. But I later learned that the University of Tokyo was leveled in a bomb raid. I never found out which bomb raid and I never asked. I guess I should have felt guilty in case I was partly responsible, presumably, for my colleague's death. But I never did. We were at war. He was as much my enemy as I was his, and I am sure that had I sent him a map of Tulane, he would have turned it over to his intelligence people, too. It was that kind of war."

Many of the men who stayed at home became something like den fathers to neighborhoods filled with wives waiting for their husbands. They were unofficial plumbers, carpenters, electricians, and spider killers. Druggists often served as paramedics and prescribed medicines for various ailments that did not obviously require a doctor's treatment. They kept in close touch with doctors and hospitals, and the responsible ones always checked with a doctor before prescribing anything stronger than an aspirin.

One druggist, Frank D. Dexter, saw an opportunity in this, and took it.

"I went to work for a drug chain just before the war. I had barely missed being called up for the First World War and was sure they'd get me for this one. But they didn't. I just kept on working and watching other guys like me with a wife and child being called up.

"So one day the owner of the chain came in and I put it to him: 'Mr. Winters, are you on my draft board?'

"He kind of laughed and said, 'Yes, I am.'

" 'Well,' I said, 'why aren't you calling me up for the draft?'

" 'I told them when your name came up that you were too important here,' he said. 'I told them you should stay in the neighborhood where the women have young kids and have to be by themselves. You can help take care of them.'

"He had a point there because druggists had more leeway then on what they prescribed. If a kid woke up sick at night they could call me and I could judge whether they needed a doctor or not. If they did, I'd call him and he would usually go along with what I thought.

"Then I got to thinking, and a few days later Mr. Winters and I had our talk. I went up to him and said that it seemed pretty important that I stay where I was, and that I had been trying to get a raise, but hadn't been able to. . . .

"The next paycheck had a raise on it."

There were a few men who had good jobs during the period, and knew it. Some of the luckiest were men in the service who were assigned to shore stations within the country and would never be sent to the war zones. Fred Ross was nearing the maximum age limit for servicemen and had gone into the navy with a solid background in newspaper work.

"I was stationed at the Great Lakes Training Center, and was treated almost like a civilian by the navy. It was just like being a civilian, anyway. I was home every night and weekend, but every morning when I went to work I put on a uniform instead of a coat and tie.

"In fact, I had it better than any civilian I knew because we lived in Chicago and the mayor of Chicago then—Kelly, I believe his name was—loved the servicemen. He couldn't do enough for us, it seemed, and the whole town was that way to a degree.

"As an example, my wife would go down to the meat market and ask if he had this or that, and he would tell her he was out. But I could go right in behind her and he would have it for me. As long as I was in uniform we never had any trouble getting any kind of meat we wanted.

"We could ride free on all the streetcars, and when I got on the bus to go to work, the driver would put his hand over the fare box.

"My job was a snap, too. After the war started, the navy saw that the marines were getting all the publicity, and they didn't like it. They decided to do something about it, and since I had been on newspapers, they got me to start the Fleet Hometown News Service. They just turned me loose and told me to get as big a staff as I needed.

"What I needed was guys who could write press releases. We started pulling service records looking for newspapermen. And we got them. I got managing editors from some pretty big papers, desk men, reporters, the works. I had some of the best journalism talent in the country assembled in my office.

"Then we got an index of every newspaper, every radio station, every weekly paper in the country and made up a card file. When we had a guy assigned to a ship, or wounded, or promoted, or when a ship just came into port after a long voyage, we hauled out the ship's roster and started flooding the mail with stories about the men. We were sending out as many as 2000 news releases a day. Pretty soon the marines were left behind in the dust. The navy always got more local publicity than any other branch of the service, and that system I set up was used by the navy for more than twenty years that I know of."

The overall impact of the war years on families at home was summed up by a woman who was weary of poverty and all its uncertainties:

"After all those years of the Depression when men had to sit around without work, it was kind of exciting just to see the rows of men going off to work at the plants with lunch pails under their arms."

The curfew ordinance, long on the statute books but for years disregarded, will again be enforced. Under this ordinance it is unlawful for children under sixteen years of age to be on the street after 9 P.M. during the winter months to April 1, and 10 P.M. in the summer season, unless accompanied by a parent or guardian or performing an errand for a parent or employer.

The ordinance is considered necessary at this time because of the increase in juvenile delinquency.

The *Seattle Post-Intelligencer*
February 25, 1945

Selective Service disclosed today broad liberation of its draft deferment policies for college students.

Affected by the revised policy are undergraduate and graduate students in scientific and specialized fields, undergraduate, pre-professional students, and students in professional schools, interns, and students of agriculture, forestry, pharmacy and optometry.

One of the major changes provides that any student in undergraduate work in approximately twenty scientific and specialized fields should be considered for occupational classification if he is a full-time student in good standing in a recognized college or university and if it is certified by the institution that he is: competent, and gives promise of successful completion of his course of study, and will be graduated by July 1, 1945.

Associated Press
March 4, 1945

4

Growing Up on the Home Front

V-Mail

Dear Dad:

Miss Chilton made us write our dads and brothers overseas this week. This is my letter to you. How are you? Mom said not to ask you for anything but I hope you can bring home a Nazi helmet or long dagger like Donnys dad sent him. We are fine.

Your son,

Jack

P.S. *I changed my name. Jackie is for kids. Mom says the man of the house should have a mans name.*

THE PEOPLE WHO WERE INTERVIEWED for this book said repeatedly they were glad they grew up in the Thirties and Forties. They were of the opinion that anyone growing up in the following decades did not feel the warmth and security of growing up in a country that was quite pleased with itself in spite of the problems of depressions and wars. More than any other time in memory, the country was convinced it was on the right course.

People who survived the twin adversities of a depression and a major war felt they had accomplished something simply by surviving both. They are also convinced that people were more likely to help each other during those years than in more prosperous times; that a common threat or danger brought them closer together.

Children of those years quickly absorbed the prevalent attitudes and carried them over into adulthood, creating a congress of attitudes that their children in turn do not always understand. Materialism and conservatism were basic to those who reached adulthood during or shortly after the war, but each generation not only refuses to learn from the past generation, it usually rebels, then turns conservative in its own time. The cycle continues.

Children of the war years remember that period as the most exciting years of their lives. They remember collecting shoulder patches; watching war movies in which the Allies always won; learning hundreds of new types of planes that constantly flew overhead; reading about new tanks, half-tracks, landing crafts, and seeing these, plus jeeps and artillery, going past on trains.

We remember starting each schoolday by reciting the Lord's Prayer and the pledge of allegiance. We remember when our favorite candy bars disappeared from store shelves, and how terrible that new gum, Orbit, tasted when Wrigley's gum was no longer available. Bananas were hard to come by, and ice cream was replaced by orange and vanilla sherbet. We ate Spam sandwiches because other meat was rationed more strenuously, and we heard jokes about Spam and meatless Tuesdays.

We remember that the Green Hornet's Oriental pal became a Filipino. Our comic books switched from *Plastic Man* to *Spy Smasher, G.I. Joe, War, Don Winslow of the Navy,* and so forth. Most of our comic-strip favorites became involved in the war, and the cartoon Nazis looked something like gorillas in helmets and the Japanese (Japs) looked like monkeys with protruding teeth and thick eyeglasses.

We earned extra spending money by selling scrap metal, rubber, and paper. Many parents of the period still wonder what happened to that cast-iron skillet or some other prized possession that their children stole to sell for a few cents. Movie theaters often had special matinees for scrap drives. A bundle of newspapers often got us in to watch cartoons, serials, and either a western or a war film. Some theaters changed their names; Victory was a popular new name for them.

The backs of cereal boxes were turned over to the war effort. Plane-spotter silhouettes or cards were common, as were the types of military headgear, squadron decals, and thumbnail biographies of heroes. Few toys were given out by cereal companies because of material shortages. For the duration, we had to console ourselves with things we could cut off the backs of the boxes.

Our schools had air-raid warning systems, especially if we lived on a coast. Drills were held frequently and we were herded down to the lowest floor, where we scrambled under tables and chairs. In schools that had the metal tube for a fire escape, the air-raid drill was a combination of both. The coastal schools had a three-bell system for air raids, one or two or three bells to tell the school how near the enemy planes were. Children had to tell the school how long it would take them to run home in case of an attack, and those who lived nearby were permitted to dash home.

In their games children acted out their defined roles: Boys were the soldiers, and girls the nurses, wives, mothers. At home, boys had to listen to their mothers' laments about raising boys only to be killed in a war in some strange land. The boys early on selected the branch of service they would enter when they were old enough, and if the war lasted long enough. Getting ready to go to war was as much a part of initiation rituals into manhood as killing the first buck deer without getting a severe case of "buck fever." Those who suffered the shakes and nausea at shooting a deer were nevertheless certain they would feel nothing of the sort when they killed their first Jap or Nazi.

These attitudes carried over beyond the war's end in 1946 and were part of the mystique that made the first years of the Korean War in the early 1950s so palatable. But as that war dragged on with no plans for conquering the whole Korean nation, the edge went off. Yesterday's child who wanted to be a war hero became disillusioned and wanted only to get out and go home. Long before that war was over he realized that there would be no more heroes.

However, the war years weren't as innocent as we would like to believe. Juvenile delinquency was at its worst in the nation's history. Juvenile prostitution was a major problem. Children were left alone for hours every day while their parents worked in defense plants, many living in those instant slums that grew up around the larger cities. They ran in packs that became gangs. Not only the Mexican-American juveniles in Los Angeles wore zoot suits.

Yet most people remember the pleasant aspects of those years, and those who were teen-age criminals do not care to talk about it. As they remember that period today, it was almost an idyllic existence.

* * *

"Gasoline was the biggest problem for a teen-ager. We still had cars, and gasoline was our biggest worry of all the rationing. We'd always pick up our dates in sequence when we had gas, and you might end up not taking your date home if it would save gas for you to be dropped off first. You'd kiss your date goodnight in front of *your* house, not hers. Some guys you didn't trust very much, and you wondered if they might not be kissing your girl also, because they would drop their date before yours. You worried about such things, and there were certain guys you didn't double-date with because you didn't want them taking your girl home. There were maybe four or five guys in the whole school who had their own cars, but most of us had access to our fathers' cars.

"We didn't notice all the young women who moved into town during the war because we were too young and weren't able to get any of that action. And I don't think any of my friends did, either. So we missed a whole field of endeavor there, you might say.

"There was a broad social line in high school; any girls who went out with soldiers or sailors were out; they were immediately sluts, and we looked upon servicemen the same way—except, of course, our own relatives. And we wanted to be in the service ourselves, so it was a very strange social line. You'd never take your girl downtown, either, because it was pretty wild down there. It was another dividing line; nice girls stayed pretty much away from there.

"We had other definite moral rules. If the boys were going to drink, we didn't drink with the girls. We didn't mix that up. It wasn't done. You played poker and messed around one night with the boys, and took your girl out the next. You didn't do both. I'm sure girls were doing the same thing, but we just didn't hear about it.

"I remember the agonizing my sister and other girls went

through during the war, and we classified them as those who waited and those who did not. I look back and it was really hard on them, and there were a lot of questions asked. Some of those poor women would sit around doing nothing for three or four years and it must have been very difficult for them sexually. That's pretty tough on anyone. Some didn't wait. Others weren't too selective about the whole thing. My sister-in-law lived with my family and they played a lot of bridge and did some pretty good drinking. That was about the extent of it. She was never the social kind. She wrote my brother about every day. But my sister was a party girl and liked to go out all the time, dances and so forth.

"And it was tough on the women, too, when the men came home after being gone a long time. They'd have to get reacquainted. They'd have it built up in their minds that the whole world was going to be wonderful as soon as their husbands came home. It wasn't always that way. It was very traumatic for the men to return. My oldest brother had a lovely wife, but they just couldn't make it when he returned. My sister and her husband got divorced. But my other brother had been going with his wife for a long time before the war and they had a pretty stable relationship.

"It was a very emotional time and so many of them got married on leaves to total strangers. Some of the guys used the line that it would be their last leave, and then got carried away with it and got married.

"We tried saying in high school that the next year we would be in the service, but it never worked. The girls would say, 'Sure, let's wait until that last week when you're here.'

"Girls were quite different then and we just didn't get any in high school. In fact, the best we had was dry-fucking; we'd just rub ourselves off against each other through our clothes. We couldn't even get the panties off most girls, and to get our hands beneath bras was really something. I'll never forget the first time I felt a girl's nipple. Boy oh boy oh boy!

"Long after the war was over, one of my friends, who had been getting it right along and never told me anything about it, then told me how he had to go through all this rigmarole to get it. He was one of the guys I double-dated with because he had a car. I don't know if he got to one of my girls or not. He wouldn't say that. But he did say he had to put on two rubbers and, even then, some of the girls would make him withdraw. The poor guy didn't know what good sex was until after he was married a long time."

Young soldiers are notorious teasers, and one young farm girl, Valerie Beardwood, whose parents became a soft touch for the local soldiers, was thrilled by all the attention the boys showered on her.

"I was about fifteen when the war started, and we lived on a farm in California. The army set up a camp not far from the farm, and I had to walk by it on the way to catch the school bus every day. The soldiers were very nice to me, and pretty soon they were calling me 'Goldilocks' and their 'mascot.' My mother took them in by the dozen, it seemed, and then they began calling our house the Farmhouse Canteen. Some of the young fellows we met at that time became lifelong friends, and my mother corresponded with a bunch of them for years and years.

"Since I was just a young girl, they treated me something like a younger sister or cousin, and I remember walking to catch the school bus one beautiful morning, and I was singing that song from *Oklahoma*, 'Oh, what a beautiful morning,' and from somewhere down in the meadow came a young man's voice: 'Oh, what a beautiful day.'

"When some of the guys shipped out to Fort Bliss,

Texas, they remembered me and I guess they assumed I'd
never get any love letters while the war was on, so they got
together and wrote me one:

> MY DEAREST DARLING VALERIE:
>
> We promised you a love letter and we always keep
> our promises, besides writing you a love letter is a honor
> and a privilege that everybody cannot share.
>
> The moment we saw you we knew you were the most
> gorgeous creature God put on earth. Your shimmering
> golden hair is beyond our poor power of description.
>
> Darling our love for you is greater than the space of
> the universe. Just to know that you think of us once in a
> while is all that we ask of life. Your slightest wish is our
> command and for you we would gladly lay down our lives.
> To make the world a safe place for you to live in makes
> the hells of war worthwhile.
>
> Your bewitching blue eyes haunt me in my dreams.
> My every thought is filled with your angel-like beauty.
> Your soft lily-white complexion is finer than the rarest
> velvet. Your tantalizing ruby red lips just beg to be
> kissed. The sensation of one kiss (each) would be greater
> than a sip of Holy wine. Your heavenly figure is beyond
> compare even to that of Cleopatra. Your exotic beauty
> is so great that we humble soldiers must bow down
> before it.
>
> The ecstasy of holding you in my longing arms is
> beyond anything that life can offer. Darling, as I lay
> staring at the stars your beautiful countenance is outlined
> in every constellation. To tell you more is impossible for

thinking of your charms puts us in a spell that is unbreakable.

God bless you and protect you always and may the man that wins your love be forever worthy of you.

xxxxxxx	*All our love,*
xxxxx	J O E C A V E G L I A
xxx	S T A N C O O K
x	J A C K S C H N E I D E R
. . . – V	

"Another fellow, not to be outdone, wrote one to me all by himself. He must have been in the paratroops because the letter had a drawing of a paratrooper falling through the air upside down and reading a book called *Instructions for Emergency Parachute Jumping*. His letter was a bit more brief":

D E A R V A L E R I E :

Darling when I see your face reflected in the mirror of the memory of my life, I can almost feel your smooth cheek pressed against mine. It is then I know victory is worth any price, a hundred lonely hours like this eve because I know when I come back the world will be bright and shiny again, for you, for us, forever.

B R U C E (Brucie)

Some feel they were manipulated by the nation's propaganda, which was nurtured by the churches at that time.

"It was no accident that Eisenhower called the book he wrote after the war *Crusade in Europe*. That's the way we thought of the war, as a holy crusade against the forces of darkness. I grew up with it and it was okay in our parish to pray that a lot of Germans and Japs got killed.

"I was in the eighth grade of a Catholic girls' school at that time and we were taught in no uncertain terms that God was on our side. And the good sisters wouldn't lower their standards for anything. They still insisted that we wear long hose. To show a bare ankle would have caused so much sin in the community that you could even kill each other getting the hose; anything so long as you didn't turn some man on with a bare ankle. So our mothers would go downtown and stand in line so their daughters could have long hose and not go to hell or cause some poor man to go to hell for getting turned on by our bare legs. Isn't that something? The feeling we had was that we could knock some poor old lady over and grab her hose, and that wouldn't be as bad as bare legs.

"So we went about helping win the holy war. The sisters did something that blew my mind when I thought about it years later. First, you simply did not date servicemen. Under no circumstances. That was a sure way to be ostracized by the school, the community, and the church. Right? Well, what do the sisters do but get a list of servicemen's names and get us to strike up pen-pal relationships with them. The one I drew is still a dear, dear friend of the family. He used to come over to the house and visit with my parents—he was twenty-three, I think—and treat me like a kid sister. But it always seemed so strange that this kind of thing was fine and patriotic and had the sisters' blessings, but we could not date them. Of course it was different when the boys from another Catholic school were drafted; then we were patriotic when we entertained them.

"And I can remember us selling war bonds, and an army officer coming to our school war-bond rally in his jeep to talk to us. Also, different rooms competed on bond sales, and I remember girls getting up and telling stories about their fathers or brothers or cousins who were in the service.

"Of course there were always one or two girls who dated servicemen on the sly and came around school bragging about it. They seemed so worldly, so casual about it, and they gave us vicarious thrills by talking about it. Of course their exploits and experiences weren't all that great, but in a convent atmosphere, wow! We were sure they were headed to hell in a hurry, of course, but now when I see one of those girls and what she has become, I'm not so sure they weren't going about life in the proper way. This one in particular is a great woman, a truly fine mother and wife, and she's useful in the community. I guess she just didn't buy the fear and the closed-mind policy we were taught.

"But I think the thing that bothers me more now than anything else was that holy crusade aspect. It took me years and years to get over my feelings toward the Japanese. I was the epitome of the good-guy-bad-guy syndrome. We sang songs like 'An Army of Youth Flying the Standard of Truth' and 'We're Fighting for Christ the Lord.' And I remember being so fond of 'In an Old Dutch Garden' and thinking of how beautiful and pure Holland was until I read that children ate the tulip bulbs because they were starving. That sort of thing begins to shake your confidence.

"It was all this mentality that got us into all the trouble in the 1950s, when they went to Korea with the attitude of 'Kill a Commie for Christ.' And it helped get us into Vietnam, I'm convinced. But if my kids are any criteria, the government and the church will never get away with that holy war aspect. No way.

"But I do want the young people to understand how it was then. They should know that we are no more stupid than they are. I'm sure each generation looks back and sees how it was manipulated by propaganda of one form or another. And I'm sure they'll be as bitter and ashamed of it as we are."

* * *

For many people, the high-school years are the most important of their lives, hence the best seller a few years ago *Is There Life After High School?* Combine this with a distinct period such as the four war years and the impact on young men like Bruce Vance is doubled.

"A kid in my class loaned me his Model A once, and that was a real thrill. I'm not even sure I had a driver's license then. I told my best friend I had the car the next Saturday and wanted him to ride with me while I drove past all these girls' houses I wanted to impress and show what a big deal I was.

"We whizzed all over town, and of course we ran out of gas. I was an expert at siphoning, but you don't siphon gas at four o'clock in the afternoon even if you are desperate. If there was one thing the police got cranky about, it was siphoning gas. You could get away with a lot of other things under the heading of 'kid stuff,' but that they got cranky about.

"You don't like to put paint thinner in a car, because it can wreck it—at least that was what the guys in the hardware store kept telling us because they always suspected something was up when a kid came in saying he'd been 'sent' to buy some thinner. Anyway, it wasn't always that easy to find. So I went to a hardware store to buy something else, then sort of nonchalantly bought a gallon of thinner, too. I was certain that guy was fish-eying me, but he sold it and didn't say anything.

"We put the thinner in the Model A and it fired up right away. I got the car back to the kid who owned it a couple of hours late, and he was fuming at me over that. I don't think he ever knew I'd given him a shot of thinner. But what the hell? Some people burned booze in their cars. Those old heaps would burn about anything."

* * *

The death of a fiancé was something thousands of teen-age girls had to learn to expect, although none could be prepared for it because death is so remote to the young:

"When I talk about the war years now it sounds like I did nothing but go to parties and dance half the night. Part of that is true because when you're a seventeen-year-old girl the seriousness of some situations doesn't sink in right away. The thing about Pearl Harbor Sunday that really annoyed me, for example, was that they weren't playing dance music on the radio. When I was eighteen I was dating a pilot who was about twenty-eight and he was very tall. He gave me his wings and we were going to be married. He wrote me from all over the world, and then he was killed in the first bombing raid over Germany. His family called me from back east to tell me. This was suddenly no fun. It brought the war home to me. It was the first time I realized the war was serious, and that there was a certain amount of truth to the soldiers' old line that they might be gone tomorrow.

"At that age deaths in the war were unreal to us. There were no bodies, no real funerals as we knew them. It was almost a disassociation. Some of the girls who were married to those fellows whose bodies were never found, but were declared legally dead seven years later, it was terribly unreal to them. There was nothing to grieve over, just a memorial service.

"Death got to be a common thing with us. Every day they'd have a big list in the paper and a friend might be on the list. At the time you'd think it was too bad, but you got so saturated with deaths and people missing that you just accepted it as natural. It went on and on and on for four years. I think it might have bothered me more had we not lived near a base, but there we saw an apparently endless supply of eighteen-year-old boys, and there is too much vitality in eighteen-year-olds to think much about death."

* * *

Most young boys are pack rats, and to have a doting father overseas was a bonus.

"There was a kid living across the street from us who became my best friend, probably the best friend I've ever had because he was honest, never expected anything from me except that same honesty, and he never once complained. He had a lot to complain about, too, but he was always cheerful, funny, and always had some project going.

"You see, his father was at war and his father was something of a wild man. He was good to the boy, treated him like a short friend rather than a ten-year-old kid, but he was always going off in all directions looking for the end of the rainbow or getting into a fight and punching up a few guys, plus the MPs, and the city police, and the lieutenant and so forth.

"His mother wasn't a woman of high morals, if you know what I mean. She sort of slept around a lot while her husband was gone, and sometimes when she got the twitch in the middle of the day, she'd bring her boss home with her for a little tumble and send the kid over to see us. We knew when that was going on because he would always arrive crying, or, if he wasn't crying, we'd see him hanging around our backyard doing nothing particular other than looking like he'd been kicked. I was more of a diplomat then than I am now and I never asked him any questions, just had enough brains to go out and play with him without really knowing what the matter was. I don't remember that well, but I suppose I thought she'd said something mean to him, or slapped him, and every kid knows how stupid parents can be and you don't have to go around talking to each other about it.

"Years later he used to jokingly accuse me of being his friend because of all the neat junk his father sent back from

Italy and Germany. His father was such a mean bastard that they kept him at the front as much as they could, I suppose, because he loved a brawl and that was what the war meant to him—a way to kick ass and get medals for it.

"He started sending junk home, and it wasn't all junk. He sent helmets, German uniforms, gorgeous daggers, binoculars, cameras, swatches of beautiful leather, and other goodies.

"Then he started sending home boxes and footlockers filled with tools and other hardware, and we started noticing that nearly every one would have a piece of a pistol or rifle, and the first thing we knew, we were in the small-arms business. Before long we had a Luger assembled, but had all these other parts lying around. A few more boxes arrived, and we had a rifle assembled, but still had some parts left over. Finally the last parts came, and I'll be damned if we didn't have one of those Italian machine pistols put together.

"His mother didn't pay a lot of attention to us until she found some ammo. She got rid of that quick.

"But we had a ball with that armory during the rest of the war, and when his father came home he had some ammo for the machine pistol—9 millimeter if I remember right . . . was it the same ammo for the Luger? I can't remember. Anyway, we had the thrill of watching his father chop down a small tree with that machine pistol, and when I told my mother, she almost fainted. That was my last excursion with my friend and his father.

"I understand he got the machine pistol taken away from him out in California after he got drunk and shot up the delivery truck he drove."

Parents are always concerned when their children have fantasies of death and destruction, but the ban on such thinking is more or less lifted during an all-out war:

* * *

"I guess most kids had fantasies of killing Japs and Germans during the war: charging through the Black Forest, picking off snipers in the towns, sneaking through the steaming jungles and knifing the yellow creeps. Maybe I had my share, too, but that isn't what I remember.

"When my aunt went away to work in a defense plant, somehow she got one of those aircraft spotter's manuals—the silhouettes as well as actual drawings—and sent it to me. I guarded that thing with my life because none of the other kids had one. And I must have memorized that thing because even today I can tell you virtually every bomber and fighter we had. I wasn't so hot on navy planes, for some reason, but those army fighter planes were my meat. The manual even had the trainer planes, too, from the tiny Pipers up to the AT-6s.

"Now for the fantasy. We had one of those cow-pasture airfields near my hometown in eastern Kansas, and one afternoon a bunch of PT-19s flew over town, circled a time or two, and headed for the field. So naturally several of us kids raced out there on our bikes to see these planes up close. It was love at first sight for me. They had two open cockpits, low wings, fixed landing gear, and, if I remember right, a sort of handle between the cockpits for lifting them at the center of balance. They weren't as noisy as the other planes because they had only about an eighty-five-horsepower engine.

"So while the other guys dreamed of flying an Avenger or a Hellcat or a P-38 or a Mustang, I dreamed of owning a sleek but slow PT-19. I drew pictures of it until I'd practically emptied the house of paper. I was going to paint mine black with white trim. The front cockpit would be covered with a drum-tight canvas cover and there I'd keep my clothing and spare parts. After the war I would travel around the country in the plane, maybe even down into Mexico or even

South America. I would be polite, mysterious, and always on the move, something of a cross between Gary Cooper and Zorro, I guess.

"But I never even learned to fly, and I was nearly forty years old before I even went up in an open-cockpit plane, and then it was in a PT-22, which is similar to the PT-19, only not made of plywood. It was nice, but not particularly thrilling.

"But it was strange the attitudes we had toward airplanes then. They represented the epitome of freedom to us. Maybe I'd read Richard Halliburton's books too many times. But for some reason I assumed that airplanes were quiet and all you'd hear would be a humming engine and the wind in the struts and that sort of thing.

"Well, about the same time I rode in the PT-22, I went up in an AT-6, which is a fighter trainer, you know. It was the most miserable ride I've taken in anything. It was uncomfortable as a horse-drawn hayrake with the team running away. The seat was just a steel slab, the cockpit was too crowded to move, and it shook and rattled before we took off, and I couldn't hear the sound of my own voice for an hour afterward. It was no wonder that they got stupid, show-off kids for pilots in those fighters. Any adult would have taken one ride and returned to the infantry."

Employers had to hire the youngsters instead of the adults they'd had in abundance during the Depression years of the 1930s; either kids or old men. Nevan McCullough, a Forest Service ranger, remembers one youth clearly:

"One kid I was able to hire, after the war was on a while and they dropped the eighteen-year-old requirement, was a hell of a kid. He was sort of a leader in the group and had a lot of talent, but he'd take them all to town and get them thrown in the can. Drinking or fighting or both. He was like Napoleon—little, smart, and tough. Pretty soon I had to get him out of the logging camp, though, and I turned him over to a tough ranger who worked him on trails and had a few talks with him. They got along swell. The ranger called him Friday, my man Friday.

"In the fall he was still with us, not going to school, and we had an old cook with one eye, a hard-looking old guy. The good eye was a whiskey eye and the other was closed most of the time. But he was all we could find for a cook and there were about eight or ten of these kids and an adult or two.

"Friday tormented that cook. He accused him of putting too much salt on his spuds or not enough, and he got the other kids kicking about the grub. Finally I had to can Friday because I knew the cook would quit if I didn't. I could get another kid easier than another cook. I went up there one morning, but knew that if I canned him in front of the other kids he'd take all those kids out of camp with him. So I said, 'Friday, I've got something for you,' and he strutted around a while and I got him in the pickup and told him to get his stuff and come down to town with me. Gosh, he felt terrible, and he begged me to keep him and said it would be a black mark on his record from here on out. He was really worried. I really liked that kid.

"But I turned him loose and never heard anything about him for years. I told him, 'Friday, you've got two choices: You can wind up in the federal pen or you can wind up amounting to something. It's up to you.'

"You know, he's practicing medicine in a town a few miles away from me. He's got a good practice, too, I hear. I'm sure he's a good doctor, and if I ever get sick, I'm going to him. It would really be a surprise to him, I'll bet, because we haven't seen each other since that morning I took him to town."

* * *

One teen-ager who worked in a defense plant had his own reason for turning out shoddy work:

"Jobs were easy to get. They'd hire anyone and wouldn't fire anyone. One summer I decided to work at an aircraft company, and they hired me at sixteen. I wanted to learn how to buck rivets, and, boy, did I learn. You'd stand on the other side from the riveter and hold a bar against the back of the metal and the impact of the rivet gun against the bar flattened the rivet. We got 82½¢ an hour and we were rich.

"We put air bolts on the B-17s as they came down the assembly line. Then they transferred me over to the B-29s on a super-secret section with engineers running around all over the place because it was only the third or fourth B-29 they'd built. One of the main reasons they brought me in was because I was so small I could get into the tight places to buck these rivets. They were learning as they went, and we were putting rivets where the engineers hoped they were supposed to be. But those things still went out and flew, which is interesting, and surprising.

"On the B-17s I was working on what you might call the keel, a big strip that went all along the bottom. I still wonder how those things flew from the way we bucked those rivets. If they didn't split too badly, we just let them go.

"I was kind of proud to be working on the bombers, but there was one problem: The riveter I worked with had bad, bad B.O., just gross B.O. We'd get in a small place and I'd want to get out and away from him so badly that I'd say it was okay whether it was or not. I didn't give a damn if the plane flew; I just wanted out of there and away from him. Today I would tell him how he smelled, but back then I was too chicken."

A country boy remembers his family's move to town, and an eerie little incident involving the supernatural.

* * *

"We were lucky. None of my brothers had to go in the service, and none of my sisters were married to servicemen. A pack of cousins did go in, and I guess they made it pretty rough on my brother because he was a 4-F.

"We had just moved to town from the farm and none of us had ever seen an electric light or a flush toilet before. What a ball my brother and I had flushing that toilet. Wow! What a blast! Here's all these wild country kids running around flicking light switches and flushing the toilet.

"My mother was very religious and was afraid of most things that weren't mentioned specifically in the Bible. There was one thing in the house that spooked her more than anything else, an Ouija board we found in the closet when we moved in. My mother hated that thing, but my father wouldn't let her burn it. He said it was just a couple of pieces of wood with some cloth and paint, and how in hell could that hurt anyone?

"We were playing with it one night and my mother was watching. If she'd been Catholic she would have been rattling beads at it, I suppose. Two of us were asking it the usual dumb questions and getting the right answers, probably by shoving the board around where we wanted it to go. Then someone asked: 'Where's Roland tonight?' Roland is one of my cousins who was in the infantry, and we hadn't heard anything from him in weeks.

"It got very quiet in the house and we sat watching that silly thing move around the board. It spelled out 'On the water.' Now that really spooked us because it made sense.

"That was the end of the Ouija board for us. My mother burned it in the kitchen stove and my father never asked about it again. That particular board simply ceased to exist..

"After the war we compared notes with Roland and found that he was, indeed, on a ship the night we asked the

Ouija board his whereabouts. Makes you stop and think, doesn't it?"

While there are plenty of statistics to prove that more young women were on the prowl during the war than before or after—and that more venereal diseases were transmitted by the teen-age free-lancers than the professional prostitutes—there have never been as many loose women as men like to think. Still, there were enough during those years to cause concern among military leaders and parents.

Some stories refuse to die, such as the clubs every high school in the land is supposed to have for girls; they must sleep (to use a polite euphemism) with a certain number of boys—or with the entire basketball team or football team—to earn membership. Undoubtedly there have been, and perhaps still are, such clubs, but certainly not in every school every year.

With these misgivings in mind, here are two stories which were probably true sometime or somewhere:

"The guys I went to work with were pretty wild, mostly Jewish boys, and they found this gal in the plant who had a whole wall at home decorated with pictures of sailors she had slept with. She kept telling us which ones were good and why, and which ones weren't and why. I was embarrassed. This other kid kept baiting her and she'd tell us about it.

"Then this clown told her my parents owned a hotel downtown, because it was the same as my last name, and he told her I tried out all the girls who worked as whores at the hotel. I couldn't shake her for about a month. I was scared to death. She wanted to work as a whore and didn't know how except to haul me into bed.

"I suppose some of the guys laid her at work. Sometimes you'd see somebody sneak off into a toolroom, or in the nose assembly of the bombers, but the thought of getting caught at that terrified me.

"You always wonder what happened to women like her. Probably a grandmother now who refuses to remember such things."

"I wish you could find some of the Victory girls and get them to talk, but none would admit it today. They were sort of like the nonvirgin clubs that came along after the war. But the Victory girls thought they were being patriotic and helping with the war effort.

"I was stationed in this little jerkwater base near a little jerkwater town in Illinois for advanced flight training. We were there only six weeks, then overseas we went. There were no weekend passes until we were almost through with training because we had a lot of night flying, a lot of early-morning calls, and that sort of thing.

"Some of the guys could hardly wait to get to town and see some of those Victory girls they had heard about from the permanent personnel on the base. The girls went out only with pilots, and each guy had to give them a picture for their scrapbook. Some of the girls even carried little Brownie Hawkeyes or something like that to take their own pictures. The guys made it sound like every girl in town was a member, but there were apparently only four or five. They'd pick up guys at soda fountains or in the movie theater and take them out in daddy's car and go at it. Some of them took on four or five guys a night, I heard.

"I went to town with another pilot one night and saw a couple of them pick up two pilots, and were they ever tough-looking dudes. I lost interest in the whole thing and didn't join the ranks. But I will always remember what one pilot said after he came back. He was a hillbilly type, and he said that girl got his buttons unbuttoned faster than a chicken-plucker paid by the piece."

* * *

One would-be hero pondered which was the safest path to glory, then ended up getting in a trifle too late and felt cheated.

"I was almost out of high school and close to draft age and was sure I would have to go in the service. I remember being a little disappointed because I was afraid the only action I'd see would be the invasion of Japan. That would be all. I was a little scared of it because we'd heard that the military people had predicted losses up to a million men to take the Japanese islands. But they dropped the atomic bomb, and that took care of the invasion I was both dreading and looking forward to.

"I remember assessing the services and not really knowing which one to take. The marines had this tactic of going straight ahead, and those who lived were heroes and the others just dead. We thought Patton was a little nuts and that he should have been a marine. The army believes in an inch at a time, and Patton would go until he ran out of gas. I hoped I wouldn't be under Patton if he managed the Japanese invasion. And my marine brother told me the hardest thing in the world was getting a GI out of his foxhole.

"The war was barely over when they took me in the service. I wanted to go through that whole routine of people crying at the train station. It didn't happen for me, because there was no war. I was gypped. 'Grab the bus to go down to the depot,' they told me. 'But I'm leaving for the army,' I'd say. 'Where're you going?' 'Maryland,' I'd say, and they'd say, 'So what?'

"But I'm glad I grew up then, when wars had a purpose. We were relatively sure of the course the country set out on. It was the last time."

Although it isn't
Our usual habit,
This year we're eating
The Easter Rabbit.

Gourmet magazine

DENVER, March 8, 1943—(AP)—"My dog can eat a horse, and I don't see why I can't eat what my dog eats," protested Senator Robert Bosworth, Denver Republican, during debate today on a bill to prohibit sale of horsemeat for human consumption.

"Your dog can also scratch his ear with his hind leg, and that's more than you can do," retorted Curtis P. Richie, Pueblo Democrat and a sponsor of the bill. "Eating horsemeat is nothing short of cannibalism."

A man walking on a dock saw another man crying for help in the bay.

"What's your name?" asked the man on shore.

"Joe Smith."

"Where do you live?"

"Four-fifteen Dexter Street," came the reply as the man slowly sank.

The man on the dock ran to the address as fast as he could and, panting, knocked on the door. "Joe just drowned and I want his room," he gasped.

"You're too late," replied the landlady. "The man who pushed him in just rented it."

WASHINGTON, March 12, 1943—(AP)—Each person, regardless of age, will be allowed sixteen points a week for the whole group of new items to be rationed. There will be no exact meat ration, although . . . the amount of meat available will average two pounds per week per person for home consumption.

Restaurants will continue to be coupon-free to the customers, although OPA will ration the supplies used by restaurants.

Bouillon cubes and beef extracts, not rationed now with canned soup, will be rationed with meat.

Not all cheeses will be rationed. Hard cheese like Swiss and American will be rationed; soft or perishable cheese like cream cheese, cottage cheese, Camembert and Brie will not be rationed.

Canned fish will be rationed, but fresh, frozen, smoked, salt and pickled fish will not be rationed.

Weekly coupons will be good for a month. If any coupons are left over from the first week, they may be used with the second week's coupons.

Because meat cutting is inexact, point costs of meat will be figured to the nearest full point. Thus a steak which figured ten and one-fourth points could be had for ten points. But if it figures ten and a half or larger fractions, it will cost eleven points.

Blue Stamps in War Ration Book No. 2 are used for most canned goods and for dried peas, beans, lentils, and frozen commodities like fruit juice. The Red Stamps are used for meats, canned fish, butter, cheese, edible fats, and canned milk. You have to give up more points when buying scarce foods than when buying the same quantity of a more plentiful one.

Red Stamps J, K, and L may be redeemed through June 20. Blue Stamps G, H, and J are valid through June 7, and Blue Stamps K, L, and M are valid through July 7.

Gasoline and tires—All pleasure driving is banned for holders of A, B, and C ration books. All A coupons are valued at 3 gallons; B and C coupons are valued at 2½ gallons. Coupon 5 in A book is good for 3 gallons through July 21. Motorists must write license number and state on back of each coupon before offering it to dealer. No coupons for new or recapped tires will be issued. . . .

Office of Price Administration directives

The OPA office in Oklahoma, a prohibition state, has ruled that ceiling prices for bootleg whiskey must be posted in all speakeasies.

The 48,750 cuspidors in Washington government buildings are slated for the scrap-metal heap, to eliminate the expense of cleaning. "It takes two workers all night to clean the cuspidors in just one building," says an official, "and there are 325 buildings."

Reader's Digest "National Newsreel"

It is a question of whether the farmer can walk out into his field next year and see a bright sun in a blue sky, with the birds singing in the treetops, with the bees making music in the flowers, with the honeysuckle saturating the air with the odor of the nectar of the gods, with hope beating high in his bosom looking forward to a happy tomorrow; or is it a question of whether the farmer will see a dull sun in a hazy sky with hope gone from his bosom as he looks sadly over the fields, meadows, and woods which he has called his home while he wonders where he can go when the sheriff notifies him that this farm is no longer his?

You, gentlemen of the Congress, have created a controlled economy. You have set up a machine of crushing power. For those who live in the space over which this machine operates, there is no middle ground. Either the farmer must ride on this machine or be crushed by it.

Tom Linder, Commissioner of Agriculture, state of Georgia, testifying before Congress on the creation of the Office of Price Administration.

ANNOUNCER: The Columbia Broadcasting System in cooperation with the Office of Price Administration presents "100 Million Questions." Day after day from all over America questions in letters, postcards, and telegrams pour into the nation's capitol addressed to the Office of Price Administration. Tonight you will hear the answer to a few of those questions selected at random from that national mailbag. The answer will be given by the man appointed by the president, the director of programs of rationing, rent, and price controls. Ladies and gentlemen, Mr. Leon Henderson!

HENDERSON: Thank you, Mr. Announcer, and good evening, everybody. By the way, before we start trying to answer some of these questions, I'd like to say that every single letter, postcard, communication of any sort that comes properly addressed to the office here in Washington is read and considered sometimes by three or four people if it is a difficult question, and an answer is sent out. Well, let's hear what the folks back home have to say.

ANNOUNCER: This letter, Mr. Henderson, comes from a woman in Kansas City, Missouri, and she says . . .

WOMAN'S VOICE WITH ACCENT: Dear Mr. Henderson, I don't know why people like us are being pushed around and no one does anything about it. My husband and I and two children live in a four-room house and pay $26 a month. The landlord, who wanted us to pay $30 but the rent control wouldn't let him, now wants us to pay one year's rent in advance. We have no money for a year's rent, but he says he has a right to do this if he doesn't raise the rent. And I want to know what—

HENDERSON (interrupting): Well, the answer to that is that the landlord is not entitled to advance rent. If she paid by the month on the maximum rent date established by the city of Kansas City, she can continue to pay by the month. A year's rent in advance would result in a substantial burden on the tenant over and above what was customary in her case. If we allowed practices like that, we'd be left a hole in the rent control big enough to drive a truck through. Now, talking about annual rent, I'd like to point out that without rent control the average tenant right now would be paying the equivalent of fourteen months' rent instead of twelve. We can chalk that up in favor of rent control.

What's the next one?

ANNOUNCER: This one comes from a man in Vermont, Mr. Henderson. He wants to know . . .

TWANGY VOICE: We are trying to help our government in every way we can. Sometimes we wonder what you men in charge of the government are doing. How does it come with all this talk of rationing that sugar and tires and gasoline are still being used to make and transport intoxicatin' beverages instead of putting them to good use?

HENDERSON: Well, Mr. Vermont, something is being done. Right now no sugar at all is being used to produce industrial alcohol except what alcohol goes right to making smokeless powder and synthetic rubber. And since late July—I think it was the twenty-eighth—uh, the tire rationing regulations that I issued cut off all new tires to privately operated trucks carrying alcoholic beverages, soft drinks, tobacco products, and a lot of other items.

What's next?

ANNOUNCER: It's from a man in Florida who says . . .

MAN'S VOICE: My wife and I and one son live in a trailer camp. We pay $3 a week for the space we have. The owner of the camp has tried to raise the rent, but we have rent control and he had to drop his rent. Yesterday he stopped his garbage collection and cut down on our water supply because he said it cost too much money. Can he get away with this? Aren't trailer camps protected? My wife and I both do war work.

HENDERSON: Answering both questions, trailer camps are protected where rent control is in effect. No, the man can't get away with deprivin' the tenants of services such as garbage collection or water supply that was customary before the maximum rent change. A case like that should be reported to the area rent director, and any local rationing board can tell you where to go.

Next? . . .

From tape in National Archives

5

Red Points, Green Points

Rationing was one of the most controversial elements of the war effort. On the one hand, people were earning more money than they had at any time in their lives—indeed, many defense plants *forced* them to earn more money on overtime. On the other hand, now they had all that money, they were restricted on how it could be spent. Some could afford steak every night, yet under the rationing system couldn't buy it. They could afford automobiles, but Detroit was producing tanks and airplanes and half-tracks, not Fords and Packards and Chevrolets. Those who owned automobiles were restricted in the amount of gasoline they could purchase, and it was virtually impossible to buy new tires. Even bicycles were rationed for a while, and people could hardly leave town because the trains and buses were jammed with servicemen and their wives, children, parents, and brothers, and sisters.

It was clearly a frustrating situation. It was enough, one former shipyard worker joked, to make you want to save money.

For all the blunders, bureaucratic stumbling, and decisions based on politics and speed rather than wisdom, the rationing system seems to have worked as planned. Few citizens were unduly inconvenienced by it, nobody starved because of it, and there was enough fuel to heat most houses.

The logistics of rationing are almost overwhelming, and the remarkable thing is that it worked at all and went into effect so smoothly and so rapidly. The Office of Price Administration, headed initially by the shambling but direct and stubborn Leon Henderson, soon established some 5600 ration boards across the nation, which depended largely on volunteer labor to distribute the books of ration coupons each month at local schools. Every family in the nation was registered for ration books, all 130 million of them, and each fiscal year some 40 million pounds of paper were consumed in the forms, coupons, directives, and so forth. It was established that more than 5 *billion* forms were printed each year.

The OPA devised two methods of determining allocation of the commodities rationed: equal sharing, and according to special needs. The latter prompted a great deal of Yankee ingenuity. Everybody wanted more gasoline, tires, coffee, and sugar than the OPA was willing to allow, and people became as adept at stretching and bending the truth as they are at writing expense-account vouchers today. But OPA officials became equally adept at spotting the real and the imagined or invented needs. It was a game of wits.

In theory, the equal-sharing method of giving out ration coupons was used in the food program. Processed foods were controlled by blue coupons ("blue points"), and meats, fats, and oils were "red points." Each consumer was granted an equal basic ration each month. The coffee program was set up for adults only. Shoe rationing was set up on an interval program, as was sugar and coffee, rather than on a monthly basis like food.

The special-needs program was applied in several ways. Rubber footwear, stoves, tires, automobiles, and trucks required eligibility for each one purchased. Fuel oil was distributed according to a formula based on the floor space and number of small children in each home.

Gasoline was divided into three main classifications: The "A" sticker was the basic ration of four gallons a week, later reduced to three; the "B" sticker was for those who had legitimate extra driving to do, such as war plant workers in a car pool, who were given additional allowances according to the distance driven each week; the "C" sticker holders needed their cars for essential activities—doctors, ministers, and so forth. Thus, an aristocracy of sticker holders developed, with each holder carefully watching those above him to be sure they deserved it.

In the beginning, gasoline rationing was based on a true shortage. German submarines had been sinking an inordinate number of tankers in the Atlantic, and the pipeline from Texas and Oklahoma oil fields to the Northeast could not be completed until 1943. Railroads could not help to ship fuel because they were already overburdened with troop trains, hospital trains, war materials, and a military and civilian population seemingly in perpetual motion.

As the war progressed, the supply of gasoline became sufficient to meet the demands throughout the country and of the war itself, but there was still another shortage connected with automobiles: rubber. Since it all came from other nations and the Japanese had cut off the supply from the Pacific, it would have been self-defeating to drop the gasoline and fuel-oil rationing; people would have worn out their tires without these mandatory restraints. So gasoline remained on the ration list until the war ended.

The OPA tried to be fair, and was in most cases. But there were some situations over which even the tough Leon Henderson had no control. One was the members of Congress who voted themselves "X" stickers, which gave them un-limited amounts of gasoline. He raised hell over that, and soon was thrown out of office by congressmen who did not like to be criticized by federal employees. They kept their stickers, but Henderson's system was so firmly entrenched by that time that his legacy of fair play remained largely in effect.

Having survived the 1930s when there was no money and precious few frills, most women were already trained for meatless Tuesdays and other aspects of the rationing. Mrs. John Keller recalls:

"It was the excitement of the period that makes it so remarkable when you look back on it, and without that excitement I think most people would have folded. Fortunately most of us had been through World War I, and after the Hooverizing of the Thirties, anything we got was better than the Depression. I knew an awful lot of ways to save and substitute.

"I looked down the ration list and found that mutton wasn't on it. Wonderful! We'd learned to cook mutton during the Depression so that it tasted just wonderful. Why it was never rationed is beyond me, but for us it was a bonanza. I asked our butcher to get me a whole mutton and he split and aged it for me, then kept one-half of it in the butcher shop for me. Luckily we had a huge refrigerator for the rest.

"I had been brought up in a rather elegant fashion for the time—my family had kept its money during the Depression, at least enough so that our Hooverizing wasn't a sacrifice to our health, and I had gone to college with orchids, the whole bit. So when my father asked me one winter during the war what I wanted for Christmas, I really unstrung him. I said I wanted a good butcher's saw. He must have seen that education and lady training going out the window."

Naturally the complex rationing system built up a vast bureaucracy, which was no more popular then than any other time.

* * *

"I think what bothered me most about those years was the bureaucrats and the patriots who didn't know how to be patriotic. For instance, I had this one nosy neighbor, which is always unpleasant no matter when it happens. Another neighbor didn't drink coffee, and I had all kinds of sugar, much more than I needed. So we traded. This nosy neighbor reported us to the ration board. Of course nothing came of it, but you can appreciate the irritation.

"But the bureaucrats—they were petty people who became even more petty. So many of them were little people who had never had a chance to exercise power before—a lot of them were little old ladies and little old men—and they were always saying dumb things like, 'Don't you know there's a war on?' and equally asinine things. Most of them were totally wretched."

Claire Vining remembered the rationing system as a little game between her parents:

"We lived in a small town near Portland, Maine, and after the war started mother got a job on the local ration board through a friend who was appointed head of the board. Mother's job included processing the applications for A, B, and C gasoline ration books, and the books for meat and sugar coupons. Mother's job was passing out the coupons. She was also the one who tore out the extra coupons that the person was not entitled to.

"Each night mother came home with a white chocolate box full of coupons she was authorized to destroy. And destroy them she did. The large black door of the coal furnace was opened and mother honestly put every ripped-out coupon in the fire and complained while they burned that there were so many people who needed those coupons. She always stood there until every scrap was burned. There was no question:

Mother was the most honest person ever employed by a ration board.

"Father, on the other hand, was honest up to a point. He felt that the rules should not necessarily be broken, just bent to his desires. Gasoline was no problem; he owned a trucking business that picked up milk to be delivered to a refrigeration plant. Whatever he needed for gasoline, the ration board gave him. He even had two gas pumps, 500 gallons each, installed on the farm to make certain his milk trucks would roll at 2:30 A.M. to the farms. Needless to say, the car had a 'C' sticker—'necessary for pleasure plus essential business.'

"Sugar and meat were father's biggest worries during the war. While mother honestly delivered our fair share of coupons from the board, no more and no less, father saw things differently. Being a trucker, he met many people and loved to entertain them with his storytelling. After he delivered the forty-quart cans of milk to the plant, he would then pick up express packages to deliver in the area.

"After the war started, he began making friends with the small grocers in the area. He would drop by the stores frequently, and it wasn't long before father asked me to come out and see what was in the back of the truck. He had brought home twenty ten-pound bags of sugar. I was told to ask no questions, just clean out the rear of an upstairs closet—and don't tell mother a thing.

"He always liked to keep little secrets from mother just to see how long it would take her to find out. That was the way he operated. She just took it in stride because it was part of the give-and-take between them. It was part of our recreation and very enjoyable for me, an only child.

"He and I stored the sugar late one fall afternoon in the closet in a back bedroom while mother was at work on the ration board. Fall passed, and so did winter while Father waited for mother to find the sugar. Spring came and she still hadn't. Father and I went to check the sugar and found it all intact, carefully placed in the back of the clothes and boxes. But now we had 200 pounds of rock-hard sugar. It was like cement!

"Father's sugar project had backfired, but he and mother were able to gradually use it up over a long period of time. Father often used it to make ice cream. He could easily pick up cream from the farmers, and he would put in the sugar and rock salt and ice and crank and crank and have a group of people over for ice cream.

"Father had better luck with his cocoa purchase. Cocoa wasn't rationed, so father bought it mixed with sugar—approximately two cans mixed with ten pounds of sugar. Mother wasn't sure this was honest, either, but she always used what he bought.

"Father had a good friend who was a meatcutter. He would go to the meat department of the store and tell the butcher what he wanted. The butcher would wink, wrap it up, and take the number of coupons father happened to have with him.

"Next to ice cream, steak was father's favorite food, and it didn't take long for him to get tired of the coupons. Pressure canners were expensive, but father bought one at a discount store and gave it to me as a present. I needed a pressure canner at sixteen like nothing! But there was a reason for it: Father had bought half of a bull from one of his farmer friends. A bull, not a steer. He and I were going to can the meat.

"He bought a bunch of quart jars and can we did. He sliced the meat and I packed the jars with round coils of meat, for hours and hours. Then we stored the jars in the cellar, back out of sight because he didn't want his friends to know what had been going on. My mother wanted no part of it. It was strictly a father-daughter operation.

"Then we opened a jar, heated the meat, and served it.

It looked great, just like beef stew. Father tried it. He didn't say much. Mother tried it. It was tough. Worse than tough. It was like shoe leather. That bull was just about impossible to eat, and mother refused to take another bite.

"We threw some out, but gave most of it to my grandmother's hired man on her farm, doling it out at regular intervals. He ate it with his dog at his feet, presumably sharing the meat."

Another woman recalls:

"Buttons caused me more embarrassment during the war than anything else. Elastic was worthless then, and you had to wear buttons on all your garments if you planned to keep them on.

"One morning on the bus I sneezed and popped a panty button. The material was so smooth—like satin—that I knew I was going to lose my panties if I wasn't careful when I got off. So I squeezed my legs together while I got down from the bus—don't ask me how I managed it but I did—and then I had to cross the street and walk a whole block. Here I was dying the death of a rag doll and hoping nobody would see me. People on the street must have thought I was crippled or something from the way I walked.

"When I got to the building I worked in—it was a windy day—the door jerked open and pulled me forward. I forgot about my knees and down went my drawers.

"Thank God there was just an elderly guard there. I picked them up, scarlet, and said, 'Excuse me,' and ran to the ladies' room. I never looked at that man again.

"I lost a half-slip that way, too, but at home."

One way to make clothes last longer was to trade bits and pieces of dresses, or wear as few clothes as possible. Mrs. Fred Ross explained:

* * *

"We learned all kinds of ways to make things stretch. We learned to take the top of one girl's dress and put it with another girl's dress because fabric was so hard to come by.

"We had one beautiful girl in our dormitory, red hair and blue eyes, just a gorgeous girl. I didn't know until after I was married that at one of the parties we had she was sewn into her dress with nothing on underneath. My husband told me years later and I asked him how in the world he knew, and he said, 'Honey, remember, I danced with her.' She ended up being a model or something in New York."

Ruining that last pair of silk hose was a tragedy for young women.

"I graduated from high school in 1943 and went down to the University of Michigan for nursing. I was in a cadet program, which meant the government paid for everything except my underclothes, shoes, and that type of thing.

"Just after I left, my grandmother stood in line for a pair of nylon hose for me to have to wear at college. Before the war we had silk hose, and lisle was very popular, too. But lisle didn't fit very well around the ankles; they were sort of like bags. So I had the first pair of nylon hose in the whole dormitory, and when the guys started coming home from the war I would lend the hose out to whichever girl had a date.

"My dearest friend borrowed them when her fellow came home from Honolulu—he brought her an orchid, I remember, and he had been gone quite a while. Well, the ten o'clock curfew wasn't good enough, so we snuck her out again. When we snuck her out, we dangled her from a window and were going to drop her down to him. Somehow or another things didn't connect just right and she fell and hit on a little prickly bush. There were six girls hanging out the window and none of us inquired how she was. We were only worried about the hose. She had ruined them, and was she mad!"

While there were enough basic food items available for everyone, some cravings could not be satisfied. Many spices disappeared from grocery shelves due to Japanese occupation of Pacific and Indonesian plantations. Worst of all, cigarettes were in short supply.

"We would listen to the radio programs and hear how some tobacco company was sending so many thousand cigarettes to different units overseas or to hospitals. That only made it rougher on us. Here we would be sitting in the parlor smoking something that tasted like dried weed, and all those good cigarettes being given away.

"Coming home one night on the bus, I sat near the back and a sailor got on. He was pretty well looped and was talking and laughing and teasing us about how easy it was for him to get cigarettes. He had a paper sack in his lap and he started hauling cartons of cigarettes out. He had five or six cartons in the bag, and he started opening the cartons and throwing packs all over the bus. He'd throw one toward the front, another toward the back, and he almost started a riot!

"I caught a couple of packs and shoved them in my pocket. Damn right!"

Even with a shortage of cigarettes, quitting was no easier then than any other time.

"It was so bad that my fiancé sometimes sent me cigarettes from his base in the South Pacific. I decided that was ridiculous and one Friday afternoon smoked my last Lucky Strike and said that would be the last one for me.

"By Monday morning I was going crazy and was ready to smoke the weeds along the sidewalk. I walked into the building I worked and went up to the cigar stand to see the little old man I'd known for several months. I almost ran to him and asked him for a pack of Luckies.

" 'Gee, I'm sorry,' he said. 'I don't have a single pack of cigarettes.'

"I was horrified and thought I would die. I felt so sorry for myself, being so far away from home with my brothers overseas and my fiancé over there, too, and I couldn't even buy a cigarette. I couldn't help myself—tears started rolling down my cheeks.

"That poor little guy saw me crying, and quickly reached under the counter and gave me a whole carton of Luckies.

" 'Here,' he said. 'I was saving them for someone else. Take them!'

"I was so embarrassed. But you'd better believe I took them."

Mrs. John Keller remembers going on scavenger hunts in San Francisco in search of shoes for her children and cigarettes for herself.

"You remember the old Camel cigarettes ad about walking a mile for one? Hell, I walked a lot farther than that looking for them—or any other kind of cigarette. Sometimes you could pick up a pack here and there or something they called Old Bill. God, it was horrible. It was a long cigarette, almost like a small cigar, with brown wrapping. I'll swear it was the sweepings from a cigar factory. Awful!

"One of my children's favorite memories is of the time we started at one end of Market Street and wound in and out of virtually every store on that street. We'd head in every place that sold cigarettes, then down the street to a shoe store. Shoes were just wretched then. The soles were made of something that resembled pasteboard and they wouldn't hold up in rain at all. They'd wear out before the kids got home from school the first day they wore them. They would even fall apart in a good San Francisco fog."

The war effort was a bonanza for those who loved to criticize neighbors. Hundreds of thousands of people were reported to ration boards, police, the FBI—anyone patriots and busybodies thought should know of suspected waste and cheating. Some people loved to torment these busybodies.

"My parents were divorced and I lived with my father, did all the cooking and housekeeping during the war years. He knew all the angles and loved to barter with neighbors or friends to get those things he loved most. One of his loves was butter, great big chunks of it on his pancakes, and we always had enough.

"A woman lived next door and we couldn't stand her. She was nosy, bossy, and was always peering in our kitchen window at us. We had a huge Russian wolfhound that we loved and she hated, even though it never bothered her. She was always complaining about it because she simply hated dogs.

"My father's greatest moment was at breakfast each day. Every morning he would take a big stack of pancakes out to that hound and, while the woman watched, slap a big chunk of butter on the pancakes and hand them to the dog. It just about drove her out of her mind, but there wasn't a thing she could do about it."

The shortages and rationing caused otherwise modest people to do things totally out of character:

"The biggest mercantile store in my little town announced one week they were getting a shipment of women's hose in, and that we could sign up for a pair that Saturday.

The store was being remodeled and expanding to the store next door, and everything was dismantled except the exposed plumbing along one wall—stool, washbasin, and all. There were a couple hundred men, women, and children queued around the room while waiting for the sign-up.

"When a goose sees water, it wants to drink, and when a child sees a toilet, they've gotta go and right now. The mothers weren't about to give up their places in line, but one mother of a nervous child solved the problem. She sat the youngster down against a wall, then stood in front of the little girl and looked nonchalantly in another direction— much like someone walking a dog—and let the child do her do-do. It was just like someone with a dog pooping on the post-office lawn."

Another small event is remembered by Don Lanskov every time he sees a former neighbor:

"I was only ten when the war ended, but I remember one event clearly. A neighbor woman, an otherwise normal, modest woman, came running down the street one day shouting at the top of her lungs: " 'There's toilet paper at the A&P!' "

Joe Nye, a butcher, said he was everyone's friend, especially to people who had been steady customers before the war.

"The law said that if you had the points you could buy meat and butter, but if you didn't, you had to wait. That was what the law *said*, but there was some skulduggery going on: You rub my back and I'll rub yours.

"Say you had a customer who had been coming in regularly for two or three years and you trusted them. They wouldn't have the right points, but you would find a way to take care of them anyway. That was the way business was done; nothing wrong with that.

"When the war started I had three kids and was exempt from the service, but they told me I had to get into a defense job or I would lose the exemption. They gave me two weeks to get that job, but my boss got me a deferment through the supermarket chain I worked for. I stayed with the chain until I retired a few years ago.

"The most trouble I had in those years wasn't the rationing but the wage freezes. The bigger store chains—Safeway, A&P, and Tradewell—were under the freeze, but the independents weren't affected. They could raise their wages anytime they felt like it, and you'd better believe they did, too. That way they could hire the best people away from the chains.

"And we were fighting the shipyards and aircraft plants and other defense projects for employees, too. That didn't leave us much to work with. When the war started, I had a young fellow working for me and he was good at his job. But he quit and went to work in a shipyard, and I didn't blame him. Then he would come in and cash his check and rub it in that he was making so much more money than I was. Of course, he was working seven days a week, and some overtime, but I was stuck because of the deferment. If I quit to work in defense, I was afraid they would snatch me for the draft.

"I had to hire young single girls as helpers, girls who were just out of school trying to pick up some extra money. Why they ever went to work at the store is beyond me because they could have made so much more money in defense plants. I would have preferred hiring men, but about ninety percent of the men available were goddamned dehorns, winos, and you never knew when they were going to show up for work.

"I had a hell of a time with the girls working for me. They just didn't work out. They were a pain in the ass. They could never learn the cuts, and I ended up doing everything in the place. It isn't that I don't like women; don't try to hang that on me. I just don't like them in a butcher shop.

"There was a hell of a lot of hanky-pank going on, too, with those young gals. Not that I was ever lucky enough to get in on any of the action, but just in the store alone I could see a lot of it going on. If their husband or boy friend was in the service, just being free, white, and eighteen meant there were no holds barred for a lot of them.

"There were a lot of small markets that didn't pay a lot of attention to ration stamps, and if you went in with the money you could get anything you wanted. Then about a year later they'd be raked over the coals for not having enough red points to cover their sales. I never heard of anything serious being done to them. A slap on the wrist and back to work.

"Sure, I worked that way some myself. I had to take care of my good customers, and there were ways to stretch meat to cover your shortage of points, to juggle things around to come out even. I was accused of being a little liberal with the red points by my supervisors, but as long as I made money they didn't really care. And I did make money for them. I think they had to get a little concerned once in a while to show their authority, but I never heard of a butcher getting fired for coming up short on ration points.

"Turkey and mutton were never rationed, and I had turkey gizzards, turkey liver, turkey hearts running out of my ears. I used to have enough to fill the display case. Couldn't give them away. The same with mutton; I sold very little of that—people just didn't know how to cook it. A friend came back from the service after being stationed in Australia, and when he walked into the house that night, he sniffed the air and said, 'Jesus Christ, don't tell me you've got goat for dinner!' He had been eating mutton about eighteen months and didn't want to touch it again. My wife had a nice roast in the oven and you've never seen an unhappier woman in your life.

"Just before the war ended I went into the buying end of the business, and by this time almost everything was on a black-market basis. If you operated on a strictly legitimate basis, you had a hell of a time buying meat. The packers had a little system that got you the meat, and it worked like this:

"You'd see a nice beef hanging in the cooler and the packing guy would say, 'I'll bet you twenty bucks that thing weighs five hundred pounds.' And you'd say, 'I'll bet you twenty bucks it weighs only two hundred pounds,' and you'd know damned well it weighed five hundred. So you'd lose your twenty bucks, then pay him the going rate for the beef and get the meat. He pocketed the money and everyone was happy. My company didn't know about this little payoff system because they were pretty straight."

Some offenders were caught and punished, although it usually was a loss of privileges rather than jail terms or heavy fines. One who was caught tells how he managed to keep driving his car in spite of having no gasoline ration stamps:

"I was working at a shipyard and hoping to be a reporter when the war ended, so I got a job writing bowling news for a local paper. A professional bowler named Paul Krumske came through from Chicago on a tour of the country, and I got the job of hauling him around and doing promotion for him. I think the real reason I was chosen was because I was one of the few single men around with a car and ration stamps for gasoline. Whatever, I wanted to make a good impression on the paper and took the job.

"We were about halfway through the tour, and out in a small town, when I blew out a tire. I called the local OPA office and told them I needed a tire. I told them the truth, too. Apparently there was a bowling fan in the office, because I got permission to buy the tire and we went on our way.

"But when the papers were sent to my hometown ration board, I got a notice to go down and see them. When I got there I saw all those stern visages around a table and knew I was in trouble. They wanted to know the details of the trip and how important it was to the war effort. The upshot of it was that they took away my gas coupons. No more coupons at all. Ever. Period.

"But they didn't take away my book. They must have forgotten it.

"So I worked out a gimmick. It didn't work every time, but I had a pretty good percentage, and was able to keep using my car until the war ended.

"I'd go to a station and order a couple of dollars' worth of gas or some other even amount. I'd have the change in my hand and the gas coupons visible. I'd strike up a conversation with the gas station attendant while he was putting the gas in, then get in the car with the motor running. Then I'd hand him the money, keep the coupons and, still talking, drive off. It worked more often than not. If he yelled at me, I'd act real dumb and embarrassed about it and fork over the coupons.

"I made the last of my coupons stretch me through to the end of the war. I don't know how patriotic it was, but I wanted to drive my car."

Gasoline rationing took its toll on vehicles, too, especially when fuel had been cached away carelessly.

"We lived on a farm, and if we went anywhere we had to use tractor gas. One time we were going to a box social and didn't have enough gas for the car. My cousins had hidden some in an old culvert. They filled the tank of our car and we took off.

"But we didn't get back. Water had seeped into the can and it almost ruined my father's car. All through the war he had to take it in once in a while to have it worked on because of that. He says to this day that his great contribution to the war effort was having to live with that car."

Liquor was another hard-to-come-by item that stretched the ingenuity of drinkers, sometimes pathetically when the drinker happened to be an alcoholic.

"We were restricted to three bottles a week, if I remember right, and a fellow I worked with was a heavy drinker and couldn't get through the week on three fifths. It would just kill him to drink beer between times.

"One evening he stopped at the liquor store and had all the liquor he was allotted in a paper bag when he stopped in the tavern where we all hung out. He sat down beside me and had the liquor in his lap. There was a brass rail at our feet, and after a few beers he got a little careless, dropped the bag, and it hit the brass rail. Every bottle in the bag broke.

"I thought he was going to die of heart failure. But he picked up the bag with all the broken glass and asked the bartender for something to dump it in. The bartender handed him a metal wastebasket, the same one he used to dump ashtrays in. My friend dumped the whole thing in the wastebasket and gave it back to the bartender.

"Then he got to thinking. He called the bartender over again and asked for an empty whiskey or wine bottle. He got the wastebasket, whipped a handkerchief out of his pocket, and made a funnel out of a piece of cardboard. He got another guy to hold the bottle while he poured this booze with all the cigarette ashes and butts. He kept stirring it with his finger and letting it slowly strain and drip into the bottle.

"Oh, man, was it murky and sickening. But he took it home with him, and said later he kept straining it until it got a pretty good color again. He was able to save one of the fifths that way. But it must have tasted fierce!"

A member of Merrill's Marauders was brought out of the jungles of northern Assam, more dead than alive.

"Man," said a hospital attendant, "it must have been hell in there."

"If you think where I've been was rough," the fever-wracked soldier said, "you should have been on Tennessee maneuvers."

A little moron was going to be drafted and he held out his hands, one palm up and the other down.

"You can't draft me," he said. "My hands don't match."

6

Defending the Home Front

V-Mail

Letter No. 55

DEAREST SNOOKIE-PUTS:

I started off in a colossally high mood 'cause I got another letter from you today—and Gabriel Heatter just came on and I'm scared stiff. There's a huge battle in the Solomons area, and Japan is putting out what even I know are impossible claims, but it's frightening. This is one of those *major* battles—oh darling, God keep you safe! I'm working and praying for us both, and I know you will be guided to protect yourself, and to guide and assist your men.

There's a sweeping order out about the draft. Dependency is no longer to be the basis, as they want men with dependents in war work, and the ones who don't want war work can get out and fight! The order in general says any man regardless of his dependents who is not in a war-essential industry by April 1 is classed in 1-A, and inducted within a month.

It's all over in Stalingrad—just *think* of *that*—one-third of a *million* of Germany's best fighters went into that campaign, and straggling hordes are left—all of whom have surrendered! That to me is the most encouraging thing that has happened yet in the war. We're *winning*, honey—we're *winning!* It's only a matter of time before Germany is out of Russia, out of Africa, and attacked in France. Days, months, years—but we're *winning!* The reports on your sector are not clear yet, and I'm praying my heart out—they just said there are Jap cruisers and planes 500 miles off the Solomons, they *think*—oh Lord! I have a huge map mounted on the wall by my desk and by measuring with my architect's scale (ruler to me) 500 miles isn't very far. I *wish* I knew where you were, and I wish you were where the scuttlebutt said you were, but I'm afraid it's closer to the combat zone than that. Oh, Al—you *must* keep yourself well for me— you're my *life!* I dream of you and me when you come home, and do my best to learn things now—collect recipes, etc. I bought some 100% wool (last in St. Louis) for a suit so I'd look sharp when you come home.

All my love,

B y MAY 1945 the war was virtually over. Germany surrendered on May 2, and American B-29s were raining
bombs on Japanese cities in the most massive bombing raids
in the history of warfare. The last Japanese troops had been
defeated in Southeast Asia and it seemed only a matter of
weeks before the Allied forces would be transported the 325
miles from Okinawa for amphibious landings on the Japanese islands. The enemy was cornered, waiting. The atomic
bombs that would be dropped in August were still being assembled. Japanese civilians, including the bedridden, were
put to work building various defense devices for the invasion
that all but the most blindly fanatic expected.

For most Americans the war was already consigned to
history. The V-E Day celebrations across the country had
given the remainder of the war an anticlimactic mood. The
defense industry was already being shifted to a peacetime
economy, and many plants were closing down. Men and
women who had been courted for jobs now found themselves
out on the street with an uncertain future.

The previous four years had been so intense that the
thought of the war ending was strange. We had become accustomed to the war and we viewed the coming peace with
apprehension. The labor market would be flooded with the
returning veterans, and there were ominous predictions that
peace would bring an economic collapse even worse than the
Wall Street crash of 1929. Reports of trouble with Russia
filtered down to us, and some hoped, secretly of course, that
we would whip the Japs, then take on the Russians, in part
because we felt invincible and had no patience with an ungrateful nation, and in part because it would guarantee the
continuance of the wartime economy.

Women wondered how their marriages, either existing
or planned, would hold up under more normal circumstances,

and parents worried that their sons would be strangers when they returned from the horrors of war. Some sociologists predicted that the returning soldiers, every one a trained and experienced killer, would create a major crime wave in America.

But on Saturday, May 5, 1945, a tragedy occurred in southern Oregon which reminded the few who knew of it that the war was by no means over, and that our country was not immune to attack even though the enemy was thousands of miles away and was unlikely to set foot on our shores at this late date. Nobody doubted that the Japanese were fanatic enough to launch another Pearl Harbor if they had the resources. So much secrecy was connected with the war effort that civilians knew nothing beyond the certainty that almost anything could be expected.

On that spring morning the Reverend Archie Mitchell and his wife, Elsye, were preparing for a fishing trip and picnic in the mountains behind the small town of Bly, just north of the California border, where they had been sent only two weeks earlier by the Christian and Missionary Church. He was in his early thirties and Elsye was twenty-six, five months pregnant with their first child. It hadn't been an easy pregnancy. The previous day she had written her sister that she felt good for a change and that her husband had asked her to go on the outing with four boys and a girl from the church. "But since I'm still pretty weak I won't be able to keep up with a bunch of boys," she wrote. "One of the boys . . . Dick Patzke, couldn't understand why I was sick so much. He was telling me all kinds of things to take and I just laughed up my sleeve. He is almost fifteen. I just about up and told him but thought I wouldn't. He'll find out some day. . . ."

When Saturday turned out to be a pleasant and warm day, she changed her mind and joined the group, which included Dick Patzke and his sister, Joan, thirteen; Guy Gifford, thirteen; Edward Engen, thirteen; and Sherman Shoemaker, eleven. They climbed into Mitchell's 1939 sedan with fishing gear and picnic lunches, including a cake Mrs. Mitchell had baked for the occasion, and drove up a Forest Service road toward Gerhart Mountain. Near a small stream they found the road blocked. A Forest Service road grader had slid into the ditch and three Forest Service employees were trying to pull it out with a pickup. They told the Mitchell party the stream was too muddy for fishing, and that the road beyond was impassible, anyway. Reverend Mitchell decided to stop where they were for the picnic, and everybody got out of the car so he could back it off the road. Mrs. Mitchell said she was feeling a bit carsick and she went with the children down to the stream while he moved the car. He got in and was backing up when he heard his wife call to him twice to come down and see what they had found.

He stopped and just as he got out, he heard a terrible explosion. He and the three Forest Service employees ran down the bank and found all the children dead, and Mrs. Mitchell barely living, her clothes on fire. Mitchell burned his hands severely trying to beat out the flames, but she died a few minutes later.

The bodies were lying near a hole about three feet across and a foot deep. Hanging from tree branches and underbrush were bits and pieces of rain-soaked and mildewed Japanese paper and string. On the ground were pieces of shrapnel, an unexploded incendiary bomb, a small demolition charge, and various pieces of metal rings and clips.

The six were the only victims of enemy bombing in the United States. Their deaths went unnoticed, except locally, because the government feared the public would panic if told the Japanese had a weapon potentially as dangerous as the Germans' V-2 rockets that had been sent against England. Also, the government didn't want the Japanese to know they had been successful in at least one balloon bomb, and nobody knew how many had been sent against us. It was a new wrinkle in our defense strategy. Nobody in this country knew if they were launched from submarines operating offshore, or if they drifted all the way from Japan. Nobody knew how many we could expect to find or how accurate and dependable these flimsy-appearing weapons really were.

The balloon bombs were ingenious. They were inexpensive to build and as easy to launch and as random in target selection as dandelion seeds. The Japanese had high hopes for them. They expected them to have a demoralizing effect on Americans. However, very few landed in North America, and most of those that did failed to explode on contact with the earth.

The British had experimented with balloons as a vehicle for delivering bombs, but abandoned the idea because wind currents were so unpredictable. But the Japanese had an advantage over the British: They had studied and mapped the wind currents and were the first nation to find the swift westerly winds of the jet stream at the 30,000-foot level. They experimented with several types of balloons and instruments, and designed a special gas-relief valve to compensate for extremes in temperature caused by the sun and varying altitudes.

The first group of balloons designed to carry bombs to America were made of rubber. About 300 of these were constructed, and about thirty were launched before a fire, presumably from a B-29 raid, destroyed the factory where they were built.

Then a research team discovered that paper balloons performed best, and were simpler and cheaper to build. The design they settled on called for balloons ten meters (32.8 feet) in diameter. They were lighter than rubber, easier to launch, and carried a bigger payload. They were constructed of laminated tissue paper made from the kozo bush, a relative of mulberry. Each balloon was made of some 600 separate pieces of paper and coated with the traditional Japanese waterproofing lacquer made of the fermented juice of green persimmons.

The armament mechanism was quite complicated—perhaps too complicated—and designed to kill with the first bomb; start fires with the second, an incendiary bomb; then self-destruct with the third bomb. More than 9000 were launched between November 1944 and April 1945. Only about 340 were recovered in North America. They landed all over the western part of the continent and as far inland as Manitoba, Nebraska, Texas, and Michigan. Some were found as far north as the Yukon Territory and Alaska, and down in Sonora, Mexico. Presumably many more are still lying in the forests of the three countries, still armed.

The experiment did not work, and American morale was unaffected. Only a handful of Americans have ever known about the bombs because of wartime secrecy and peacetime disinterest. But there were other incidents throughout the war with Japan that the government couldn't keep secret because bombardment of coastal cities was too much of a spectator sport to hide from the public. Since no lives were lost and damage was minimal in each case, the attacks only confirmed Americans' attitude of invulnerability to attack and our low opinion of the Japanese as a threat to our nation.

When the Pacific war opened with the attack on Pearl Harbor, the Japanese had nine submarines lying in wait off the West Coast, stationed from the Strait of Juan de Fuca on the north to San Diego on the south. One sub spotted the *Cynthia Olsen*, a 2140-ton freighter, a few minutes before the Pearl Harbor attack was to begin. The submarine skipper obeyed his strict orders to launch no torpedoes until the exact minute of the Pearl Harbor strike. Then he sank her and her load of lumber.

Three days later the Matson liner *Mauna Loa*, laden with Christmas turkeys for Hawaii, was ordered back to port. In the run for safety she ran aground off the Columbia River and most of the turkeys washed ashore, bringing Christmas dinner to beachcombers.

Then on December 20, the tanker S.S. *Emido* was running empty between Seattle and San Pedro when a Japanese submarine attacked her off Cape Mendocino, California. Five of the six shells struck the ship, and the crew abandoned her. The tanker didn't sink and eventually drifted northward onto the rocks off Crescent City, California.

Four days later, on Christmas Eve, a B-25 patrol bomber attacked one of the subs off the Columbia River bar, but failed to sink it. Interestingly, the B-25 was one of those chosen for General Jimmy Doolittle's daring raid on Tokyo, a primarily psychological raid to show Japan it wasn't invulnerable to attack, either.

After the nine submarines ran low on ammunition and stores, they returned to Japan and things were quiet on the West Coast until the evening of February 23, 1942, when a submarine returned and fired twenty-nine shots at the Signal Oil & Gas Complex at Goleta, California. Damage was minimal and assessed at only $500: a damaged shed, catwalk, and walls peppered with shrapnel. Long after the war an interesting footnote to this raid was discovered in Japanese records. The commander of the submarine had called on the Goleta complex before the war as the captain of a merchant vessel. While he was being escorted through the refinery, he slipped and fell off a pathway and sat down on a prickly pear, a painful and humiliating experience. Historians speculated he attacked Goleta as an act of revenge to restore face lost in the fall.

The night after the Goleta raid, February 24, 1942, brought one of the war's most embarrassing moments. Suddenly, with no command from anyone, the sky over Los Angeles erupted into an inferno of antiaircraft fire as intense as that faced by Allied bomber pilots over Germany. When the firing finally stopped, 1440 rounds of ammunition had been fired. At nothing. The unofficial but widely accepted explanation was that a "green outfit was firing at its own searchlight beacons." America had a very itchy trigger finger.

These attacks, both real and imagined, brought the civilians into the defense mechanism along the coasts. While block wardens, aircraft spotters, air-raid wardens, and drills were common throughout the country, the efforts were doubled along the coasts. Camouflage became an art form, and defense plants were so cunningly concealed that, from the air, factories looked like suburban housing projects or downtown business districts, complete with lampposts, barber poles, and trees.

Harold Chriswell, a Forest Service ranger stationed in the Olympic Mountains of Washington, remembers those years with a mixture of exasperation at the military mind and admiration for the civilians who worked for him.

"I still don't know what was going on in the rest of the world at that time. I was just a forest ranger trying to keep about fifty aircraft warning stations going twenty-four hours a day.

"The army would put a finger on a map and tell us to put a station there. Sometimes they picked peaks that were impossible to climb and still expected us to plant a cabin and two civilians in it. So we would have to scout around and find an alternative for the army to consider. We were able to use many of our existing fire lookout towers, most of which were used only in summer months. It was our job to winterize them for the hard winters at high altitudes. We had to put double walls on them, haul in a supply of wood and grub and whatever else would be needed for the winter.

"It was a struggle. The main problem was getting anyone between the ages of sixteen and seventy. The others were already at work in the shipyards where the pay was good, or in the service. We fought fires and manned the lookout stations with everything from sixteen-year-old kids to old men. Occasionally we got lucky and found a good 4-F. My lead man had asthma so bad none of the services would take him, and he was a lifesaver to me.

"The kids were absolutely marvelous. I couldn't believe that boys that young could do the job they did. Not only were they good workers, they were tireless. They'd come in from a tough day in the woods, dog-tired and starved. After they got some food in them, they were raring to go again and played roughhouse football on gravel roads."

The aircraft lookouts were spotted all along the coast and inland a few miles as a second line of defense. They were manned during the first few years of the war, and the personnel were constantly reminded of the importance of their duties, even though not one saw an enemy plane during those years atop the peaks in the lonely cabins that roared and swayed in the storms, and were often struck by lightning.

"The people who went into that kind of work had to be dedicated," Harold Chriswell continued:

"They were away from home over long periods of time, stuck alone on a mountaintop. They had to really believe in what they were doing. Some even sold their homes so they wouldn't be encumbered. Most were getting on towards elderly and they were doing a job for their country, and not a well-paying job at that. There were a lot of man-and-wife combinations, and they took turns staying up all night to keep a watch.

"We hired a relief crew that went from lookout to lookout, giving the others a week off at a time. They usually took a pack train in with grub and other necessities, and the crew being relieved brought the horses and mules back out with them. Everyone had training in identifying enemy planes as well as our own, but they were supposed to call in all planes they spotted to a central exchange. Our communications equipment early in the war was pure junk. But somebody managed to patch together a telephone apparatus to all the lookouts that wasn't much more than sophisticated tin cans and pieces of string.

"We couldn't build cabins on a lot of peaks the army wanted manned. We just couldn't get the material up there without a helicopter, and I don't think they were even in use then. The best we could do in some places was pitch a tent at a lower elevation, then have the lookout climb up with his little firefinder and binoculars. On one of those sharp peaks we had a length of Number 9 telephone wire strung up to the summit for the lookout to pull himself up on.

"On that particular peak we finally got a wall tent at the summit, then started building a cabin. I hired a carpenter, but he didn't know what he was doing so I fired him and got another one. I hired a packer to haul the lumber up, but the material never arrived. He was an experienced packer and I couldn't figure out what was going on. Finally I caught him. He was using his pack string to haul out illegal elk meat. And it was a government-owned pack string at that.

"When October came I still had a crew of kids working up there trying to finish it before winter. One weekend the kids took off to town, but the cook, an older man, wanted no part of that trip to town. It was too far for him to walk, he said, because they had to hike several miles to the railroad, then take a handcar about ten more miles, then load onto a truck and ride nearly forty miles on into town. The cook knew what he was doing and said he wasn't budging from that mountain until snow fell.

"When the kids got back that Sunday night, they couldn't find the cook. They looked all around the area, shouting for him, and no cook. They called me on the phone and I told them to keep looking because he had to be there. I told them to work in ever-widening circles, to crawl between boulders or whatever, but to find him.

"They found him all right. He was dead. He had fallen off the lookout and fell right in a yellow jackets' nest.

"Remember, these were just kids. Finding his body scared the wits out of them. They panicked and ran all the way back down to the railroad, pumped the handcar back to the truck, and came to town. Three of us had to go up and bring out his body. He had fallen off the opposite side of the mountain from the trail. It appeared he had just walked out in the evening to look around or something. They had been blasting the top off the peak to build the cabin and left some loose rocks and dust. He probably slipped on that and went over.

"We didn't know how to get him out, so we finally wrapped him in canvas and tied a rope around him, then hung a block and tackle from a tree above. Then we tied the rope to a saddle horn and took it down the trail like we were yarding logs. Winter was pretty close, so we just shut down the project until the next spring.

"We naturally had a lot of false alarms. After sitting up there for months without seeing much of anything, you want to see something so badly you create it in your imagination. Occasionally the army sent P-38s down the canyons, trying to sneak up on the lookouts, but once they sent a group out for a strange report. A lookout said he had spotted a barrage balloon that escaped. The army had no reports of wandering balloons, but the lookout was stubborn about it. They sent the P-38s up and they saw nothing. 'I can see it with my glasses,' he insisted.

"Finally, two days later, a captain and I drove out and hiked in to the lookout to see what he was talking about. He had found Venus. On really clear days Venus could be seen with the naked eye in daylight. Mystery solved.

"People saw Japs everywhere. An army colonel came into camp once in one of those little command cars with a canvas top and side curtains and said he and his driver were investigating a strange report. Some guy living up there said he saw a strip of trees pointing directly toward the Bramerton Navy Yard. He figured that some spy had left that strip standing as an arrow for the Japanese when they invaded America. The spy would set it afire. Hard to believe, but people were pretty nervous in those years."

Fear of spies, "fifth columnists," and of giving accidental aid to the enemy was common during those years of threat. Rumors of cornfields planted so that the rows pointed toward military targets were in continual circulation, and nervous citizens were prone to finding enemy aids wherever they looked for them.

In addition to the lookouts scattered along the West Coast, and concrete bunkers planted on cliffs overlooking the coastline for shore batteries, the Coast Guard was called in to patrol the coastline itself. On foot. Beach patrols were established to watch for secret landings, such as those attempted in Maine and on Long Island. It was almost an exercise in futility; if Americans couldn't navigate the remote beaches and headlands, how could an enemy force land on the rugged and miserable shore to establish a beachhead? From their vantage point of offices in the cities, planners assumed an enemy could land anywhere it wanted, and even those who knew how difficult it would be to launch an attack from such places preferred to take no risks.

The Coast Guard was under orders to patrol the coastline on foot, horseback, or however else possible to keep the coast under surveillance. Some stretches of coastline, particularly California, had been settled with a string of towns along busy coastline roads. But the remote Oregon headlands and the entire Olympic Peninsula in Washington were another matter. That was, and still is, a roadless jungle in a temperate zone with an annual rainfall of more than 200 inches, dense underbrush, and rocky headlands impassable except on foot.

Some hardheads insisted mules could navigate anything, including the rain forests. But when a colonel went in with ten pack mules and emerged several days later with his clothing in shreds and only one mule still alive, the military came to the conclusion that only men on foot carrying backpacks could negotiate the rougher sections of the coast.

In the areas with miles and miles of unbroken sand, the Coast Guard rode horses that were shipped out from the Midwest. But, like their backpacking counterparts, they found nothing to report other than an occasionally grisly piece of flotsam washed up on the beach from sunken ships, and their routine was broken only by the infrequent rescue they helped perform.

One piece of driftwood frequently found by patrols intrigued the military leaders, and gave them some hope that their enemy in the Pacific was a little silly. Japanese submarines used a diversionary tactic that could have raised havoc had it worked. But, as with the fire balloons, the vastness of North America worked against the plan. Submarine crews built false periscopes by tying a stone on one end of a stick to hold it upright in the water. On the other end they affixed a small mirror that was supposed to resemble a periscope when the sunlight reflected off it. Large numbers of these phony periscopes were tossed into the ocean just offshore, but there are no recorded incidents of planes bombing them or shore batteries firing on them.

One shore battery, however, had its hands full on the evening of Sunday, June 21, 1942. It happened at Battery Russell, part of the Fort Stevens complex at the mouth of the Columbia River in Oregon. The gun station was equipped with obsolete ten-inch disappearing rifles, which were designed for warfare in 1900, before the world had to contend with airplanes and submarines. In order to keep a low profile from enemy guns, the rifles were designed so that the recoil of each shot drove the gun backward and down out of sight, where it was locked while it was cleaned and reloaded. Then it was raised back up again into firing position.

The ten-inchers had their drawbacks. In addition to their Rube Goldbergish raising and lowering, their range was only slightly more than 16,000 yards. At Battery Russell they lost several of those precious yards because the guns were installed inland behind the first set of dunes. The shallow surf ahead of them kept vessels at almost the full 16,000 yards.

On that evening one of those cruising Japanese subs, the I-25, surfaced about 20,000 yards offshore and leisurely fired seventeen rounds onto the land, "walking" them up and down the beach, seeking the battery and trying to attract its fire so a definite target could be found. Wisely, the commander of the battery refused to give the order to fire. There was one tense moment when a soldier forgot his orders and turned on the headlights of a truck, but he was well away from the battery and no damage was done.

"There was no reason to fire—to give our position away," said Colonel Carl S. Doney, the commanding officer. "We had tracked them all the time and they were from five hundred to a thousand yards out of our maximum range. A big flash from shore would have given them a pinpoint and would have been absolutely useless."

Max Shafer, a newspaper editor from the nearby resort community of Seaside remembered the aftermath of the shelling as almost a festive occasion, especially since nobody was hurt (except for a few bruises among soldiers manning the guns who stumbled around in the blackout, bumping into each other and walls).

"My God, if the Japanese had wanted to take the coast, all they had to do was walk ashore and say it was theirs.

There was so much confusion that they could have been over the Coast Range and in the Willamette Valley before we knew what happened.

"But I'll give the battery people credit for holding their fire. The only way they could have hit that sub was for it to run aground right in front of them, or skip the shells out like a flat rock.

"That was all there was to it. The sub fired into the sand dunes. The battery people laid low. The sub went away. Period.

"But the next morning when the story hit the Portland newspapers, people began driving down to the beach in droves to look at the battlefield. There wasn't much to see. Nearly all the shells exploded in the sand and left little potholes that the first breeze or rain shower would fill.

"Then a bunch of local kids got an idea. They found an old cast-iron stove and broke it up into little pieces with a sledgehammer and took the pieces out on the highway and sold it as Japanese shrapnel. I'll bet there are still people with chunks of that old stove lying around that they show people as war souvenirs. That's what I call war profiteering."

When the war ended and the two former enemies exchanged information, it was found that these attacks, and those that followed, were in retaliation for the Doolittle raid on Tokyo in April 1942.

After firing on Battery Russell, the I-25 returned to Japan for yard work in Yokosuka. While there, the former vice-consul to Seattle went aboard to brief the crew on the next mission, which was to drop bombs in the dense and vast Northwest forests and start forest fires. A Zero-type reconnaissance plane was put aboard in a deck hangar, and the sub departed again for America.

In September 1942 the sub was back in U.S. waters,

and on September 9 the plane was catapulted off on its first mission. The pilot flew east under cover of darkness and dropped two incendiary bombs in the forest a few miles east of Brookings, Oregon, just north of the California border. Fires were started, but Forest Service crews put them out before they spread, and nobody knew they were started by the Japanese.

The I-25 lay offshore a few more days and patrolled the coast until September 29, when the plane was launched again off Cape Blanco, north of Brookings. Two more bombs were dropped east of Port Oxford, but no fire resulted. No more attempts were made. The I-25 headed back to Japan and never returned to America.

German submarines had been operating in American coastal waters along the Atlantic seaboard since before the war really began for America. The U-boats had been picking off British freighters with distressing regularity, and people who lived on the beaches soon became accustomed to finding bits and pieces of ships, cargo—and bodies—washed up after the sinkings. Some military and civilian defense officials had begged for months to institute blackouts along the East Coast because the city lights, visible for miles and miles at sea, served as a lighted backdrop for the German submarines while searching for ships to attack. The most difficult city to darken was Miami, a resort capital that depended on its night life for its income. But after several sinkings just off the beach, the city at last agreed to darken itself at night to save lives of seamen.

Apparently the Japanese made no efforts to put spies ashore on the West Coast—their racial characteristics would have made them easy targets for anyone. But the Germans did succeed in putting spies ashore in rubber rafts launched from submarines off Long Island and Maine. All these spies and saboteurs were caught eventually in New York City where they bungled their assignments, argued among themselves, and made a mess of things in general.

The American public wasn't too aware of these things due to a shroud of secrecy thrown over the captures by the FBI and military leaders. But some information leaked out about the spies who landed on Long Island, enough to convince the East Coast that it was being flooded with "fifth columnists," and since more German immigrants settled on that coast than other parts of the nation, the fears did not make life more comfortable for those who simply wanted to live their lives in peace.

Not all such immigrants were dedicated Americans, of course. A Long Island resident tells of one such case:

"We had some neighbors of German heritage, one born over there and the other in this country. We were at their house one night playing pinochle when a B-17 flew overhead. One of them looked up and shook his fist at the sky and shouted: 'Ach! What is the matter with Goering? Vere is the secret weapons? Dose are de ones that are bombing our homeland. Vhy don't they do zomething about it?'

"That was the last time we spoke to them. I still don't know why they weren't rounded up with the other Germans and Italians who were Axis sympathizers."

Inevitably the blackouts and dimouts and other civil-defense operations brought out the eccentrics:

John Chapman recalls: "I was going to an Ivy League school during the war and we had a very well-known professor of Far Eastern history and philosophy on campus, who was also a little strange. I won't tell you his name, but, for the sake of the story, let's call him Markham Philip Law. He had gone to school in the Far East, and had even studied to be a

Buddhist monk in India, which was pretty unusual in those days.

"We were having a blackout drill and the school's security police were making the rounds to see that everything was zipped up tight and dark, and they saw a light in the window of an apartment on the top floor, just glaring out into the darkness. Not a shade pulled.

"They trudged up the stairs and knocked on the door. No answer. They pounded on it and still no answer. They had a brief consultation and decided they were going in even if they had to kick the door in. The country was at war, wasn't it?

"They tried the door and it was unlocked. They walked in and stopped dead in their tracks. Seated on the dining-room table in the classic lotus position and apparently in a trance was the professor. Stark naked. Not a stitch on.

" 'Jesus Christ,' one muttered.

The professor opened one eye and raised one finger and wagged it. 'No,' he said. 'Not Jesus Christ. Markham Philip Law.' "

And they led to rather grim jokes:

"They used to tell the story about a couple awakened by the air-raid siren. While they were dashing to the air-raid shelter, the husband was pulling on his pants with his suspenders trailing on the ground behind him. His wife stepped on them and they snapped and hit him in the back of his head.

"He sank to the floor saying, 'You go ahead, Martha, I've had a direct hit.' "

For the most part, however, Americans were very serious about the threat of invasion. Rosair Earley remembers:

"The block warden in our area owned a hardware store and he was very serious about his job, very efficient. He came in frequently to check and be sure our store was stocked with the things we were supposed to have, such as buckets of sand and so forth. He came around every night during the blackouts right after Pearl Harbor to be sure we were concealing all the light.

"We had a flat roof and I don't know how many times a night he climbed up there on his patrols because he was convinced we were going to be bombed. Nobody bucked him, because we were afraid of the Japs, and when he told us to get something, we got it.

"But later in the war the fear wore off and finally even he gave up on spotting the Japanese fleet offshore."

Truth, the philosopher said, is the first casualty of war, and, as correspondent for a wire service in the wilds of the territory of Alaska, Fred Ross learned quickly that information, no matter how trivial, can be great cause for alarm in military circles.

"I was in Sitka, Alaska, when the war started, working as assistant paymaster for the contractor building the airfield up there. When the war started, I went over to the navy base and told them I was the United Press correspondent and asked what kind of credentials I needed. The main thing they told me was that all news releases had to be cleared through the office before I sent them outside. That was fine with me.

"A few days later I heard that a little patrol plane from Sitka had spotted a sub, dropped a depth charge, and scored a direct hit on a whale. I thought that was pretty funny so I wrote it up and took it over to the navy office and gave it to a lieutenant. Pretty soon he rushed out of the base commander's office and said, 'Oh, no, you can't send that!' I said okay and went back to work.

"Pretty soon the commander came down to the boss's office and they called me in and started jumping on me and accused me of trying to send stuff that shouldn't go out. I denied it and didn't get anywhere. The commander said only the Associated Press was accredited on the island and not United Press. They both were pretty hot about it, and finally the commander said that a man couldn't keep his mind on two jobs at the same time, and my boss seemed to agree. I told them not to worry; since it was obvious I was going to be fired, I was going outside on the next boat to enlist.

"I went back to work, and pretty soon the head of naval security came in and told me that he hated to do it but he had orders to run me off the island. I went. Right away.

"When I got over to Juneau, I wrote the whole thing up again, with an explanation of what had happened to me, and mailed the whole thing to United Press, with particular emphasis on the part about the Associated Press being the only recognized news agency in Sitka. To put it mildly, they were a little upset over that, and they went straight to the Thirteenth Naval District and accused the Sitka commander of showing partiality in giving out the news.

"A few years later I ran into the pilot who had dropped the depth charge. He was one of those early bush pilots who went to Alaska in the early 1930s, and a hell of a nice guy. I still see him once in a while. Anyway, he told me he thought sure he had a sub until he saw blood and fins rising to the surface, then shouted on the radio, 'Belay that!' But it was too late.

"But the punch line on the whole thing is that the station commander who threw me out of Sitka also got himself thrown out of Russia after the war, and after he became an admiral. He was, then, Commander Jackson Tate, who got a lot of publicity when his Russian daughter came over to this country in 1975."

The war was brought close to home all over the country, not only through fear of invasions along the coasts but inland where armies marched, where war planes flew overhead (and sometimes crashed in towns and fields), where troop and hospital trains wailed through the nights. In a few select parts of the country, entire states were declared war zones while troops were trained in simulated battle conditions.

The state of Tennessee was declared a war zone with its own Army Post Office (APO) number. They sent entire armies there to practice for the invasion of France, while bomber crews peppered the Mohave Desert, eastern Colorado, the Texas Panhandle. Mountain troops destined for the Alps trained in Colorado and West Virginia, and there probably weren't more than a handful of states that didn't have some kind of military maneuvers conducted in them during those four years.

The civilian population enjoyed the war games played in their backyards and down Main Street. It was exciting after the long drought of the Depression, and it gave them the sense of participation in the war, a vital element that has since been lacking in selling a war to the public.

This was especially true in Tennessee, where preparations for the invasion of Europe were under way. Gene Sloan, a schoolteacher and part-time journalist, saw more of the maneuvers than most civilians:

"I spent three summers and one Christmas season as a correspondent for the Lebanon, Tennessee, *Banner* covering the maneuvers all over Tennessee, and sometimes I'd go out with them on weekends when I wasn't busy with my job as schoolteacher. Toward the end of the war a colonel named Huller, who was a public-information officer for the Third

Army and a former International News Service correspondent, asked me to go overseas with them as a civilian correspondent, but I decided against it.

"The armies would establish a field headquarters at Cumberland University in Lebanon, virtually taking over the whole campus. I remember the Second Army used the gymnasium as a message center, and the motor pool was in the football field. The officers were billeted in the women's dormitory.

"There were two major army camps in Tennessee then: Camp Forrest near the Alabama border at Tulahoma, and Camp Campbell up on the Kentucky border. They'd usually bring in two infantry divisions and sometimes a division of tanks, and they'd split them up between the two forts. They'd divide them into armies and move out for about four weeks of a series of battle problems. One time they would work on a north-south axis with the Red army moving up from Tulahoma to meet the Blue army from Fort Campbell.

"Since it was war simulated as closely as possible, they would simply run over farmers' land, knocking down their fences and roaring right through towns and having battles on the town square. The whole state was declared a war area, and the only places off-limits were churches and cemeteries. But they moved through with no regard for fences or land.

"They did set up a board of Rents and Claims and they kept in touch with the farmers and put up the fences they'd torn down. They would compensate farmers for lost crops, and reseed their crops. Several farmers' animals were killed and lost, and towns had streets repaired from the damage of heavy vehicles. They were reasonably generous in their recompensation.

"They chose Tennessee because the terrain here was so similar to that in north France and the Rhine Valley, and some of the maneuvers were held over in West Virginia where it is even rougher. After one unit was sent overseas, I received a letter from a colonel saying that if I joined them, it would look just like the area around here. They used most of the state at one time or another, and had some maneuvers up around Nashville in the hill country.

"We were all under censorship, of course, and all our stories had to be cleared before they were turned in to our newspapers or wire services or magazines. On one occasion I had to appeal a censor's decision all the way to Washington to get the story released. It concerned a statement made several times by a Turkish officer.

"There was a group of foreign observers down for the maneuvers, and during a press conference something was said about the possibility of the Germans sending a flanking movement down through Turkey and up to relieve the Germans at the Battle of Stalingrad, which was being fought at that time.

"One of the correspondents asked the Turk what they would do in that case. 'We'd fight,' he said. Turkey had declared itself neutral, you know. That was all he said, and after a few more minutes the press conference ended. I thought I might have myself a story and followed the Turkish officer out and caught up with him at the PX.

" 'Sir,' I asked, 'you said that if the Germans moved across Turkey you would fight. Suppose that the Russians swing around and try to outflank the Germans?' 'We'd fight,' he said again.

" 'Well, what if the British or Americans sent out an expeditionary force like they did at Lafayette during World War I?'

" 'We'd fight.'

" 'You mean you will resist invasion by any army that moves in on Turkish soil?'

"Again he said, 'We'd fight.'

"I went to the PIO (Public Information Officer) and asked him to clear the story and he said he couldn't; the Turk was a neutral observer and we couldn't quote him saying something like that. So I told him I was going to appeal his decision. Washington at first wouldn't give me an okay either. I didn't give up. I asked the PIO to Teletype the story to the military attaché in the Turkish Embassy in Washington and see if they would clear it. The PIO did, and the Turkish Embassy approved the story, and it was released. That illustrates how well we correspondents were treated.

"The wire service picked up the story that night and I got a call from Reuters in Brazil asking for more information, but that was the whole story. The Turk said they'd fight anyone who came into their country, and what else could be added?

"River crossings were the most difficult problem for the army, and that is where they lost a lot of men. But they were to learn, and pretty soon they had the pontoon bridges pretty well perfected. At one time ten soldiers were drowned when their assault boat swamped in the Cumberland River. Others drowned when tanks ran off the pontoon bridges.

"I made a study of the maneuver casualties after the war was over and came up with a total of 268 soldiers and nine civilians killed during the war games. Most of the civilian deaths were from vehicular accidents, and 127 of the military deaths were from the same cause.

"Strangely, only nine were killed in the fighter planes, gliders, parachuting, observation planes, and cargo planes they brought down there. Two dozen were killed while swimming, six were killed in railroad accidents, five were struck by lightning, three from burns, and there were three murders and a few suicides. A tornado killed one, and twenty-six died from natural causes.

"I spent many hours tracking down weird reports of fatalities that were just rumor. One of the most popular rumors was 'dozens of men freezing to death.' All were untrue, but there were cases of men being found in a coma because of either the cold or booze.

"That reminds me of the cold winter day when the creeks were out of their banks and we were plodding along through rain and sleet two days before Christmas. We topped a little rise and saw a desolate scene that beggars description. From a clapboard shanty some men were bearing a coffin towards a waiting wagon that served as a hearse. I'm not sure that it was the rain that the nineteen-year-old kid wiped from his eyes while we watched the scene, but we heard his sincere statement: 'Boy, that corpse is sure a lucky devil!'

"I think nearly everybody made lifelong friends from the maneuvers. I still correspond regularly with several of the soldiers I met, and a lot of them came back to settle in Tennessee after the war. And we also estimate that the maneuvers resulted in more than 300 marriages to local girls."

Civilians pitched in to help the soldiers in a variety of ways:

"One afternoon a battalion of engineers was trying to build a bridge, and a group of teen-age girls were downstream a little ways watching the process, which wasn't working too well. One of the soldiers walked out on one of the shaky pontoons and fell in. He was swept downstream, and just as he passed the girls, one of them flipped her dress over her head and dove in after him. Her friends were squealing because she was half naked and they were afraid she'd drown, too. But the girl grabbed the soldier and kept his head above water until an assault boat was launched and sent downriver after him.

"They hauled the soldier aboard and the girl screamed something and took off for the bank. Later they asked one of the soldiers on the bank what she had said, and he told us she said, 'Take him quick.' She had forgotten she didn't have any pants on. She didn't stay around for congratulations or a medal."

* * *

The hill people didn't take kindly to the city folk assuming they were all ignorant Hatfields and McCoys:

"Some army wives followed their husbands down to Tennessee, and it was obvious that they were accustomed to getting what they wanted. They soon became very familiar around the Red Cross headquarters, where I worked, from their unusual requests.

"One day one came in and asked our receptionist how far she'd have to drive to see a real Tennessee hillbilly. The receptionist got out a map and made a tracing to Washington, D.C.

" 'I think you'll have to get out of the maneuver area to find a hillbilly,' she said. 'I suggest that you just drive up to Washington and call at the secretary of state's office. Cordell Hull, you see, is a genuine Tennessee hillbilly and proud of it.' "

Few Tennesseans enjoyed the maneuvers more than local high-school girls, who were showered with attention from the young men. Mrs. George House remembers:

"We lived in an old farmhouse that was built before Tennessee became a state and was still part of North Carolina. It had ten rooms, and each family that owned it evidently had expanded over the years, so you stepped up and you stepped down as you went from room to room.

"There were four of us in the family, two girls and two boys, and I was in high school during the war years. We had a great time. The army took over our woodlot out behind the barn and they bivouacked up there, and of course you couldn't go in or out the back of the farm without going through their sentries.

"I hadn't learned to drive yet—we couldn't get any gas

anyway—so the guys would come over to the house in a jeep and give me the key. They didn't care if I wrecked it or not. I'd go out in the field with a bunch of kids and I'd drive, and get stuck. We'd start up a hill and it'd stop. We had a sink-hole in the bottoms and everybody would get out and let me drive in and out of it and it would stall, you know? That's how I learned to drive. They'd bring all kinds of jeeps and trucks and tanks around to show us, and one time this guy said we'd seen everything on our farm except an amphibious jeep. We had a pond down by the barn, you know? He brought that amphibious jeep up and took it across the pond for us.

"They had mail call at the barn, and one day a bunch were sitting around talking, a bunch of nice country boys and a few New York guys who had never been south. This one New York guy was an artist—I can't remember his name, but mother would—and he sketched my little sister's picture, then did mine: us sitting out there in the woods. He did some of this comic-book stuff after the war and we'd see his name on them.

"They'd come down to Tennessee to fight their wars, you know? The wars between the Red and Blue armies. They'd wear red or blue stripes on their uniforms and we'd have to get off the road when they were in a battle. They looked like they were playing for real, you know? One night my friends and I and my mother made about twenty-five or thirty little cakes and we took them down to the boys and gave them all a piece of home-cooked cake and they were tickled to death. They came up to the house the next night, knocked on the door, and came in the house to talk to us, you know? And here comes the other army. We saw them coming up the road in a jeep, so we had to hide these fellows and turn out the lights so they wouldn't get captured. We had some real good times.

"Of course gas was hard to get and we were in high school and wanted enough to get to the movie on Saturday nights. So one of the boys on a farm near us said he'd furnish the chicken if we girls would cook them. I'd never cooked any chicken. His parents were gone off somewhere, so he and the other boys went over and stole some chickens from his mother, you know? And we about half-plucked them, the way kids do, and left about half of the feathers on them. And the soldiers gave us two five-gallon cans of gasoline for those chickens. They liked their fried chicken, feathers and all.

"That went on about three years, off and on. They'd come down here for like six months on maneuvers, then another group would come in. Convoys would go by and they'd throw out their names wrapped around pennies or a stick or a rock as they passed us while we were waiting for the school bus, asking us to write to them. And we did. When they'd come back this way, they'd come by or call us, but we never did go to town with any of them or have a date except to come out to our house.

"You didn't go out with servicemen. It was a kind of good time and a bad time because we didn't have any boys in our class except, you know, 4-Fs. We had about sixty kids in our high school and like seven boys graduated. So there was really nobody to date. If you didn't date somebody in the service, you didn't date. And you didn't date them, either. They were just here for a short time, see, and they didn't seem to have anything good in mind, you know? All we got was what we called three-day love affairs, which was really a big thing because they were shipped out tomorrow or the weekend and would be gone two or three years, if we ever saw them again.

"I don't know how country you are, but we had this one soldier that didn't understand about those little black pills that came from the back end of billy goats. This is really true.

And one boy from New York asked which teat we got the chocolate milk from. He was not joking. Really! Some of the other guys told him about the pills. You just can't believe that some people know so little. It really is kind of sad. And of course they'd always come down to watch us milk.

"We had an old jenny called Mae West and they always wanted to ride a horse. We had an old horse named Darlin' and they'd get on her and she wouldn't move. She'd be stubborn and just stand there. They'd get off and push and one would pull and one would be trying to ride. We had a time. We really did.

"When they would move out of the area, they would tell daddy the day before they left that they had to throw away everything, but that they were going to mark the place they buried the food. He'd go out there and there'd be sugar, coffee, bread not ever broken open, canned goods . . . everything. So we didn't really do without a whole lot. They didn't tear up much and they were real good about fixing up anything they broke, fences and things."

The adults were almost invariably kind to the young soldiers, and many competed to see who could do the most for the boys away from home preparing to go off to war.

"The maneuvers were quite an experience for all of us, and I'm sure it was for the boys, too. Murfreesboro was about eight or nine thousand at that time—it is around 35,000 now—and the town just opened its arms and doors and homes to them. And our churches. Some of the boys came here from as far away as Fort Knox and Fort Campbell because they couldn't find hotel rooms in Nashville.

"In an eating place one evening we invited some boys to come and sit at our table because the restaurant was crowded. They told us during the meal they were trying to find places to take baths, so those two young boys came to our home at our invitation and they spent every weekend they could with us. They were just part of our family. Up to a few years ago we had contact with those boys, but the last few years we've sort of lost touch. But it was quite a friendship.

"Our churches here, particularly our First Methodist Church, opened its doors to those men on maneuvers. There were hundreds and hundreds, and we served them sausage, biscuits, and coffee. And those were homemade biscuits, too. So many of those young men had never eaten one and they didn't know what southern hospitality was. We took them into our homes on Thanksgiving and on special occasions, and if they couldn't get off duty, we'd prepare them meals and carry them to them. It was real touching because so many of the boys were from Brooklyn and up in the Far East, you might say, and just hadn't experienced that.

"There were some sad experiences, too. We'd need the food that was destroyed when they left. There were so many people that could use it and that was the dumbest way of getting rid of surplus commodities. It was just one of their rules. People out in the country got the food, I understand, but not us town folk.

"On one occasion the companies were going down our main street and a beautiful home was on fire, and the fire engines couldn't get through because of the convoy. The home was just full of antiques and heirlooms, and those boys left their trucks and got that furniture out of that house. Carried the china out and didn't break a piece.

"We just tried to give them a little touch of home and let them know that people were caring for them. It was the same way all over town. People were very hospitable and understanding. It could have been annoying in a lot of ways, but we didn't take it that way. The boys were trying to do their duty, and none of us felt any inconvenience even though we were surrounded by them. You didn't know when you were going to walk out and see a huddle of them in the backyard. We just expected it."

The matter of the free food left behind by the soldiers was obviously a bone of contention between some farm and town people, but one farmer saw it as a definite benefit:

"The food they left behind for us was one of the most successful public-relations campaigns the army could undertake. They were supposed to bury it when they pulled out, but they seldom did. I can remember seeing a corncrib just filled with bread. They just backed up six truckloads of bread and dumped them into that corncrib. They'd also give coffee to people, something we couldn't get without ration stamps.

"I know it helped a lot of people because most of us were far from wealthy in those days."

Mrs. Coil Branson, a young woman who went away to school, had the military around her no matter where she went, and those four years were very special years for her.

"I attended Stevens College in Columbia, Missouri, during the war and spent the summers and vacations—most vacations anyway—back home in Murfreesboro, Tennessee. I say 'most vacations' because getting home by train was really a chore, and sometimes we stayed at school rather than sit on our suitcases two days and nights in the aisle of a crowded car. It isn't really that far from Columbia to Murfreesboro, but it took an awfully long time on trains in those days.

"Murfreesboro, as you know, was a center of the maneuvers for the army and it wasn't at all unusual to go downtown and see the two armies fighting it out in the streets, running in and out of the stores on the square, shooting blanks at each other. Or we'd go out in the backyard for something and there'd be a bunch of soldiers in a pup tent.

"We always got a big kick out of mother because she always felt sorry for the boys on maneuvers and she always fed them. If it was in the morning, she wanted to fix breakfast and take it outside to them, which she did. When we'd get up we would find soldiers all over the lawn, and sometimes we'd wake up to the rumbling of the tanks coming down one of the main streets and great long, long lines of heavy weapons and artillery.

"Murfreesboro was the scene of a famous Civil War battle, the Battle of Stone's River, and of course they were always comparing the two wars and how our town was under siege again after nearly a century. Windows shook, pictures fell off walls, and walls cracked. I imagine a lot of people didn't even put in for reimbursement for damages because that was back in the days when people didn't think too much about that. We didn't think a thing about it. We were all so grateful that it was mock warfare and that these guys were going to keep the enemy away from us.

"We lived in town, and the army never cached supplies around town like they did in the country, so we never got in on any of the free food they left behind. For years afterward, though, people out in the country would dig up sugar, lard, and lots of other things the army buried.

"The maneuvers always kept us reminded that there was a war on, and of course we knew they had loved ones somewhere worrying about them. Then sometimes when we did get acquainted with the fellows, we would invite them over to supper. Sometimes they would say they would be there and we'd never see them again. Then we'd know they got orders and had to leave, and they would write to us later. There was a lot of that.

"One time I asked this fellow and his friends to come

over. He was a good dancer and I had met him at Jefferson Barracks, near Saint Louis. He was supposed to come over and take me to the most exciting dance of the year. And he never did come. And I never heard from him. So I don't know if he got sudden orders or whether he was married and didn't want to tell me. I never did hear from him. He was such a nice fellow that I have always thought he was married. It wouldn't have made that much difference because we were so carefully guarded that we couldn't even go outside the building except to go on the porch for a breath of fresh air.

"My parents kept in touch with most of the guys we met during the war, but, since most of them were boy friends at one time or another, I just keep in touch with them through my mother. Of course my husband always has a good time teasing me and saying, 'Have the Christmas cards come from so-and-so?' Because they always tell her to say hello to me and that they love me, you know? He's a big tease, anyway, and has a great time with my old maneuver boy friends.

"When I went to Missouri to school, they really thought I talked southern and I didn't even know I was going up north to school. I thought that was a southern place. Those Brooklyn boys were something else. They loved to hear us talk, and we put on a little bit, I'm afraid. We'd really bear down and give them a good dose of that southern accent. The cook at Stevens was from Nashville and he was real cute. He would cook us black-eyed peas and things like that, you know? We just loved him for that.

"Before I started to Stevens, I worked in an airplane factory where they repaired biplanes. I worked in the office and it was one of those factories that seemed to just spring up overnight after the war started. What did they call them? I believe they were BT-something and I believe they were the Stearmans. But what a conglomeration of people we had there: fat people, old people, young people, just all walks of life working together, from the highest to the lowest. I remember one in particular I thought was old at the time and she is still working as a volunteer at the hospital and she's up in her seventies. But she was younger then than I am now. And there was one very elegant lady working in the office with me, very aristocratic, you know, but she was just as down-to-earth as anyone and friendly to all these people. We still see each other and laugh about that plant. She had been wealthy at one time.

"There were a good many men and we always wondered if they were 4-F or if they got out of the war some way. I'm afraid we weren't too sympathetic to people who tried to get out of it. A lot would tell you why they weren't in the service, but now that I'm older I don't really know if they were being honest or not. But we believed them at the time. It seemed to bother some of the men.

"We had all kinds of projects at Stevens College and went all out for the war effort. We sold war bonds—you'd be surprised how many we sold to students. Of course students now have lots of money, but we didn't have very much then. But we were very patriotic and we saved our money to buy the bonds because we thought that was one thing we could do for the war effort. When we went to school we had to hand over our ration books to the school, and of course we had lots of meatless and sugarless and different kinds of days because we felt that helped, too. The college did a good job feeding us in spite of the shortages and we never once felt deprived.

"It was a lonely, helpless feeling. We had so many friends that were fighting and lost a lot of friends. One of my schoolmates lost a fiancé, and it seemed there were a high number of girls there who lost brothers and fiancés. We hadn't been through anything like that before, so anything would have been almost too much. And we'd watch the mailboxes at the school and if we'd see one of those V-mail letters to someone we knew was waiting for a letter, we could hardly wait to get to them and tell them. Of course there were lots of telegrams, too, most of the time with bad news. They had ways of softening the blow, though. They usually told the dorm mother, and if you had a note to come and see the dorm mother, you knew something was wrong.

"My husband—my fiancé at the time—sank a Japanese destroyer and it was announced over the radio in Murfreesboro. My mother called and was so excited about it. While I was working in the dining room one night, the other girls on my floor put up all kinds of posters and signs on the outside of the dormitory saying that this was the 'Home of the Hero's Wife-to-be' and those were strung up all over the south campus."

It wasn't enough that civilians were subjected to tanks and other vehicles roaring through their farms, terrifying the milk cows and tearing down the fences. Some towns and farms were victimized by unintentional bombing attacks.

"Yeah, I bombed Turkey, Texas, and may its citizens forgive me. I was training as a bombardier in the old AT-11s, flying with this crazy lieutenant who wore cowboy boots all the time. He told me one day he'd show me how to fly below ground in Texas, and dropped that damned thing down in an arroyo. Jesus! Sure enough, we looked out and there was the ground level above us and the wingtips less than two feet from the banks. Great fun.

"So he hauled back on the wheel and almost stood it on its tail, climbed a while, then peeled off on one wing and had me bouncing all over the damned plane. We had the Norden bombsight with a toggle switch, and my leg or something must've flicked it, because one of the guys in the rear lets out a yell.

" 'Lieutenant, somebody just bombed Turkey!'

"We looked around and nobody else was flying, so it had to be us. The lieutenant asked me if we still had our bombs and I said, 'Sure—I think.' I went back and started counting: 'One, two, three, four, five.' They were all in that rack. So I started counting the other rack, and sure enough a bomb was missing. Gulp.

"It was one of the M388z bombs, eighty-five pounds of sand and fifteen pounds of black powder so they'd show up in photographs. And I dropped one on Turkey.

"Some guy claimed I'd killed one of his cows, and I had to fill out stacks of forms. Then they sent me out for a few days to stack bombs.

"But the sequel is that a friend on a newspaper wrote a column about it, and a month or two later some guy called me and asked if I was the guy who bombed Turkey, Texas. I admitted I was and he said, 'So did I. Jesus, Turkey must have been filled with bomb craters by the time the war was over.

"My wife and I drove through the Panhandle once and I saw this blue and white sign saying Turkey thataway. I kept going."

Some stories of military training and maneuvers have been told so many times and in so many versions that they have entered American folklore. Here is one:

"It was spectacular fun when I took my training in B-25s in La Junta, Colorado. These were all war-wearies that had been stripped of the equipment except the lighted gunsights and would just barely stay in the air. We were doing a lot of night flying then, and one of our favorite forms of recreation was to find a lonely car out in the middle of nowhere. We'd turn off all our lights, peel off, and dive down at this car. When we'd get only a few feet from him, we'd turn on the landing lights and every other light on the plane and roar just over his hood. I don't know how many people in Colorado must have dirtied their pants because of us.

"One pilot even went so far as to find a stretch of railroad that didn't have all the power lines running beside it, then bided his time until he found a train rolling along. He lined up on the railroad track about twenty feet off the ground, came in dark, and then turned on the lights and scared the hell out of a train crew."

Famous Lines from Radio Shows

"Whatcha doin', huh, mister, whatcha doin'?"

"That's purty good, Johnny, but that ain't the way I heerd it."

"Somebody bawl for Beulah?"

"Love that man."
                    —"Fibber McGee and Molly"

"That's a joke, son."
           —Senator Claghorn on "The Fred Allen Show"

"Lee-ee-ee-ee-roy!"
                    —"The Great Gildersleeve"

"He hunts the biggest of all game, the public enemies who try to destroy our America."
                    —"The Green Hornet"

"Good evening, friends. This is your host, inviting you through the gory portals of the squealing door. . . ."
                    —"Inner Sanctum"

"Of what material is a silk dress made?"

"Who is buried in Grant's tomb?"

"I have a poem, Mr. Howard:
    "I eat my peas with honey,
    I've done it all my life;
    It makes the peas taste funny,
    But it keeps them on my knife."
            —"It Pays to Be Ignorant"

"Wave the flag for Hudson High, boys,
Show them how we stand;
Ever shall our team be champions,
Known throughout the land."
        —"Jack Armstrong, the All-American Boy"

"Hi-ya, Jackson!"
            —Phil Harris to Jack Benny

"Psst! Hey. Bud . . . c'mere!"
            —Sheldon Leonard to Jack Benny

"Stop da music! Stop da music! There's something wrong wit da orchestral harmonics."

"Everybody wants ta get into da act!"

"Goodnight, Mrs. Calabash, wherever you are."
            —Jimmy Durante

"Pardon me for talking in your face, señorita; thirty days hacienda, April, June, and sombrero—I theenk."
                    —Mel (Pedro) Blanc to Judy Canova

"I doggies, Lum. . ."
                    —"Lum and Abner"

"Goodnight to you, and I do mean you."
                    —Jimmy Fidler

In like Flynn.

Zoot Suit Slang

Construct for me a sadistic cape with a murderistic shape, shoulders Gibraltar, shiny as a halter. Drape it, drop it, sock it and lock it at the pocket. Give me pants that entrance; a frantic thirty-one-inch knee that's draped lightly, politely and slightly to a twelve-inch cuff, making it *eeeemperative* for me to grease my Garbos to slip 'em on. As for the color, Jack, let the rainbow be your guide.

7

The Entertainers

WE LISTENED TO THE RADIO and heard Kate Smith sing "God Bless America" more times than we recited the Lord's Prayer or pledge of allegiance in school each morning. We heard Doris Day sing "Sentimental Journey," and the Glen Miller band playing "Chattanooga Choo-choo," and "Smoke on the Water," and "I'll Never Smile Again," and "Don't Sit Under the Apple Tree," and the biggest hillbilly hit of them all, "Pistol Packin' Mama." Waiting for the "Hit Parade" each week was excruciating for us because we developed loyalties to certain songs and wanted them either to become first on the charts or remain there once they arrived.

We went to the movies to see John Wayne whip the Japs, and we wondered if our parents realized that Betty Hutton was impregnated by several servicemen in *Miracle at Morgan's Creek*, then wondered why our parents didn't have the movie banned if it was that sinful. We often paid our way into movies by bringing in scrap metal, and were treated to a cartoon, the march-of-time newsreels, a western or Mandrake the Magician serial, previews of coming attractions, and finally the main feature.

We listened to Bob Hope's jokes, to the residents of Allen's Alley give old Fred what-for. We tried to anticipate when the crazy lady on "It Pays to Be Ignorant" would finally get the joke and bray her laugh. We tried without success to imitate the American Tobacco Company's auctioneer, Johnny the Bellboy, who could never get Philip Morris to answer his page. None of us could master Mel Blanc's Mexican on "The Judy Canova Show," or even the fellow who "came to court Ju-u-u-u-dy."

Many of us didn't know of Errol Flynn's rape trial until long after the war was over, because our small local papers didn't carry such news. We had to wait until the servicemen came home to learn the new phrase "In Like Flynn," and to find out that the trial had provided the boys overseas with nearly as much amusement as the USO shows.

Nearly every town had a Victory Square where during lunch hours entertainers, both local and national, performed while encouraging us to buy more war bonds. The USO established Stage Door Canteens in all major cities, and servicemen would suddenly find themselves being handed a cup of coffee from Jack Benny or a doughnut from Dorothy Lamour.

An adequate entertainer could always find work during the war, and with the men between eighteen and nearly forty in the service, the 4-Fs, older men, and young people could be on the road earning a good salary all during those years. The government recognized the importance of entertainment for both military personnel and civilians, and went to great lengths to make transportation available for them.

Thus, Betty Lee Johnson, a young girl with some talent and a lot of ambition, was able to go right to work after high school and have some adventures, until, like the Rodgers-Hammerstein song of the era, she saw a stranger across a crowded room who changed her life:

"I was orphaned at fifteen and I had wanted to be a journalist or an attorney or a schoolteacher. But a fifteen-year-old orphan doesn't have that many options. I had sung since I was a little girl, loved to sing, so that was what I became. I was just eighteen when the war started and had just graduated from high school, was engaged, and, luckily, everything was brought to a sudden halt. I would have been very unhappy if I had married that man, so the war did me a favor.

"I was working in a little German café in Chicago on North Avenue, a German neighborhood. I don't know how Chicago is now—haven't been there in years—but then it was a whole bunch of little foreign towns all put together. Each neighborhood had restaurants and cafés from that country, mostly family places where you'd dance to a string trio or a quartet. I was working in a place called the Hunting Lodge as a singing waitress. We had about two waitresses and three waiters, and one of the waiters was a Bavarian yodeler. I sang with a young waiter, duets and then solos.

"Then I got a chance to work with a traveling road show, and for the life of me I can't remember what they called this particular show, but we traveled the county-fair circuit one whole summer, all across the West—Minnesota, the Dakotas, Montana, Idaho, Colorado, Nebraska. There were somewhere between fifty and a hundred people in the show and we usually had a whole railroad car to ourselves. But sometimes they'd have to split us up and we'd share the cars with other people. We got to be experts at tearing those cars apart and making beds of them. In no time flat we would have the backs off those seats and spread out so that the whole car was one big bed. Sometimes we'd be in a car so old that it still had kerosene lamps and potbellied stoves. They must have found cars that even the railroads had forgotten they owned.

"We were generally in each town a week, but occasionally we'd have a split week—three days here, then three days at another town. I was paid the magnificent sum of $100 a week, big money in those days. Out of that I had to pay my hotel and food bills, but rooms cost something like $5 a week, and if you spent more than a dollar on a meal, even dinner, you were really splurging. And a lot of local guys would take us out to dinner between shows. So that $100 went a long ways.

"I was billed as Bettina Liandra and the Singing Commanders. The Commanders were eight men and they were really something. One was an old queer; another had a deformed hand that kept him out of the service; another was an old bass singer past his prime; and there were some teenagers not old enough for the service.

"It was quite a production. We had a trained-horse act, a tightrope act, trained dogs, a ballroom dancing act—every show had ballroom dancing in those days. We had the basics of an orchestra, about six permanent members, and we'd pick up the rest in each town and train them real fast with a couple of rehearsals. There seemed to always be good musicians in each town.

"It was work, but I was young. I celebrated my twenty-first birthday in Lincoln, Nebraska. In fact, the day I was old enough to drink legally was the first day in my life I was asked for identification, and of course I had none.

"When we hit Great Falls, Montana, I met a cowboy who really fell for me. He followed us to every town the rest of that summer. I'd get to a new town and he'd be there at the depot. How he beat us every time is beyond me, but there he'd be. It got to be a joke, of course. He was a very nice guy and I liked him as a friend but didn't have any other feelings toward him. He followed me from Great Falls to Billings; then to Pocatello, Idaho; Pueblo, Colorado; and when we returned to Chicago, he was there, too. And there he stayed.

"With the fair circuit over, I decided to make a try at the big time in New York. I subleased my apartment in Chicago to this cowboy and took off for the Big Apple. And almost starved to death. If it hadn't been for picking up some modeling jobs, I would have starved. I would be down to my last 20¢ and the rent would be overdue and I'd land a job in modeling—fashion and photography. One time I had to sell a pint of blood. I was already a member of the Gallon Club and had the pin and ribbon or whatever they gave us for donating a gallon of blood during the war. But I heard that a Catholic hospital not far from Forty-seventh Street, where I lived, was paying $5 for a pint. Well, $5 would buy a whole lot of those 20¢ pot pies in the Automat.

"I had been trying out for singing jobs, stage work—anything in show business—and had a chance to go down to Norfolk, Virginia, to work in a supper-and-gambling club. So I worked there a while to get enough to pay the rent and live a while longer. I suppose gambling was illegal then, but the sheriff turned his head, or was paid to.

"When I went back to my hotel in New York, there was a message to call this production company where I'd tried out for a part. I called, but they said they had already cast the part I could have had. It was as the understudy for the lead in *Up in Central Park*. I had just missed my big chance.

"It was really a blow. But I finally landed a job in a joint called the Nineteenth Hole—and it *was* a hole. It was run by a guy who used to be a golf pro, and I couldn't remember his name if I heard it today, but it was a little bar with a miniature golf course down in the basement. It was just a hole in the wall. I worked there a week and earned enough on salary and tips to pay my hotel bill and go home again.

"While I was gone, the cowboy had apparently given up on me and had sublet my apartment to some girl and returned to Montana. I got her out of the apartment and had one big mess to clean up, then went looking for a job in Chicago. There was a new entertainment tax that really killed off the live entertainment in clubs and lounges, and hurt small-time musicians like me. But I finally got a job in this nice little cocktail lounge down near the depot on the border between the good and bad part of town. Sometimes a bum would wander in, and someone would grab him and wander him right out again.

"They hired me first as a cocktail waitress, and I hoped to sing later, but after I was there about a week I met my husband and had a whirlwind romance. My husband had been in the Pacific for fifty-six months and was right at the end of his six-year enlistment. So they put him on shore patrol. I looked up one night and this guy comes in. He isn't a big man—in fact, he reminds me of a banty rooster. He was standing there in the doorway with his legs spread apart and a big .45 on his hip. He had curly hair and a little curl was hanging down over his eye, and I told myself, 'That's the guy!'

He saw me and talked to me a while, and asked if he could take me home after work. The next afternoon we met and had dinner before I went to work, and he took me home again that night. The third night he asked me to marry him. We called his parents and told them we were getting married the following Saturday. We went to Kansas City and got married that Saturday. That was thirty-one years ago."

Magicians were among the most popular entertainers in those years, particularly in hospitals, since their performances were quiet and demanded concentration. One magician wound up with a tough assignment through one of his shows.

"I'm a professional magician and I used to go out to the army hospital where they were bringing men in from the war. . . . I probably went out twice a week, and the Old Gold cigarette company told me I could have all the cigarettes I wanted for this one trick. You know, it was the one where I'd show this little round tube empty, then pull enough cigarettes out for everybody. The boys were very pleased with this because they were short on cigarettes.

"Then one night a captain told me that I did a good magic show but if I wanted to see some real magic to come with him. He took me over into the ward where the boys were that had their ears blown off or their noses or their hair. They were grafting new skin on from other parts of the body to make them new noses and new ears, you know, and anything else that was needed.

"A little later I was selected to go to New York to take a course of a month in post-exchange work, so before I went I stopped by the hospital and asked the boys from New York if they wanted me to look up their parents or relatives. There was only one, who said he had a father working for the city as a subway inspector.

"Well, I looked all over New York, I think, before I finally found this old gentleman and told him who I was. I said I'd seen his boy and that he was all right and getting along fine.

"Well, sir, the first thing he did was to bawl me out and his boy, too.

" 'Tell him when you see him to send us some money,' he yelled at me. 'We're having to take care of his family.' He didn't seem to appreciate me coming there at all.

"Well, it was a little embarrassing for me to tell the boy when I went back to Texas, but it didn't bother the boy.

" 'Yeah, that's him,' the boy said, and laughed. 'Still rough as a cob. I'm going to send some money to them, don't worry.' "

Many of us dreamed of getting on a radio show, or at least having our names mentioned on one for providing a question or an answer.

"The radio was very important to us and we listened to the news as if our very lives depended on it, which they actually did. We were dependent on it also for much of our entertainment and one of my favorite shows was 'Information Please.' We listened to it faithfully.

"It had Franklin P. Adams, Oscar Levant (who was asked on a show if the first year of marriage was the hardest and he replied, 'No, the last year,' and that is so true), and that real smart Irish guy whose name escapes me now.

"I had a question I never did send in, and should have: Define candling, noodling, and kindling as they related to animal husbandry.

"Candling is sorting eggs according to freshness and fertility with a light behind them, originally a candle.

"Kindling is the word for a rabbit giving birth.

"Noodling is when they nail a goose's feet to the floor of a crate and force starchy noodles down his throat by massaging it. It is very popular among the Germans and Slavs."

One young wife discovered how remote some husbands were from the American mainstream when she mentioned a relatively new singer in a letter.

"I'll always keep that letter because it has one sentence that still gets a laugh when I mention it:

" 'Who the hell is Frank Sinatra?' he asked."

Red Kelly is a well-known jazz bassist who played for many major bands, beginning during the war, and still leads a group in the Pacific Northwest. Kelly is famous for his bass, his warmth, his extended-family life-style, and wacky sense of humor. Here he talks about how he became interested in music and what his life was like during the war years.

"I went into an orphanage when I was seven and lived in it until I was about twelve, when things got a little better for my parents. I could spend the summers on my grandparents' farm in Idaho and there was a lot of singing around

Wallace, ethnic music, and my grandparents spoke Gaelic, which itself is a musical language. If you hear it spoken, you're going to start thinking music.

"The orphanage aroused a taste for music in me, for which I'm grateful, but it also aroused a great distaste for laundries and kitchens, and in order to get out of working in them, I figured that if I could get to play in the drum and fife corps the orphanage had, I could get out of all that other stuff. That is what I did. I played the drums and then really got interested in the noises and sounds of music.

"Then when I started high school in Seattle I heard a live band and it really intrigued me. I heard Jimmy Lunceford was going to play at Victory Square in Seattle at noon, so I skipped school and went down to listen. The minute I heard them, it was all over. School held no more interest to me. I decided on the spot that was what I was going to do. I didn't know what I was going to play, but that was what I was going to do. Years later when I went with Harry James, Willie Smith, who had been the lead saxophone player with Jimmy Lunceford at the time I saw them, was with Harry James and became a close personal friend. I told him about all that, and that if it hadn't been for him I wouldn't be there.

"I went back to school and wanted to play drums, but there already was a guy in school who played drums real good anyway and I could see I wasn't going to get asked to play. But there were no bass players, so I got a hold of a bass, and that was it.

"As a matter of fact—I suppose the statute of limitations has run out—there was an old bass in the high school that was all beat up and standing in the corner. Had been there for years. So I just confiscated it, took it home and got some strings and that was that. After the orphanage and finding that bass, everything was straight up. I never finished high school. I had no interest in it and I wouldn't have missed all those years on the road for anything.

"There was a great demand for entertainment during the war. Everybody wanted to be entertained. We even played breakfast dances. You'd play until two o'clock in the morning and then you'd find out that somebody else was going to start at six in the morning, so you'd go out and play from six until two in the afternoon. It was a great time to learn, because you were playing all the time. It was that way until I was in my mid-twenties, from the time I was fifteen. It seemed like everybody was playing all the time. Every chance you got you found some guys and went someplace and played.

"Most of the war I was playing around in kid bands and things like that. I call them 'kid bands' because that was all the leaders could get, other than older men. The conditions then were so much different because there were a lot of minor-league bands traveling then, not only the name bands but those that survived because they traveled so much. It was a very good opportunity because I was quite young and the older fellows were getting drafted, which created an opportunity that hasn't been the same since.

"There were a lot of very good bands, what you'd call B-class bands; Bob Chester, Teddy Powell were a couple. The first band I went with, when I was fifteen, was Tiny Hill, kind of a Dixieland society band. Later I went with Ted Fiorito, who had a swing band comprised of six or seven older fellows and a whole bunch of young kids. Doc Severinsen was one of the kids; and Bob Manning, the drummer; Don Trenner, who later accompanied Steve Allen; Ward Swingle, who later started the Swingle Singers, was our vocalist—many people like that.

"We played a lot of military bases, and with the kid bands we played some USOs, shipyards, and so forth. Lord knows, when you think back and try to remember how those bands must have sounded, I really don't know how good they were for the morale of the shipyard workers, but evidently they thought there was something there. I know we were pretty awful, though.

"There might have been maybe 200 bands in those days, including what we called 'territory bands,' those that would work the Midwest in particular, or New York or Texas. A band out of New York would work around there and up in New England, down to Washington, and never any farther west than Youngstown, Ohio, maybe. Sam Donahue, who was in the service, had a great service band. So did Claude Thornhill. And there was Georgie Ault, Lawrence Welk, Jan Garber, Guy Lombardo . . . there was a lot of activity. People were making money in the shipyards or whatever. I know guys who worked in joints and had days off. They'd work in the shipyards and then work most of the night in a joint to feed the kitty. It would be just a dive next to the shipyards. I know two or three who built lavish homes out of that kitty.

"There were many times when most of the people in our band would be under draft age, and when we played in army camps, especially at officers' clubs, there would invariably be some guy just mad as hell at us for not being in the service. We were too young, damn it! But he would be just convinced we were draft dodgers. There were some ugly incidents over that, and it was just bewildering to us. We didn't know how to combat that. Here's a guy who is supposed to be mature and he's an officer, but it was obvious that a lot of things I'd heard about a lot of officers are true. This guy is a nitwit! They'd yell at us from the dance floor, kick the drums. One time our drummer was putting his drums away in a big fiber case and this guy goes over and kicked it and called him a dirty 4-F and all that. In the first place, if you're a 4-F, what are you going to do about it? Go sneak on a troopship?

"The enlisted men didn't bother us that much. We were kind of thrown in with them because the bandleader would often stay in the officers' quarters while we usually got the

barracks. The enlisted men figured that since we ate pow-
dered eggs with them, we must be all right. It was a lot more
fun that way because the officers I ran into, with some exceptions of course, made me think I'd rather hang out with the
enlisted men. They were a little more down-to-earth.

"But all things considered, we had it very good, especially
compared with the Depression years. The lengths the band-
leaders had to go to to stay in business, the conditions, were
fierce. There were many cases where they played eight or ten
hours with five or six guys. One fellow would go off and take
a smoke or get a cup of coffee and they'd never quit playing.
That wasn't unusual at all. I missed it and I'm glad I missed
it. Just doing what we were doing seemed hard enough because you're always concentrating so thoroughly that it gets
very tiring.

"But the war opened up a whole new world. We were
finally out of that Depression and now there was money plus
the frantic air to have some fun. People started working, and
recording contracts were all revised and much more lucra-
tive. There was such a desperate feeling to the period. People
were expecting submarines to surface anytime, even in Lake
Erie, and there was just that feeling that maybe there would
be no tomorrow and to hell with it.

"Joe Venuti was working all during those years and he
was one of the great nuts of all time. He had a piano player
who was pounding his foot and distracting the other guys.
And he wouldn't stop. So Joe went backstage and got a hammer and nail and nailed his shoe to the floor. And he used
to send one guy a single cuff link for Christmas. There are a
hundred stories about Joe, and they're all true.

"Practical jokes are part of the musicians' society. We
were always pulling jokes on guys. One came on the road
with us, a kid who is playing the studios now, and we told
him he'd have to bring a lot of towels and soap because
there weren't any in the hotel rooms. So he brought a whole

suitcaseful and realized he had been had when we checked into the first hotel.

"Another time we told him we had a girl for him and one of the saxophone players hid under the covers. Of course the whole band, with the exception of the older fellows, hid in the room listening to the dialogue, which was fantastic. Here's a sixteen-year-old kid trying to be cool.

"I've always felt sorry for the older fellows because they were thrust on one-night stands with these young kids, a horde of young children. One of the older guys became a homicidal maniac and I'm sure we had something to do with that. They'd just lost their buddies to the draft and here they're stuck with this mob of kids. I look at my sons and nephews now and they're around that age. I think, Good God, if I had to go on one-nighters with a bunch like that . . . The time to be goony is at that age, and we were no exception.

"It is a mistake as far as musicians are concerned to keep young guys from playing clubs, because they are marvelous music schools. They have the regular schools where they learn all this technique, but they're running before they learn how to crawl.

"When Corky Corcoran went on the road with Harry James, he was about sixteen and he always looked nice and shiny like an aspirant to the presidency of the senior class. Harry had to adopt him legally to get him in those clubs. I was never questioned because I always looked older. I started drinking when I was fourteen and to this day nobody has ever asked me for my ID.

"Transportation was interesting at that time. We had to use trains, buses, and there were even occasions when they stuck us on cattle trucks. We just crawled under blankets and that was that. We were just young kids and it was all great.

"There was one time when we were on one of those tiny army airplanes with bucket seats and we ran into foul weather and had something wrong with an engine. The older fellows were quite concerned, and when the pilot told us to put on the parachutes because we might have to jump, this made the older guys even more uncomfortable. For a young kid, this was great. Put on the parachute and let her go! The older guys were afraid these young maniacs might go up and take over the controls.

"We traveled all over the country. My first trip was with Tiny Hill and we were out six months, from Seattle to California, then down to Texas and up into the Midwest and into Chicago. Then I took a train back to the Coast with my bass fiddle in the seat beside me. We had a great time. The train was loaded with servicemen and their wives and they were all very nice. There was a spirit of camaraderie the war produced. Everybody thought it was a just war. But I haven't seen that kind of unified spirit since.

"But most of the time traveling was pretty grim. We worked mainly through bookers, and the guy would tell the bandleader that he had one spot for him and would try to line up others, and of course those spots would be so remote that we'd have to ride on a navy bus or something, which was second to a bed of nails. Later on, when I worked with the big names, we did a lot of flying, but even then, if it wasn't over 500 miles, you'd go on that bus anyway.

"When you go on the road, you rarely go at scale. Everybody makes their own deals. When I was with Tiny Hill I was making $90 a week and I had all my clothing from high school. My idea of a great meal was a cheeseburger and half a pint of whiskey, which was never hard to get. A half-pint would do me fine. I've never seen that much money since. I've made a lot more than that, but it never seemed to go so far again.

"For amusement, we'd sleep on the bus. After the first two years I'd heard all the questions and all the answers, and heard all the musical stories and all the legends about the old players. It was the same thing day after day: The young guys would talk about everything and the old guys would conk out—or pass out, whichever the case might be.

"There were always girls around. We called them 'Band-Aids.' Talk about being in good hands . . . that's always part of the band scene. Every area of entertainment has its groupies. It was really unbelievable with the girls, though. It was a picnic. I had red hair and the girls thought I looked like Van Johnson. Oh, God! Boy! I had a great time. Until I opened my mouth. Then they said, 'Oh, forget it!'

"I've heard tapes of me and some of the others from that time and I don't think being good had anything to do with my being hired. I think having a body there was more important than being good. I'm sure it is about the same in any profession; you don't really become proficient at what you're trying to do until you've put in enough time, as we say, to pay some dues. At that point we hadn't paid any dues. We were just out there trying to make the older fellows pay some more dues.

"It was a great experience because we got around the country and had a chance to hear some of the great bands. There was one case when we had no idea this band existed. Billy Eckstein had a band in Louisville and we had not heard of him or his band. One afternoon my friend Don Manning and I went walking around and saw this black theater and the marquee said 'Billy Eckstein and His Band' and we went in. It turned out he had all the big names then: Charlie Parker and Dizzy Gillespie, one great after another. It was an astounding band. And for never having heard a band like that, it was really avant-garde. We were going around talking to ourselves for two weeks. '*What was that?*'

"I played with Bob Wills for a while, but it was just complete confusion to me because I was into Duke Ellington and Count Basie, and what on earth is all this? There were so many guitars and amplified zithers and accordians playing. Good Lord, I couldn't make any sense of it. I'm sure that was one of the requirements—that it didn't make any sense.

"The vocalists hadn't started taking over just yet. Perry Como was with Ted Weems, Rosemary Clooney and her sisters were with Tony Pastor, Betty Grable was with different bands, and June Haver sang with Ted Fiorito—before I was there, damn it! Every band had to have a vocalist, but it didn't necessarily follow that the vocalist was any good. On rare occasions they were, but in many cases they just stood there and howled out the words and everybody was dancing and they didn't really care to hear Caruso, they just wanted to dance. There was a festive feeling, a kind of desperate festivity. After they found that the war wasn't going to be over in two weeks, they kind of settled in and decided not to let themselves get too grim. There was a kind of desperation not to get grim, flaky.

"By the end of the war we had enough experience that we could compete to a degree with the other guys coming back, and we also got into the pattern of finding the good guys and picking their brain. It is a pattern, a tradition, that hasn't changed or even slowed down today. When someone comes around that you respect and they've got something figured out that you want, you're going to find out how they do it. It is a real tradition. I remember one time we had an old drummer with us, Dave Topp, who was playing for Woody Herman at the time. He gathered that I was voracious to learn, so he took me under his arm and took me to all the hot spots where there was knock-down, drag-out jazz, and I heard some great stuff and learned from it. That's what you do because there were no schools, just this tradition.

"The top bassist in my mind was a young man, Jimmy Blanton, who died when he was twenty-one. He played with Duke Ellington and he revolutionized the whole bass. Of course Chubby Jackson was alive then and he was better known as far as the people were concerned because of his exposure with Woody Herman. But Jimmy Blanton was my idol. He made the bass important. It hadn't been before. It had been just a percussive instrument and Jimmy made it very much a front-line instrument. My experience was that playing for Charley Barnett, Woody Herman, Stan Kenton, and of course Harry James were just marvelous schools. You could learn more in those bands than in any real school. Practical on-the-road touring where you've got your neck on the block every night.

"When I started, most bands had the drum solo and it was usually 'China Boy.' I didn't venture out for bass solos. I had to stick pretty close to the basics then. But the war period produced some really great bassists—Oscar Pettiford, for one. But Red Mitchell is the world's greatest living bassist for my money. He lives in Sweden and comes over once in a while. He calls me from Stockholm like it's just down the street and we'll talk for forty-five minutes.

"When I first went back to New York as a kid, he and I had an apartment together and decided then to call ourselves Red because we both had red hair. His name was Keith and he detested it, and my name was Tom, which I hated. The phone was down on a landing below our apartment and when someone would call with a job for us, they'd ask for Red. Whoever answered the phone would holler up, 'Red!' and whichever one of us didn't have a job would answer the phone and take the job. It worked out very well, except one time Red Norvo called for Red Mitchell and got me. He picked me up in front of the apartment building and we were way the hell and gone somewhere over in Jersey before he realized he had the wrong Red.

"Mitchell and I were together about a year, and later on when he got TB and was in a sanitorium, he heard I was out of work and almost starving and sent me to Woody Herman. That's the way it works. After the initial part, you look after each other. There's a profound underground.

"I have a Rogers and Hart songbook here, and all you have to do is read the titles. They're absolute masterpieces, every one of them. Every time somebody comes in the club and talks about how the Beatles revolutionized songwriting, I hand them the book and tell them to read the titles and tell me how the Beatles revolutionized songwriting. Forget it! They write good tunes, sure. But the poetry part I find lacking now. Read the lyrics to 'All the Things You Are.' 'You are the angel glow that lights the star. The dearest things I know are what you are.' Good Lord, you tell a girl that instead of 'I'm drunk out of my head in a car going ninety miles an hour' and I think you're going to get a lot more points."

Norma Barthel's case is slightly different. She was as committed to music as a professional musician, but she was a listener, a collector of music, instead of a performer. Her story is not unlike that of many lovers of hillbilly, or country, or country-western, or whatever it is being called at any given moment. The war was almost directly responsible for introducing the music from Memphis and Nashville and Wheeling to America. Although it would take at least two more decades for that music to arrive in New York and Los Angeles, its acceptance across the nation was insistent.

The loyal fans, like Norma Barthel, were as dedicated to that music and the performers as the average citizen was to the concept of America during the war. Mrs. Barthel was the founder of the Ernest Tubb Fan Club.

"We were in Arizona picking cotton when the war broke out. We were just getting ready to return to eastern Oklahoma because it was getting late in the year and cotton picking was about over. I was fifteen that year, and it was the first time we followed the cotton pickers to Arizona. We followed the wheat harvest north several years, but only the cotton that one time.

"My daddy always liked the traveling, and could always find a job, but my mom didn't like it very well. She went along with him, but she didn't feel she had a base to work from. We'd just pull up stakes and go every spring. We never had anything to come back to or anything like that. My daddy liked it that way, and my mom just had to go along with it. It seemed like I always enjoyed the traveling and meeting new people, but I was always wishing that if I ever got in one place, I'd stay there. When I got married twenty-eight years ago, when I was twenty-two, we did just that. We're still in the same place. I still like to go, but I like to have a place to come back to.

"I started working in the fields when I was twelve years old. My brother and I worked in the cotton patch, and when I was about fourteen I could get jobs cooking for harvest hands. Daddy would always go back to the same places year after year because he was a good worker. Mama never worked because it seemed like she always had a small child to care for. After a couple of years the places we'd work would hold a job for me when we got there each year.

"Daddy and my brother worked driving tractors in the wheat harvest. We would follow it from Oklahoma up into the Dakotas. Daddy always wanted to go into Canada, but it would start getting cool and we'd go back south. He didn't like the winter. He spent one winter in Kansas and he couldn't hardly stand it because it got so cold. He said the wind blew right through him. We stayed a summer and a winter, then another summer on that farm, and then he said, 'Boy I've got to go south with the geese.'

"We would usually come back to Arkansas for the winter. When I was seventeen we went to Oklahoma and there was

a lot of work down there in the rice fields. We picked straw-
berries and tomatoes; we had a lot of field work in those
days, I stopped traveling by the time I was eighteen and
started working in factories or offices.

"But all during my early teens we traveled the Great
Plains working in wheat harvest. Daddy liked harvest because it paid better. In cotton you were kind of on your own,
and if you didn't work very hard, you didn't get paid very
much. In harvest you got paid by the hour.

"We really enjoyed it because everybody laughed a lot,
talked, and just had a good time. There were lots of them
from Arkansas, where we stayed, and eastern Oklahoma. A
lot of them would take truckloads of people, usually just men,
and several truckloads would leave every year from around
Mulberry, Arkansas.

"Daddy had a Model A truck. He would plow gardens
with it, and I think it cost him about $28. There were four
of us kids and we'd pile our belongings in that pickup and
away we went. We'd stop alongside the road and camp, build
a fire and cook over it. We had a little tent we'd put up and
mama and the little kids slept in that while my brother and
I slept in the back of the truck. It was really roughing it. I
didn't really like that—it was a little too rough for me—but
that's the way we did it.

"By the time I was in my teens I was already interested
in hillbilly music. Roy Rogers and Gene Autry were my
favorites until I heard Ernest Tubb sing 'Walking the Floor
Over You' in the small Arizona towns we visited during our
cotton-picking days. My brother and I liked to walk along the
streets while mom and daddy did the grocery shopping. We'd
listen to the jukeboxes blaring from the honky-tonks that lined
the streets. We weren't allowed to stand at the doors, of
course, but there was nothing anyone could say about us walking down the street real slow. We could hear 'Walking the
Floor' all the way through as we walked around the block, up

and down the streets. It was playing on every one of the juke-boxes, or nickelodeons, as I think they were called in the Southwest. It was the biggest record Ernest ever had, and was a big hit all through the Forties and early Fifties. Back then songs lasted longer. Now we will have a song that is number one for a few weeks, where it used to be that one would go for months and months. 'Walking the Floor' was a big hit all during the war and after.

"Every year when we got ready to go to Kansas, my daddy would write a couple we knew out in western Kansas around Dodge City. They owned a store way out in the country and they had a gas pump. Towns were so far apart then that people would flock from everywhere to that store. So they sold a lot of gas. Somehow they could get spare gas coupons, and they would save them through the winter and send them to us. Otherwise we couldn't have gone as far as we did every year. We had relatives who weren't going anywhere and they'd save theirs, too. Tires were hard to get, of course, and he used to stack three or four real old ones on top of the cab and tie them down. He'd get as far as he could on one, then switch to another old one.

"During the winters when we were back in Arkansas or Oklahoma, we had soldiers all over the place. Oklahoma was supposed to be off-limits to the soldiers at Fort Chaffee near Fort Smith, but Fort Smith itself was wide open. I didn't know any soldiers—they were off-limits to us girls—and parents tried to keep us as far away from them as possible because they were on the loose, away from home, lonely. I remember that a girl or two couldn't go to a movie matinee without a soldier working his way over to any empty seat nearby and starting a conversation. I was afraid of them because of my mother's warnings.

"I didn't happen to have any relatives in the war, or even any close friends. But my very first boy friend went to war. I lost track of him almost immediately. This boy told me repeatedly that he would be waiting on the doorstep when we came back that fall from Kansas. I don't remember his name today, so you know how serious I was. But the thing I remember is that we hadn't been gone two weeks before I got word he had been drafted and had married my fifteen-year-old cousin. She wanted the allotment check and the possible life insurance. She barely knew him. She followed him around a little while, then came back home and eventually divorced him. Things like that were quite common during the war.

"I remember Ernest Tubb's 'Walking the Floor Over You' more than anything else about that period. He went to the Grand Old Opry in the latter part of 1942 as a guest and 'Walking the Floor' had already been out two years. He sang it there and got four encores. They liked him so well that they took him on for a few more appearances, and by January 1943 they made him permanent.

"Another one of my wartime favorites was Bob Wills. He played Cains Ballroom in Tulsa regularly and was at the Winter Garden Club in Fort Smith once a month. People just flocked to every performance. One of his big wartime hits was 'Silver Dew On the Bluegrass Tonight.' Then of course he had 'San Antonio Rose' and 'Faded Love.'

"But of course the biggest wartime hit of them all was Elton Britt's 'There's a Star Spangled Banner Waving Somewhere.' By that I mean a song related to the war, because the biggest hit of them all was Al Dexter's 'Pistol Packin' Mama.'

"Some time after the war I founded the Ernest Tubb Fan Club. It has been so long ago that I almost forget how I started it, but I had a lot of pen pals and I'd heard Ernest's records but didn't know him. There was a Gene Autry Fan Club and a Roy Rogers one, so I wrote around to all my pen pals and asked them what they thought about starting a club for Ernest. They were all for it, so I wrote Ernest and told him about it.

"I didn't think he would even see my mail because he was getting so awful much mail. But it wasn't too long before he wrote back and told me to go ahead and start it. He told me years later that he had gotten a lot of letters at that time from girls wanting to start a fan club, but thought mine was the most sincere. So he gave me the okay on it and his wife got busy and helped me with lots of names and addresses of his fans. She sent them to me by the boxload, and it wasn't long before we had 2000 members all over the country. I don't have that many members now; it got to the point where I couldn't keep up with them. But I sent out a monthly letter on Ernest and all that. We still have around a thousand members.

"It is so funny. Fans really stick with country singers. About half our members have been with us for twenty years.

"I see Ernest rather often, not as much as I did, but when he comes to Oklahoma within driving distance I always try to make it. He's just an old friend. He's been very helpful, very cooperative, very appreciative. I handle a lot of things for him. I send his records to the DJs that don't get them, and he sends me lots of mail he gets, because he says I know more about him than he does himself.

"I don't know. When I look back at those war years, I remember the good times we had. You didn't want as much in those days as you do now. When we were traveling we didn't go into cafés or restaurants to eat; we would just go to a bakery and get day-old bread. A loaf of bread and bologna. I don't know. I wouldn't want to do it now, though."

Most of the male Hollywood stars of heartthrob age went into the service. Some fought, while others were assigned to Special Services and entertained the troops. Bob Hope began his famous war-zone trips with a large band and a bevy of beautiful girls. Errol Flynn, the Tasmanian-Australian hero of action films, was a 4-F, and he did his part inadvertently for the war effort by entertaining almost the entire English-speaking world via his trial, and acquittal, for rape.

For actors too old to serve, it was business as usual in Hollywood, but with a few changes. With fewer leading men available, lesser-known stars got the leading roles. Many, many films were made for propaganda purposes. Chinese and Filipino actors had almost as much work as they wanted portraying Japanese soldiers.

Things didn't change that much for a character actor named Charlie Arnt. He was married to a publicist named Pat, and they had their own quiet adventures during the war years:

CHARLIE: "My first play was in a small Indiana town junior high school. Then I went to Princeton, where we had a little theater and a tiny little stage that was operated entirely by the students, no faculty supervision at all. Princeton didn't even have a drama department then, so we students built the scenery, made the costumes—the whole thing.

"Then we formed the Triangle Club, which did musicals. I think the Triangle Club in those days was the best college show of all the schools in the country. Then a group founded the University Players. That was Josh Logan, Hank Fonda, Margaret Sullivan, and Millie (Mildred) Natwick. We played in the summertime and had a permanent theater. Our stock town was Baltimore.

"This was in the Depression and it finally caught up with me when I was in New York. During one year there were two plays on the boards, and I was in one that lasted a month. Then Jimmy Stewart got in *Goodbye Again*, and that lasted a bit longer. My play was *Carrie Nation*. I was rehearsing for another play that Josh Logan was going to take to England. I rehearsed for six weeks, I guess, and then we got a message from England that they wouldn't allow any American actors in parts that could be cast in England. That cut us off and we got nothing. Actors weren't paid for rehearsal then.

"My entree into Hollywood was Frank Tuttle, who was a Yale graduate and a director at Paramount. He came through and did quite a few of the early Crosby and Bob Hope pictures. And he came to Princeton while I was there to do *the* college picture, a silent. Nobody had really done a college picture before. So he did *Varsity* with Buddy Rogers as the leading man and Chester Conklin as the character lead. Chester was the Mack Sennett comedian with that big walrus moustache. He was very funny in silent pictures, and I played his son at Princeton as an undergraduate. They also hired Phillips Holmes, a very, very handsome boy who was the son of a well-known New York actor, Taylor Holmes. Phil got a very nice part in the picture and we were all supposed to go out to Hollywood that summer. But I had to go to ROTC [Reserve Officer Training Camp] that summer. Phil went and never came back to Princeton. He stayed in Hollywood and made a big hit.

"Chester Conklin was like Ernest Torrance at that time. Both were fantastic actors, and Chester had reached the point where he could name his price and pick his parts. So they took *Varsity* out to Hollywood, and sound came in before the picture was released. They went back and shot the end of it with sound, and Chester Conklin never had a job after that. It was his end. Later on, when I was at MGM, Chester was playing extra parts, trying to get about $7 a day. He was through.

"After things got tough in New York in the Depression, I went to Hollywood to see Frank Tuttle, my only contact there. He got me a job as technical director of a Crosby picture, *She Loves Me, She Loves Me Not*. Josh Logan was the stage manager, and it was about college, about Princeton. They had one big dormitory scene with Oriental rugs in the dorms, and big potted palms, and so on. Since I was supposed to be the authority, I told the director he couldn't do those things, that nobody would have Oriental rugs in a college.

" 'Don't say anything, Charlie,' the cameraman said. 'It photographs better and looks so much better this way.'

"So they didn't pay a lot of attention to my expertise.

"During the Depression there weren't double features. You had a single feature and a cartoon and a newsreel—"

PAT: "They had those Pathe newsmen who went out and risked their lives, I thought. They'd take pictures of all those disasters and you'd wonder why they didn't throw away their camera and go and help save somebody."

CHARLIE: "During that time there was a shortage of makeup people in the business and I was working at RKO. We had greasepaint in those days, actually a grease-style makeup, and since I played character parts I almost always made myself up. You've got much more realistic makeup these days. You put on pancake and use your own wrinkles— bring your own wrinkles!"

PAT: "I met Charlie when we were both working in summer stock, and he said, 'Come on into the dressing room and I'll make you up, so I—' "

CHARLIE: "It was a good line."

PAT: "It worked. Suddenly I looked at myself in a mirror and I was looking like an old hag. 'What are you doing?' I asked Charlie, and he said, 'I just thought I'd like to see what you'll look like when you're old.' "

CHARLIE: "A lot of actors worked in defense jobs during the war. I worked in a factory for a while drilling holes in airplane parts with a drill press. I wasn't very good at it, but when you're out of a job—in pictures you'll be out of a job most of the time. I wasn't under contract, and even if you were, you wouldn't be working most of the time. How those airplanes stuck together I'll never know, because all these people didn't know what they were doing and they were making parts. There was constant turnover in the plants. Some draft boards thought actors were expendable, but where we lived they thought an actor would do more by staying home. I wasn't very good at war work, so I decided I could do a lot better in the war effort by raising produce. So I raised chickens, turkeys, and sold eggs."

PAT: "I came home on Friday nights from my job as a publicist and helped dress chickens. On Saturday mornings I'd deliver the chickens to various people around Pasadena where we lived. It was a very affluent neighborhood, and one day I took the children to the country club to go swimming and I met one of our chicken clients and she was *so* nice, so pleasant. You could just see her thinking how nice it was that the peasants got to swim, too.

"I did publicity for Standard Oil of California as well as motion-picture work. I worked at the Century House in Pershing Square, where they sold war bonds. People with various talents would come down and entertain and we would sell war bonds. People would contribute things to the person who bought the most bonds or stamps. They gave them handmade quilts and all sorts of things. It was amazing the number of people who came with these things, little old ladies usually, and donated them to the cause. We had Judy Garland, Spike Jones, and even Rudy Vallee came down one time.

"The magicians were just darling. I'd be left alone in the office, doing the booking or whatever, and while I would be there concentrating on my typewriter, suddenly I'd feel a presence in the office with me and look around. There would be a magician pulling handkerchiefs and rabbits out of a hat. He would perform his tricks, not say a word, lay his card on my desk, and say, 'Anytime,' and walk out. So we always had magicians."

CHARLIE: "As you know, there was a major transportation problem then because of gasoline rationing and Detroit not making cars anymore. The government lowered the speed limit to thirty-five miles an hour, which was just wonderful for me. I never did like to drive fast. But Pat needed a car to work down in Pershing Square, and we had to have a car for me because if you lived anyplace in Los Angeles you were a long way from the studio. The studio was at Culver City, twenty miles from us. Then out in the valley was Universal, and Columbia was in town. RKO was in town. So we had to have two cars.

"A friend of ours in a Ford agency kept an eye out for one, and one day called and said he had something in but we'd better come down and look at it first. So we went down, and it was a great big twelve-cylinder Lincoln—"

PAT: "Custom-built—"

CHARLIE: "—town car with a windshield between the front and back, a speaker system between the chauffer, a liquor cabinet, silver mirror, two great big spare tires—the works. I said we couldn't afford anything like that, and our friend said we could have it for $150. It had belonged to the president of a gas company who died, and his wife wanted to get rid of it. So we bought it."

PAT: "And I delivered chickens and eggs with it for a while. But we finally gave it up because I had to fill the tank going into town and again coming back home.

"The Victory House people were so nice, and everybody felt we were in the war together. With the exception of the refugees. We had a lot of trouble with the displaced people because some would just walk up and try to carry off the things people had brought in to buy war bonds. When we stopped them, they'd snap, 'Well, this is a free country, isn't it?'

"I sat next to an Austrian DP at the symphony and one day she was complaining to me that Los Angeles didn't have anything to offer a cultured person. 'In Vienna we would have . . .' and she went on and on telling all the things Vienna had. I was fed up with that and got up my courage and said, 'In Vienna, *now.*'"

CHARLIE: "I was the chief of the volunteer fire department in our area and we had to patrol the streets at night to check for light leaks and that sort of thing. One particular night was a big scare. We were about 2000 feet above the valley and all of a sudden we could see big flashes going up in the sky toward Palo Verde. The Japanese are attacking! They're bombing us! The coastal guns are shooting at them! It was quite a show until they figured out they were shooting at each other's shell bursts."

PAT: "We could have made a fortune in real estate then. Everything on the Coast was going for absolutely nothing. Then in 1946 everything doubled, then quadrupled in price."

CHARLIE: "Places like Newport and Balboa. They were all scared to death that the Japanese were going to arrive. I never could figure that out myself because it was completely unrealistic. After all, the war had been going on so long . . . the Germans weren't able to go twenty miles across to England, and here we expected the Japanese to come 2000 miles and drop in and land and take over California."

PAT: "Talk about driving thirty-five miles an hour. I was just about to have our second child and I told Charlie I had to go to the hospital. I kept telling him not to spare the horses, don't spare the horses, and he was driving a sedate thirty-five. Finally he got tired of my yelling at him and snapped, 'I hope you have a good excuse when we're stopped for speeding!'"

"CHARLIE: "I was getting a lot of work during those years. I played all kinds of character parts. A lot of heavies, strangely enough. During the war, for some reason, psychopathic heavies were very popular.

"I worked for all the studios, Columbia quite a bit, and

then at Paramount, where I spent more time than in any other studio. The psychopathic heavies caught on and I played them steadily. Before that, I was playing comedy roles—the henpecked husband, the fussy little guy—and if I did play a heavy, it was a heavy that didn't appear at first to be a heavy: a nice guy who became a heavy.

"I made several Bing Crosby pictures and loved working with him more than anyone else. One particular film was always a favorite role for me, and at the moment I can't for the life of me think of the title. Anyway, I played a crazy man with Bing, and the gag was that we were playing tic-tac-toe in a restaurant booth. I brought in two bottles of seltzer and gave him one while we played tic-tac-toe. He lost the first game and I picked up a seltzer bottle and shot him in the face.

"That sounds pretty easy, but if you've ever tried to shoot somebody with one and you aim normally, it will shoot you in the foot or something. So before we started filming, Bing and I were out on the sound stage drawing faces on a board and taking target practice—*psssst!*—with the bottles.

"Frank Tuttle was the director, and we did the first take with all the camera crew around. We had a big audience. It was relatively easy to get on a set then, and very often something was going on that would draw a big audience. The whole crew was anxious to see what would happen when I let Bing have it in the face.

"In those days Bing wore a hairpiece and his ears were glued back, and of course we had greasepaint and mascara on. Bing also wore a corset and built-up heels. He was a wonderful person and my favorite in the whole business.

"Anyway, everything was going on and the camera rolling and a big crowd watching. I took the seltzer bottle and—*pow!*—hit him a beautiful shot right between the eyes on his forehead. You have to be careful with those things because you could put an eye out. Nobody seemed to think of those things then.

"So there was Bing with all the greasepaint running down, and his mascara. He was a mess. A total disaster. The scene went on and I lost and he shot *me* in the face, and my line was: 'Oh, you've played before.'

"They had brought seltzer bottles in by the truckloads and they had a great big dining-room scene with the girls in evening gowns and the men in tuxedoes, and when they saw Bing and me shooting each other, somebody grabbed a bottle and shot somebody else, and pretty soon the whole dining room was full of people shooting each other. The extras had a field day. The girls who had on the silky dresses were getting shot the most.

"During this seltzer orgy, Jack Oakie came on the set to see what was going on. By that time everyone had gotten enthusiastic with the seltzer and everybody was getting it. As soon as Jack walked on the set, some guy—*pssst!*—gave him a shot, and somebody else handed one to Jack, and then some guys crawled up on the catwalks above and really doused Jack. He took off out of there and about half an hour later came back wearing slickers, a crusader's gauntlet and helmet, hip boots, and carrying two seltzer bottles. 'Okay, boys,' he told the crew, and got ready to do battle. But the grips and so forth grabbed him and hauled him outside to a big swimming pool where they did the miniature sets, and threw him in with his whole regalia.

"We used to say that what we needed in the business were efficiency experts. Well, we got them, and now it's no fun.

"I was playing a comedy Nazi policeman right at the beginning of the war, with a big German star, whose name escapes me now. It was a great part, a lot of fun, but the war came along and my part was cut down to nothing. All the comedy was taken out."

PAT: "Everyone at the studio was very nervous about Errol Flynn's rape trial because he had a big film just coming out [*Gentleman Jim*]. It opened in a theater right across from Victory Square where I worked, and on opening day a line went all around the block. It was a smash hit."

CHARLIE: "I did one of Busby Berkeley's pictures, *Cinderella Jones*, during the war, and it was the only Busby Berkeley flop. He conceived the idea for one particular scene that was a convoy of trucks and tanks. We got the army to supply them. The convoy was about half a mile long, and it was a musical, and the music had to be in sync with the caravan going by and people singing from the tops of these tanks. It was a heck of a hard thing to do, and if somebody made one little error, they had to go up the road about five miles to turn around and come back and start all over again. It took us I don't know how many weeks to film this one sequence.

"Edward Everett Horton, Chester Klute, and I made up the three comedy characters. We were lawyers and the thing was so haphazardly written that none of us knew what we were doing.

"One morning Buzz Berkeley, Eddie Horton, and I were sitting on a sound stage that had a lake, trees, and a little boathouse and dock on it. Eddie had figured out that since the stars of the film were such poor actors, he, Chester, and I were the real stars. During one of those bull sessions by the lake, Eddie and Buzz were joking, and Buzz, wanting to take advantage of Eddie's famous double take, came up with a great idea:

" 'Wouldn't it be funny if Eddie was swimming across the lake and a white horse came by going the other direction with a guy riding it? Eddie could do his double take and keep swimming.'

"Everybody said, 'Yeah, that would be funny,' and so help me Buzz did it. The horse swam by and Eddie did his double take, but you can imagine how many takes they had to get to have the horse and Eddie in the right position to show the double take while he was swimming.

"That was Berkeley's swan song at Warner Brothers. The picture was such a turkey that he couldn't get another job there.

"I didn't do any war films. People seemed to want things bright—lots of comedy and happy endings—during the war. They didn't want to be depressed.

"I'm not sure of the exact number, but I made somewhere around 250 films. Every once in a while I'll see where somebody said they made thirty films, and I'll say that's pretty good but . . . However, they probably had better parts than I did."

A Jap's a Jap. It makes no difference whether he's an American or not.

Lt. Gen. John L. DeWitt

We have not, however, uncovered through these searches any dangerous persons that we could not otherwise know about. We have not found among all the sticks of dynamite and gunpowder any evidence that any of it was used in bombs. We have not found a single machine gun nor have we found any gun in any circumstances indicating that it was to be used in a manner helpful to our enemies. We have not found a camera which we have reason to believe was for use in espionage.

Memo from Attorney General Francis Biddle to President Roosevelt, May 1942, released after the war

I am for immediate removal of every Japanese on the West Coast to a point deep in the interior. I don't mean a nice part of the interior either. Herd 'em up, pack 'em off and give 'em the inside room in the badlands. . . . Let 'em be pinched, hurt, hungry and dead up against it. . . . If making one innocent Japanese uncomfortable would prevent one scheming Japanese from costing the life of one American boy, then let the million innocent suffer. . . . Personally, I hate the Japanese. And that goes for all of them.

Newspaper columnist Henry McLemore,
January 30, 1942

Associated press—(Jan. 31, 1942)—Sixty-nine additional areas in California from which all alien enemies are to be excluded on and after February 15, were announced today by Attorney General Francis Biddle.

"You are fools to suppose you can win our friendship with good food and fine buildings," snorted a Wehrmacht veteran to a guard at a Michigan camp. By the record he would not seem far wrong—unless both the army and the American public wake up to the realities which this war should have made self-evident. Overseas our soldiers fight and die to break the hold these men and their fellows have fixed upon a continent sheltering more than 300 million people. That grip they have cemented with an array of thoroughly documented atrocities staggering to the civilized mind.

James H. Powers, "What to Do with German
Prisoners: The American Muddle"

8

The Victims

IN RETROSPECT it is almost miraculous that the war wasn't used more widely by political groups as an excuse to suspend individual rights, and by bigots to settle old quarrels between religious and racial groups. An event as devastating as World War II was to the societies of Europe, Asia, and America gave the dominant Christian, Caucasian peoples license to subjugate, even eradicate, minority groups of which it disapproved. The definition of patriotism like interpretations of the Bible, can be reshaped and stretched to mean almost anything a dominant group wants. Yet, compared with the actions of our enemies in the war, our treatment of minorities was mild.

Before we offer this restraint as reason for tribute to our leaders and ourselves, however, it must be remembered that we had the totalitarian regimes of our enemies as a counterpoint for our policies. We had to be their opposite; it was to our advantage to remain an open, compassionate society for the majority of our citizens. If we portrayed the Germans, the Italians, and the Japanese as evil, we had to be compassionate and just. If we were fighting a war for personal freedom throughout the world, as we said in our propaganda, then we had to have a free society ourselves.

The victims and potential victims on the home front were many. The most obvious were people of German, Italian, and Japanese descent, no matter how long they had been in America. The others included religious groups, such as the Jehovah's Witnesses, who were an irritant to other religious groups and patriots; the Mennonites, Hutterites, Quakers, and other, smaller religious groups that did not believe in war and refused to kill; the blacks because they were a traditional target for professional haters; and almost any political party other than the Democrats and Republicans.

The German- and Italian-Americans had something of a built-in immunity: They looked like the dominant Caucasian group. Darker-skinned Italians, of course, were much more visible than the Germanic people, but important political leaders and commentators were quick to point out that Italian-Americans were fine people, indeed, and that some of the greatest baseball players in America, the three Di Maggio brothers, were of Italian descent. Next to our warriors, baseball stars were the greatest American heroes of the period.

Thus Germans and Italians living in America escaped most of the patriotic wrath. Other Americans tended to sympathize with them and treated the war led by their native countries as a source of embarrassment, something like an uncle who had become a petty crook.

For many German- and Italian-Americans, the war was indeed a source of shame. Nancy Meyers remembers:

"It really embarrassed my dad when the Italians joined the Germans. He came over from Italy as a little boy and still spoke with a heavy accent. We heard some comments about being Italian, but he was so involved in community activities that we didn't get much sarcasm.

"All during the war he was worried about his family still over there. His father was still living and he had two sisters and four brothers in Italy, some of whom were in the Italian Army. I had a cousin, American, who was sent to North Africa and fought there and went on up to Italy. He couldn't speak a word of Italian, but as soon as he had a chance he looked up my grandparents and other relatives who lived in one particular district. He found them and introduced himself, and joined the village in a week-long fiesta. At one point my grandfather sidled up to him and said they had girls for him if he wanted one, but I don't know what my cousin said.

"When he came home and told my father, I remember my father crying because it was the first time he had heard from his family since before the war started. It wasn't until 1948 that he took his first trip back to Italy after more than forty years in this country.

"I was always ashamed of being Italian. We were in an Irish neighborhood, all through grade school, high school, and part of college. We were made fun of and called wops and dagos. Not long after the war it became suddenly very campy to be Italian. But during the war there was nothing worse than being Italian-Catholic-Democrat."

The Japanese-Americans did not fare nearly so well. They were alien to the Caucasians. They looked different. They could not blend so easily into the society, and their native tongue was not spoken on the streets of New York, Boston, and Chicago. Our relatives had not married their children. For a variety of reasons, they had remained apart. While the German- and Italian-Americans received sympathy, the Japanese-Americans were more often treated as local units of the Japanese military apparatus.

In time of war, the most dangerous weapon of them all is patriotism. It is the club that bullies can use to ignore constitutional law, and to intimidate political and court leaders who would interfere with their missions of greed and hate pursued under the umbrella of patriotism. Judges, all the way to the Supreme Court, can yield to the most vocal proponents of drastic actions and later explain it away by blaming it on "the times." No one is better at convincing themselves that morality and the common good is on their side than these plunderers marching under the banner of whatever faith or political philosophy is in power at the moment. War creates victims, they say. Someone always has to suffer for the common good. Time heals all wounds. To suffer for one's country is a sign of nobility. Life will return to normal when the war is over.

Yet in spite of America's propensity for violence and injustice, it is one of the few nations in history that almost invariably suffers from a delayed national guilt after the fact. Thus, the Indians, the blacks, the Chicanos, the Puerto Ricans, and other minority groups who have been showered with money and economic opportunities after long suffering. That is part of the rationale that led America to rebuild Germany and Japan after the war. Some Indian leaders have joked that Hitler was one of the best friends they ever had, because shortly after World War II ended, the American government granted many concessions to these minority groups to further remove any taint of injustice similar to that found in Europe and Asia during the war years.

Ironically, the group that suffered the most in Europe, the Jews, didn't really become a cause until the European war ended and their suffering, which transcends our worst nightmares, became known. America was very, very slow to take action on their behalf, even when the first reliable reports came out of Europe that Jews were being massacred simply because they were Jews. We were told that thousands, if not millions, of Jews could be saved from extermination on the edges of the war zone—in Rumania and Hungary, for example. Yet we did nothing while many died, until Eleanor

Roosevelt began making speeches and pressuring government leaders on their behalf.

The European war was not fought to save the Jews, any
more than the American Civil War was fought to free black
slaves. The Jews were an issue, but a very minor one. It was
mainly the efforts of American Jews raising funds for their
European counterparts that helped bring the survivors out of
the battle zone to safety. When several thousand began arriving on America's Eastern Seaboard and were placed in
camps to await sponsorship and jobs, the vast majority of
help came from other Jews, not the government or the population as a whole. The horrors of the concentration and death
camps were not fully known until after the European war
ended, but few Americans would have been willing to send
troops to Europe simply to help save the Jews from extermination.

Constance Stirrup Lackey tells of her town's experience
with the refugees when she was a teen-age girl living in Oswego, New York:

"Fort Ontario was just outside of town, and I remember
two traumatic experiences because of that fort.

"The first was the arrival of the all-black 369th Battalion.
Nobody knew what to do with them because we'd never been
around blacks before, and here they were by the hundreds
suddenly. They got a very nasty reception. There were street
fights between the whites and blacks, and the taverns were
forced to serve them in face of a boycott by the entire fort.
So the tavern owners did serve them. But whenever a black
downed his drink, the bartender would break the glass rather
than let someone else drink from it.

"Then, as the war progressed and they used the fort less
and less for soldiers, we had a large influx of Jewish refugees
from Europe. They were called 'Eleanor's Folly,' because

Eleanor Roosevelt worked so hard to bring refugees into this country, and the locals called them refuJews.' It must have been very hard for those people to become part of the local economy with this prejudice against them, but several did. I never became acquainted with any of them, except one who opened a tailor shop. But these people were usually intellectually superior to the ordinary Oswego citizen, and many were from the intellectual cream of Europe."

The blacks' suffering was about on a par with that of the Japanese-Americans. They were still subjugated, obviously, and many whites who weren't known as racists were convinced that black soldiers were naturally cowards. It would be a long time before the military services decided to try them in combat due to this attitude.

"Mrs. Roosevelt was the best friend the Negro ever had and they pretty well had the run of the place in Washington, D.C. They kept them in their place pretty well in Virginia, though. We lived in Washington then, and I remember one time I got on a bus that crossed over into Virginia, and there were big signs on those buses: 'Negroes Sit in the Rear,' or 'Colored in the Rear.' Something like that.

"Well, this big Negro got on and sat down behind the driver's seat. When we crossed the Potomac, the driver stopped the bus and told the Negro to get in the back. The Negro wouldn't, and the driver told him to get in the back or get off, and the Negro said, 'Nope.' So the driver called an MP who was directing traffic and the MP told him the same thing. So the Negro got off rather than sit in the back."

George DeMerell told a similar story:

"I was deputy chief of staff of the Charleston Port of Embarkation and we had two battalions of black soldiers training to load and unload cargo, which was about all they'd let blacks do in those days. At the same time we had a group of Italian prisoners of war working there, too. The prisoners were allowed to go downtown in groups of three or so accompanied by guards. When the Italians got on the bus, they could sit anywhere. When the black soldiers got on a bus, they had to sit in the rear.

"I didn't think it was right and discussed it with the commanding general. He agreed it wasn't right but said a post commander had to be very careful not to 'fly in the face of local custom.' And that was that."

Walter Hundley, a young black growing up in Philadelphia during the war, was more fortunate than most; he had dedicated high-school teachers who gave him a sense of direction, and a supportive family.

"Our high school had a lot of very activist-minded faculty members, and had several Quakers among them. Interestingly enough, several of them had Ph.D.'s, and I think that was due to the fact that they had earned their degrees during the Depression and colleges were not hiring. We got a hell of an education as a result and were exposed to social concerns more than most kids.

"Through the Quakers we became aware of the Japanese-American problem, but other than a rather small series of meetings and protest activities—maybe picketing and writing letters to the newspapers and perhaps a petition to the president—we didn't do much about them. Most of the people in Philadelphia, particularly the black community, seemed to be unaware or unconcerned.

"At that time the city had a practice of not hiring blacks to drive streetcars, and because of the war the real manpower problem caused them to start hiring women. But they even ran out of women. So the federal government finally said,

'Look, we've got to keep those streetcars running and if you don't have the manpower, hire a minority.' The union really rebelled at that and I remember seeing stories in the paper to the effect that the next thing we knew blacks would be marrying our sisters. There were fights and a lot of violence over it.

"Finally Roosevelt put soldiers, armed soldiers, on each streetcar. There sat a guy in uniform with a rifle and bayonet on it sitting in front, and another in the rear. They were on every streetcar in Philadelphia.

"The shipyards wouldn't hire minorities either. So the federal government intervened again and ordered blacks in there and gave them jobs. When violence flared they put machine guns up on the roofs and other emplacements around the shipyards and threatened to shoot if they didn't work together peacefully.

"But when the war was over there was no more government intervention like that. The attempts to continue these kinds of gains were a very messy affair.

"I became a very straight arrow and before the war was over I had been interviewed by the FBI and all that kind of thing. They couldn't believe that a black was a pacifist. When I entered divinity school, the draft board that had refused to give me a conscientious-objector classification now gave me a ministerial classification. I sent it back and told them that if ministers believed in fighting, they ought to fight; that they shouldn't get a special exemption. I haven't heard from the Selective Service since. Not one time.

"It was awfully tough being a high-school pacifist. I didn't go around flaunting it, because even the kids on the block didn't understand it. I was very, very lucky. I don't know how I ever got out of that neighborhood alive. A whole lot of others didn't. I mean that literally; they did not get out alive."

* * *

While the suffering of these innocents can easily be summarized under broad racial or religious categories, the experiences of individuals within these groups cannot. Each individual was subjected to different experiences, and, in spite of the injustices, many emerged stronger than when the war began, if only in their determination to never be a victim again. In the case of the Japanese-Americans, it was also a determination to merge completely into American life, to become professionals instead of laborers, to become part of the dominant group.

Decades after the fact, many Japanese-Americans are still amazed that they weren't treated even worse than they were. Fortunately most lived along the West Coast, in "Little Tokyos," and were not familiar sights along the East Coast where the political power and media are centered. When the war began, there were millions of Americans who didn't even know there were Japanese-born people in this country with children who were American citizens, with all the rights guaranteed by our constitution. Since there were fewer than 200,000 in the nation, they had not been a political or social force. They had not produced entertainers or athletes or national politicians. They sought to remain invisible, which was impossible on the West Coast, particularly in California where 80 percent of the estimated 127,000 Japanese-Americans on the West Coast lived.

Since so many of them were concentrated in one area, it was popular long before the war to hate Japs. They had been imported to America, like the Chinese, to be little more than slaves or indentured servants. Some laborers had managed to save their meager pay and return to Japan, but most—like the European peasants and poor Irish fleeing the potato famine—chose to remain in America. Even with its terrible injustices and reputation for random, indiscriminate violence, America offered more opportunity than their homeland.

The Japanese-Americans had a reputation for industriousness that enabled them to succeed and become property owners, which made the dominant Caucasians even more resentful of them. No Oriental immigrant was permitted to own property under the terms of the Oriental Exclusion Act of 1924, and as early as 1913 a law had gone into effect preventing Orientals from leasing land for more than three years. Yet the supporters of these blatantly racial laws could not find loopholes or introduce laws barring second-generation Orientals from automatic citizenship with full rights, and this became a loophole for the Japanese-Americans: They couldn't own property, but their American-citizen children could, so they were able to purchase property in their children's names.

For the most part, this property was marginal at best, land that Caucasians did not want—desert, swamps, land beside railroad tracks, beneath power lines, or hillside land. When the Japanese-Americans turned this land into lush gardens and orchards after a few years of hard labor, many Caucasians interpreted their success as almost an insult. Like the successful blacks, these people were getting "uppity." They refused to either go away or remain subjugated.

The attack on Pearl Harbor was the catalyst to put the Japanese-Americans back in their place, and the impact of the raid that December Sunday of 1941 was felt immediately by residents of Little Tokyos all over the West. Ben Yorita remembers:

"I was out for a drive in the family car with my sister and her girl friend. We didn't have the radio on and didn't know about the attack, but we knew something was wrong because of all the dirty looks Caucasians gave us. Usually they looked right through us as if we didn't exist, but that day they were staring at us, giving us mean looks.

"We were a little frightened by this and went home. When we got there, our parents were gathered around the

radio and they told us what had happened at Pearl Harbor.
Then we understood."

That day changed the lives of Japanese-Americans completely. In most cases, it would be less than a month before
they were removed by the government and placed in camps
far inland and behind barbed wire. Photos of them being
herded by armed soldiers into fairgrounds and racetracks,
then aboard trains bound for remote camps, bear a frightening resemblance to photos of European Jews en route to extermination camps. The basic reasons and the first chapter
of their forced migrations were the same.

It is easy to select targets today for our after-the-fact
anger. There were newspaper columnists such as Westbrook
Pegler and Henry McLemore, California attorney general
Earl Warren, army general John L. DeWitt, and numerous
congressmen and governors of western states who led a campaign of hatred against these innocent people. It is interesting
to note that none of these public figures attacked either the
German or Italian immigrants, and after the battle of North
Africa was won and more than 250,000 German and Italian
soldiers were brought to camps in America, there was no out-
cry to execute them.

Yet the indictment against Americans for the treatment
of these people cannot be total. Forgotten, or never known
by the public, were those Caucasians who worked on behalf
of these pawns, men and women who remained loyal to them
as friends, often at the risk of their personal safety. Obviously
there weren't nearly enough such people to have much effect
on the so-called relocation program, but there were some,
and they were able to make a difference.

Two examples of this were men in Seattle, who did so
for humanitarian and religious reasons. One was a Quaker
and the other the pastor of a Baptist church with a congregation composed almost entirely of Japanese-Americans.

The Quaker was Floyd Schmoe, a native of Kansas who had moved to the Pacific Northwest as a college student before World War I and was the first naturalist at Mount Rainier National Park. During World War I, Schmoe had worked with refugees in Europe, and once was held captive with a group of Quakers and Red Cross workers en route to Poland with food for the refugees. Schmoe worked as a teacher at the University of Washington after 1928, but when Pearl Harbor was attacked he quit his job and went to Philadelphia to talk to the general secretary of the Quaker organization and told him he feared there would be a situation in Hawaii similar to the Jews in Europe. "Except in this case it would be American citizens," Schmoe said. He recalls:

"I had been in Honolulu a year earlier while Japan and the United States were exchanging ultimatums, because I thought the Japanese-Americans there would be hit the hardest if war came, and we were already working against an evacuation in Hawaii, which we fully expected. But it didn't turn out that way. It was amazing to me how little the Japanese in Hawaii suffered. The teachers at the university there didn't lose their jobs, and the businessmen continued operating their businesses. A few were picked up and sent to detention camps, but there was no general roundup like there was on the West Coast.

"It was a different story there. We helped the Japanese fight it at first, but when it became apparent there was no way of stopping the roundup, we concentrated our efforts on helping them. We went to the camps with them, and I got involved with some college students, trying to help them stay in school. We would get them accepted in the schools with scholarships and that sort of thing so they could make it on their own.

"Of course the Quakers looked to their own colleges first because we have several in the East, and they took as many as they could. The first students we sent back went to Guilford College in North Carolina, and we were worried because of the attitude toward blacks down there, and didn't know whether the kids would be considered black or white. Fortunately, one of the kids was a very good baseball player and he opened things up for the other kids. There was one church college, not Quaker, in Idaho Falls that wouldn't take any of the kids, but nearly every school in the East was open to them."

The evacuation process began swiftly after the war was declared on Japan on December 8, 1941. Although some apologists have since insisted it was a sound military decision to evacuate all suspected Japanese aliens from the potentially dangerous coastline, the overwhelming evidence indicates it was a purely racial decision. The matter of these people was under discussion before the Pearl Harbor attack; and in spite of absolutely no evidence that they were still loyal to Japan, and reports had been made to the State Department to that effect, they became a convenient target for military rage at the attack.

The military declared the entire Pacific Coast, from the Canadian border to the Mexican border, off-limits to anyone with Japanese blood. The area even extended around the Mexican border to include all of southern Arizona. All people of Japanese blood, no matter how little, were to be interned and shipped inland away from the coast, and this included Japanese-Americans living in the Alaskan wilderness, and even children of Japanese-Eskimo heritage. The Latin-American nations followed suit: Mexico, Costa Rica, Brazil, and other nations agreed to intern their own bewildered Japanese immigrants as a favor to the United States.

None were given an opportunity to dispose properly of their homes, businesses, farms, and belongings. They were ordered to report to assembly centers—such as fairgrounds and racetracks—on a specific day with only those belongings they could carry. Obviously thousands of them lost nearly everything they owned in the process. They had to sell their property to anyone who would buy it, and it was a buyers' market. Caucasians made the rounds of Japanese homes looking for things to buy at fire-sale prices—pianos, radios, furniture, farm equipment, clothing, anything the people could not carry to the assembly centers.

Some Caucasians worked on their behalf, but not many. In an effort to at least delay the evacuation a few months, some newspaper columnists pointed out that Japanese-American vegetable farmers supplied entire cities or communities, and to pack them off and leave the farms abandoned was not in the nation's best interest during a war. But no exceptions were permitted, except a few children who were in hospitals. The elderly who were bedridden were transported to the assembly centers by truck or ambulance.

The government established fifteen such assembly centers in the three Pacific Coast states, one each in Washington, Arizona, and Oregon, and the remainder throughout California. Then ten relocation camps—a polite term for concentration camps—were established throughout the West: Manzanar and Tule Lake in California, Poston and Gila in Arizona, Minidoka in Idaho, Heart Mountain in Wyoming, Granada in Colorado, Topaz in Utah, and Rohwer and Jerome in Arkansas.

In addition, the Justice Department had five camps for suspected Japanese sympathizers: at Santa Fe, New Mexico; Bismarck, North Dakota; Crystal City, Texas; and Missoula, Montana. Naturally some Japanese-Americans still felt a certain allegiance to their homeland, but these were few. Many gathered in these camps were taken there on a hunch or to fill quotas, or because they had been commercial fishermen and were suspected of planning to help Japanese submarines off the Pacific Coast. It was to one of these camps that the father of writer Jeanne Houston was sent, and he gave one of the most poignant replies the military received in response to the loyalty questions. He told his interviewer that when a mother and father are fighting, the children don't take sides; they just want their parents to stop fighting.

The indignities heaped on these people were almost uncountable and certainly incredible. One of the worst was a loyalty questionnaire all had to fill out that was called "Statement of United States Citizenship Ancestry." It was question 28 that rankled the most and came closer to causing a rebellion than almost anything else. The question was:

Will you swear unqualified allegiance to the United States of America and faithfully defend the United States from any or all attack by foreign or domestic forces, and forswear any form of allegiance or obedience to the Japanese emperor, or any other foreign government, power or organization?

To the first-generation Japanese-Americans, the *Issei* who were born in Japan, this question was particularly insulting because all Japanese nationals were asked to forswear allegiance to the country of which they were citizens and to give their allegiance to a country that would not grant them citizenship. A "yes" answer could conceivably mean they would become legally persons without a country. Finally, after several Caucasian employees at the camps complained loudly and often, the question was rewritten and softened, but by that time the worst of the damage had been done.

The basic plan of the camps, which was carried out to a degree, was to remove the people from the coastal areas and put them in the relocation camps until they could be placed in other parts of the country. Some argued that this was for their own good as much as for the national security because it was feared blind patriots would attack the Japanese-Americans out of frustration over the Pacific war. This, however, was nothing more than another method of rationalizing a bad decision. The fact is, many were relocated, particularly the younger people of college age or just older who could enter the work force easily. The older people had little hope of finding places to live inland, and most were essentially prisoners until the war ended and they could be returned to their hometowns.

Still, people like Floyd Schmoe and Baptist minister Emory Andrews stayed with them throughout the whole ordeal. Says Schmoe:

"When the evacuation began, we helped get them to the trains and drove them to the camps. But one of the best things my wife and I found we could do was try and help the people left behind. There were more than 100 children left at hospitals because they had tuberculosis. Some were teenagers and even younger, and we maintained a contact between them and their parents. If they died, as several did, we sometimes were able to get their mother or father to come to the funeral—always under guard, of course. There was even one case where the camp commander expected the family to pay for the guard on the trip.

"We carried things back and forth between our Seattle homes and the camp at Minidoka, Idaho. My daughter got involved in the evacuation the same time I did, and took several cars over to the camps for people after the War Relocation Authority permitted them to have cars and trucks to drive back and forth to jobs on farms in the area. One of the first trips she made was driving a truck for a fellow who was a big strawberry grower on Bainbridge Island. She was about seventeen then, and she undertook to drive this truck 700 miles to the camp. She became fascinated with the whole situation, and fell in love with one of the boys and married him.

"I ran into some pretty sad cases in the camps. There were several second- and third-generation descendants of Japanese whalers or cooks on vessels that were sent to Alaska during the 1860s and 1870s. They brought these kids down to the camps and they didn't speak English or Japanese, and didn't even know where Japan was. Absurd, most absurd.

"But most things were absurd then. Before the big roundup, we were in very close contact with the FBI. Very close. We lived in a modest house near Lake Washington on a low hill and we had some *Nisei* [first-generation American born] girls from the Yakima Valley living with us and attending the university with our kids. They were with us at the time of Pearl Harbor, and some of our neighbors who had seen these Japanese kids going and coming had reported us to the FBI. They told the FBI that we lived on a hill that was full of tunnels and the tunnels were full of Japs. So the FBI came to investigate and some of the other neighbors told the FBI it was crazy. Most of our neighbors were pretty good about it.

"The whole period was one of absurdities. One Japanese-American family was able to get out of Seattle before the evacuation and move to Spokane. He was a dentist and went over there to practice. They lived in a nice, two-story house in a nice section of town, and sometimes we went over there and stayed with them, and [we] became well acquainted with them.

"Down the street was a Catholic church, and down the street the other way was a tavern. The gang that hung out in the tavern began organizing a vigilante group to drive the Japanese family out of Spokane. The priest heard about it and

told us at the Friends Service Committee in Seattle to see if
we couldn't do something about it. So my wife, one of my
daughters, and I drove over.

"The priest had been keeping his ear to the ground and
found out when this raid was going to take place. So we had
a big party that night. There were three or four of us from
Seattle, and some friends from Spokane, and all were Caucasians except the Japanese family. When the gang at the
tavern got liquored sufficiently . . . about ten o'clock that
night, they came down the street with clubs. They were going
to break down the house and drive them out. Most of the
gang stayed down on the lawn, but they had a spokesman with
a little more courage—a little more liquor, perhaps—and he
came up and knocked on the door.

"Mrs. S., a beautiful woman, went to the door and invited him in. He stepped into the hallway and saw all these
people and the priest and the rest of us. I don't remember
what he said but he was fumbling for words, mumbling something, and then excused himself and went back out to talk
to the rest of the gang.

" 'Why don't you all come in,' Mrs. S. called to them.

"They sort of mumbled among themselves awhile and
walked away. Nothing more was heard after that."

The experiences of the Reverend Emory Andrews were
similar, but his involvement with the Japanese-American
community of some 10,000 was more direct. He became pastor
of the Japanese Baptist Church in 1929 and served in that capacity for twenty-six years, including the time spent with his
congregation during the war years.

"I don't know of any other racial group that became
citizens when they had the chance like they did," Reverend
Andrews said shortly before his death. "The Italians and the
Swedes and a lot of other European groups came here and
stayed many, many years without becoming citizens. Not

the Japanese. I don't know why except they just considered this their country."

Andrews never expected the evacuation, he said. He feared something unpleasant would happen, but he lived so closely with the Japanese-Americans that perhaps he couldn't imagine the rest of America not respecting them as much as he did.

"Mother's Day 1942 was the first Sunday my church had ever been empty. Everyone had been taken to the fairgrounds at Pyallup by then. [This temporary camp, where the families were placed in sheds used for show animals during the annual fair, was named Camp Harmony.]

"The evacuation happened because there had always been a minority group in California who wanted to get the Japanese off the Coast for economic reasons. This fact, combined with the fact that General John L. DeWitt had a personal prejudice against the Japanese, was what really brought it about. I've always said that if there had been any other army commander on the West Coast, the evacuation wouldn't have happened.

"I just took it for granted that my family would go along with the group. My daughters actually cried because they couldn't go behind the barbed wire with their friends. Our whole family had been brought up in the Japanese community and all their friends went to the camp. Of course we couldn't go behind the barbed wire; only employees of the government could.

"But it was better this way because we moved to Twin Falls, the largest town near Minidoka, which was nineteen miles away, and we rented a house larger than we needed for our own family. We turned the house into a hostel so the Japanese could use it. There were young men working on farms and in town who stayed with us during the week and went back to the camp on weekends. And there were Japanese-

Americans in uniform coming to visit their families before they were sent overseas. Others were people who came down for baptismal services, weddings, and things like that. We had a guest book at that time and we had an average of 167 visitors in the house *per month!*

"I made fifty-six round trips back to Seattle from Twin Falls to pick up cars, trucks, and belongings for people in camp. Most of the trips were to Seattle, but a few were down in Oregon and California. I almost always went by train or bus, and if I was going to Seattle it was an 850-mile trip each way. If I was driving, my route depended on the kind of car I was driving, what condition it was in. But several times I went by way of Spokane, which was a 950-mile trip, because there were relatives or friends of people in the camp that I picked up to take with me so they could visit and see what the camp looked like. They were out of the military zone, which was roughly along the crest of the Cascade Range, so they were free to travel."

When Reverend Andrews traveled with Japanese-Americans, they almost always encountered some form of racial prejudice when they stopped for fuel or meals. To his surprise, he found that many people along the route had never heard of the evacuation. Some service-station owners refused to sell gasoline; others, who knew what was going on in the country, were extremely kind.

On one trip he went to Spokane to pick up a girl the church had helped get a job so she could stay out of the camp.

"We stopped in a little Idaho town for lunch. We sat down and waited and waited. Finally a waitress came over and took our orders, and we waited and waited some more. The owner of the restaurant finally came over and asked me if the girl was Japanese. I explained that she wasn't Japanese, she was Japanese-American, and her brother at that moment was fighting in Europe in a United States uniform. It didn't make any difference. They wouldn't serve us.

"So we went down the street, and the woman from the restaurant stood out front watching us the whole time. We went into another restaurant and didn't realize until we were inside that it was Chinese. The young Chinese manager was so gracious, so kind, and so different from across the street that I felt at the time he went out of his way to correct the situation. We could have left town after the first incident and said they all were prejudiced, but maybe that lady in the first restaurant was the only prejudiced person in town."

There would be many other examples of this blind prejudice, especially around Twin Falls because many there felt the Japanese-Americans had been forced on them. When Reverend Andrews first arrived in Twin Falls, he stayed in a hotel while looking for a house to rent. One evening he was eating in a local restaurant when he saw a "No Japs Allowed" sign, and commented on it to the owner.

"He knew I worked with the people in the camp, and told me I couldn't eat there," Andrews said. As he was leaving, the owner gave him a shove out the door.

"I didn't fall down, but he gave me a good shove. About a month later he had two FBI men there from Portland and he told them about me. I spent about three hours with them answering their questions. They left and didn't bother me anymore.

"My family moved in with me, and once we were settled in, the café owner came by and stood on the sidewalk shouting at me, calling me names. Soon afterward he bought the house and told us to move. He must have had a lot of hate in him to go to all that trouble. Anyway, we got out and found another house across the street that was nicer, larger, and better suited for our needs. Ironic, wasn't it?"

* * *

Reverend Andrews's problems weren't restricted to local bigots or insensitive bureaucrats by any means. He also had to ward off criticism by his own church.

"Because I was gone so much making trips to and from Seattle and the rest of the Coast, the church criticized me quite often. They thought I should be teaching and preaching in camp and doing counseling and all that. It bothered me for quite a while, then the director of missions came out two or three times because he was so interested in resettling students. I told him I was getting all that criticism, and he told me he thought I was doing what had to be done, and that it was better work than preaching in camp. So I felt better after that.

"But he lost his job. The church told him he was spending too much time with the Japanese. Think of it—a Christian organization."

Before he left for Idaho, Reverend Andrews had turned the church into a storage building for the congregation's belongings they couldn't take with them. The Andrews family marked off the gymnasium into ten-foot squares with a two-foot aisle between, and filled the entire gymnasium with personal belongings. The government had promised to provide warehouse space for the evacuees, but it hadn't been built in time.

"Every time I went back to Seattle to get something out of the gym, it was always sitting on the bottom of the pile, and the piles were very high. When they left things with friends, who said they would take care of them, I'd almost always find them used or broken or sold or given away. It was terrible." Still, he said, "I think they had some true friends, and I think a lot of people realized the evacuation was wrong."

Reverend Andrews wasn't certain what would have happened had the Japanese-Americans been permitted to remain in their homes, although he was reasonably sure there would have been some incidents. He told of one incident in Spokane, where many were able to find jobs and avoid the camps. A doctor had just moved there when a rock was thrown through the living-room window one night. Nobody was hurt, but to everyone's relief, and delight the entire neighborhood was up in arms over the incident and was ready to lynch whomever threw the rock. There were no other such incidents in that neighborhood.

Most Japanese-Americans today are solid members of the American middle class. They are attorneys, doctors, teachers, engineers, scientists, dentists, businessmen and the like. They are no longer huddled together in single neighborhoods, and can be found living in suburban neighborhoods, townhouses, and condominiums. Many are still farmers and landscape architects. As much as their physical characteristics will permit, they have blended into the fabric of American society.

Yet almost without exception, these middle-aged and middle-class citizens all share a common memory—that of being imprisoned from 1942 until 1945 or 1946, then having to start their lives all over again. Many do not discuss that experience, even with their own children. But a few do, if for no other reason than to keep Americans alert to the fact that such things can and do happen in this society. Nobody who went through that episode emerged untouched, unaffected. It was one of the most important things that ever happened to them, and, as we shall see, the end result in many cases was a freedom their parents could never have anticipated.

A typical case was that of Ben Yorita, who was a student at the University of Washington when Pearl Harbor was attacked.

"Students weren't as aware of national politics then as they are now, and Japanese-Americans were actually apolitical then. Our parents couldn't vote, so we simply weren't interested in politics because there was nothing we could do about it if we were.

"There were two reasons we were living in the ghettos: Birds of a feather flock together, and we had all the traditional aspects of Japanese life—Japanese restaurants, baths, and so forth; and discrimination forced us together. The dominant society prevented us from going elsewhere.

"Right after Pearl Harbor we had no idea what was going to happen, but toward the end of December we started hearing rumors and talk of the evacuation started. We could tell from what we read in the newspapers and the propaganda they were printing—guys like Henry McLemore, who said he hated all Japs and that we should be rounded up, gave us the idea of how strong feelings were against us. So we were expecting something and the evacuation was no great surprise.

"I can't really say what my parents thought about everything because we didn't communicate that well. I never asked them what they thought. We communicated on other things, but not political matters.

"Once the evacuation was decided, we were told we had about a month to get rid of our property or do whatever we wanted to with it. That was a rough time for my brother, who was running a printshop my parents owned. We were still in debt on it and we didn't know what to do with all the equipment. The machines were old but still workable, and we had English type and Japanese type. Japanese characters had to be set by hand and were very hard to replace. Finally, the whole works was sold, and since nobody would buy the Japanese type, we had to sell it as junk lead at 50¢ a pound. We sold the equipment through newspaper classified ads: 'Evacuating: Household goods for sale.' Secondhand dealers and everybody else came in and bought our refrigerator, the piano, and I had a whole bunch of books I sold for $5, which was one of my personal losses. We had to sell our car, and the whole thing was very sad. By the way, it was the first time we had ever had a refrigerator and it had to be sold after only a few months.

"We could take only what we could carry, and most of us were carrying two suitcases or duffel bags. The rest of our stuff that we couldn't sell was stored in the Buddhist church my mother belonged to. When we came back, thieves had broken in and stolen almost everything of value from the church.

"I had a savings account that was left intact, but people who had their money in the Japanese bank in Seattle had their assets frozen from Pearl Harbor until the late 1960s, when the funds were finally released. They received no interest.

"They took all of us down to the Puyallup fairgrounds, Camp Harmony, and everything had been thrown together in haste. They had converted some of the display and exhibit areas into rooms and had put up some barracks on the parking lot. The walls in the barracks were about eight feet high with open space above and with big knotholes in the boards of the partitions. Our family was large, so we had two rooms.

"They had also built barbed-wire fences around the camp with a tower on each corner with military personnel and machine guns, rifles, and searchlights. It was terrifying because we didn't know what was going to happen to us. We didn't know where we were going and we were just doing what we were told. No questions asked. If you get an order, you go ahead and do it.

"There was no fraternization, no contact with the military or any Caucasian except when we were processed into the camp. But the treatment in Camp Harmony was fairly loose in the sense that we were free to roam around in the camp. But it was like buffalo in cages or behind barbed wire.

"There was no privacy whatsoever in the latrines and showers, and it was humiliating for the women because they were much more modest then than today. It wasn't so bad for the men because they were accustomed to open latrines and showers.

"We had no duties in the sense that we were required to work, but you can't expect a camp to manage itself. They had jobs open in the kitchen and stock room, and eventually they opened a school where I helped teach a little. I wasn't a qualified teacher, and I got about $13 a month. We weren't given an allowance while we were in Camp Harmony waiting for the camp at Minidoka to be finished, so it was pretty tight for some families.

"From Camp Harmony on, the family structure was broken down. Children ran everywhere they wanted to in the camp, and parents lost their authority. We could eat in any mess hall we wanted, and kids began ignoring their parents and wandering wherever they pleased.

"Eventually they boarded us on army trucks and took us to trains to be transported to the camps inland. We had been in Camp Harmony from May until September. There was a shortage of transportation at the time and they brought out these old, rusty cars with gaslight fixtures. As soon as we got aboard we pulled the shades down so people couldn't stare at us. The cars were all coaches and we had to sit all the way to camp, which was difficult for some of the older people and the invalids. We made makeshift beds out of the seats for them, and did the best we could.

"When we got to Twin Falls, we were loaded onto trucks again, and we looked around and all we could see was that vast desert with nothing but sagebrush. When the trucks started rolling, it was dusty, and the camp itself wasn't completed yet. The barracks had been built and the kitchen facilities were there, but the laundry room, showers, and latrines were not finished. They had taken a bulldozer in the good old American style and leveled the terrain and then built the camp. When the wind blew, it was dusty and we had to wear face masks to go to the dining hall. When winter came and it rained, the dust turned into gumbo mud. Until the latrines were finished, we had to use outhouses.

"The administrators were civilians and they tried to organize us into a chain of command to make the camp function. Each block of barracks was told to appoint a representative, who were called block managers. Of course we called them the Blockheads.

"When winter came, it was very cold and I began withdrawing my savings to buy clothes because we had none that was suitable for that climate. Montgomery Ward and Sears Roebuck did a landslide business from the camps because we ordered our shoes and warm clothing from them. The people who didn't have savings suffered quite a bit until the camp distributed navy pea coats. Then everybody in camp was wearing outsize pea coats because we were such small people. Other than army blankets, I don't remember any other clothing issues.

"The barracks were just single-wall construction and the only insulation was tar paper nailed on the outside, and they never were improved. The larger rooms had potbellied stoves, and we all slept on army cots. Only the people over sixty years old were able to get metal cots, which had a bit more spring to them than the army cots, which were just stationary hammocks.

"These camps were technically relocation centers and there was no effort to hold us in them, but they didn't try actively to relocate us until much later. On my own initiative I tried to get out as soon as I could, and started writing letters to friends around the country. I found a friend in Salt Lake City who agreed to sponsor me for room and board, and he got his boss to agree to hire me. I got out in May 1943, which was earlier than most. In fact, I was one of the first to leave Minidoka.

"Of course I had to get clearance from Washington, D.C., and they investigated my background. I had to pay my own way from Twin Falls to Salt Lake City, but after I left, the government had a program of per diem for people leaving.

"I got on the bus with my suitcase, all by myself, my first time in the outside world, and paid my fare and began looking for a seat, then this old guy said: 'Hey, Tokyo, sit next to me.'

"I thought, Oh, my God, Tokyo! I sat next to him and he was a friendly old guy who meant well."

Yorita's friend worked in a parking garage across the street from the Mormon tabernacle, and the garage owner let them live in the office, where the two young men cooked their own meals. One nearby grocery-store owner wouldn't let them buy from him, and a barber in the neighborhood hated them on sight. Yorita parked a car once that had a rifle and pair of binoculars in the back seat, and he and his friend took the binoculars out and were looking through them when the barber looked out and saw them studying the Mormon tabernacle. He called the FBI, and two agents were soon in the garage talking to the young men.

Yorita wasn't satisfied with his job in Salt Lake City, and soon left for Cincinnati, then Chicago, which he enjoyed because most Chicago people didn't care what nationality he was. He and a brother were able to find good jobs and a good place to live, and they brought their parents out of the Idaho camp to spend the rest of the war in Chicago.

Philip Hayasaka was a teen-ager when Pearl Harbor was attacked. Unlike most Japanese-Americans, his parents had been able to find a home in a predominantly Caucasian neighborhood because his father was a wholesale produce dealer and most of his business was conducted with Caucasians. Consequently, when the family was interned, Hayasaka was a stranger to most of the other families.

Still, he and his family understood well the rationale of the Little Tokyos along the West Coast.

"If you could become invisible, you could get along. We were forced into a situation of causing no trouble, of being quiet, not complaining. It was not a matter of our stoic tradition. I've never bought that. We did what we had to do to survive.

"There was a lot of hysteria at the time, a lot of confusion, and the not knowing what was going to happen created such a fear that we became supercautious. We would hear that the FBI was going into different houses and searching, and we would wonder when they were coming to our house. We just knew that they were going to come and knock on the door and that we wouldn't know what to do when they came.

"A lot of people were burning things that didn't need to be burned, but they were afraid suspicion would be attached to those things. All those wonderful old calligraphies were destroyed, priceless things, because they thought someone in authority would believe they represented allegiance to Japan. One time I was with my mother in the house, just the two of us, and there was a knock on the door. My mother had those rosary-type beads that the Buddhists use for prayer, and she put them in my pocket and sent me outside to play and stay out until whoever was at the door left. She was afraid it was the FBI and they would take them away from us. It sounds silly now, but that kind of fear was pervasive then. It was tragic.

"When this happened, my dad's business went to hell. Suddenly all his accounts payable were due immediately, but all the accounts receivable weren't. People knew the guy wasn't going to be around much longer, so they didn't pay him. I knew at one time how much he lost that way—we had to turn in a claim after the war—but I've forgotten now. But it was a considerable amount. Those claims, by the way, didn't give justice to the victims; it only legitimatized the government. We got about a nickel on the dollar.

"It was kind of interesting how different people reacted when they came to Camp Harmony to see friends, and how we reacted in return. Friends from Seattle would come down to see me, and we had to talk through the barbed-wire fences. [Note: Nobody was permitted to stand closer than three feet to the fence, which meant conversations were held at least six feet from each other, with people standing and watching]. There was one instance when I saw a close friend from high school just outside the fence, and he had come down to see me. He hadn't seen me inside, so I hid rather than going out to see him. The whole evacuation did funny things to your mind.

"All the leaders of the community were taken away, and my dad was interned before we were and taken to the interrogation camp in Missoula. It was one of the greatest shocks of my life when the FBI came and picked him up. Here was a guy who had followed all the rules, respected authority, and was a leader in the company. And all of the sudden he was behind bars for no reason. He stayed there several months before they let him join us at Minidoka."

Hayasaka's two brothers and two sisters all went to Philadelphia to work and sit out the war, and he got a job in a defense plant making parts for half-tracks. He lived in a Quaker hostel, and "Most of the time I was the only Japanese in a large setting.

"Most of the time there was no problem, but if more than one Japanese were seen together, then we might get some name-calling. Alone, it didn't happen. Apparently one of the foremen liked my work, because he made an effort to recruit more Japanese in his section. Eventually there were four of us working there and we quite naturally gravitated together."

When the war ended and the camps were closed, about the only people left in them were young children and the elderly. All who could leave for jobs did so, and the experience had a scattering effect on the Japanese-American communities across the Pacific Coast. Several families settled on the East Coast and in the Midwest, and when those with no other place to go, or who didn't want to migrate away from the Coast, returned to their hometowns, they usually found their former ghettos taken over by other minority groups. Consequently, whether they wanted to or not, they were forced to find housing wherever it was available. It was difficult returning to the cities, however. Everybody dreaded it, and some of the elderly people with no place to go of their own were virtually evacuated from the camps. They had become accustomed to the life there and were afraid to leave.

Some Caucasians, such as Floyd Schmoe and the Reverend Emory Andrews, worked with the returning outcasts to help them resettle as smoothly as possible. A few farms had been saved for the owners, but four years of weeds and brush had accumulated. Schmoe was back teaching at the University of Washington by that time, and he organized groups of his students to go out on weekends and after school to help clear the land for crops again. Some people returning found their former neighbors had turned against them in their absence, and grocery-store owners who had become Jap-haters during the war would not sell them food.

The farmers who did get their crops growing again were often so discriminated against that they could not sell their produce, or get it delivered into the marketplace. Schmoe was able to solve this problem for one farmer by talking a neighbor, a Filipino, into taking the Japanese-American's produce and selling it as his own. Hayasaka's father was able to get back into the wholesale produce business by becoming partners with a young Japanese-American veteran of the famed 442d Regiment, the most highly decorated group in the war. The veteran put up a sign over the office saying the business was operated by a veteran, which made it difficult for buyers to avoid it.

"The older people never recovered from the camps [Yorita said]. The father was the traditional breadwinner and in total command of the family. But after going into the camps, fathers were no longer the breadwinners; the young sons and daughters were. Most of them couldn't even communicate in English, so all the burdens fell on the second generation. And most of us were just kids, nineteen or twenty. Consequently there was a big turnover of responsibility and authority, and the parents were suddenly totally dependent on their children. When we returned to the cities after the war, it was the second generation again that had to make the decisions and do all the negotiating with landlords, attorneys, and the like."

Obviously, most of the people chose to remain in America. Their children were American citizens, and the elders' homeland was almost a wasteland with no promise of stability for years to come. However, there was a tiny trickle of people going back to Japan, and one was Alta Ellert, a young girl from Seattle who was so devastated by the internment program that she fled in shame. A Caucasian woman who knew her followed her case with great interest and love.

"She was a tiny little thing I met in a department store downtown. I used to go there every lunch hour to shop and I got interested in a hooked-rug demonstration and decided to learn how to do it. While I was practicing, this tiny, tiny little girl came up to watch, and we became acquainted. We became friends and met almost every day for lunch after that.

"She told me she lived on a farm outside town and rode a bus to work each day until she could find a place to live in town. At that time my husband and I lived in his mother's house, an impossible situation because she was European of the old school. But we had no money and no other choice. But my mother-in-law was taken with this tiny Japanese-American girl and invited her to live in the house with us since there was plenty of room. She lived with us off and on for eight or nine years, and became almost a big sister to our little girl. She helped with the housework, made clothes for our daughter, and started attending the university. Some people innocently referred to her as our maid, but we always put an immediate stop to that. She was our friend, nothing less. A dear, dear friend.

"Then the war came. Then the internment. We put her on the train and haven't seen her since. She refused to come back home when the war was over. We corresponded, but she wouldn't come back to the Coast, no matter how much we begged her. She felt ashamed. She went to Texas after the war, then asked permission to emigrate to Japan, where she had never been, of course. She wrote us that she didn't want another thing to do with the United States and she was going to return to her own people.

"She wrote me often over the years, and she is a woman in her sixties by now. She had a terrible time in Japan. They treated her like an outcast because she was neither Japanese or American. They wouldn't let her work in the city, so she managed to get a tiny plot of ground and grew vegetables on it. She didn't have electricity in her little shack. Her brothers and sisters, who stayed in America, told us she wouldn't accept money from them, even though she sometimes was so broke she couldn't afford candles for light.

"Several years ago a friend went to Japan and I asked her to look up my tiny friend. That is how we came to know so much about how she lives. But she wouldn't accept money and wouldn't reply when my friend offered to give her money to come back to America.

"Since she left, my hair has turned white and I'm a widow. All these years I've always kept room vacant in the house for her because I was certain she would return one day. She's so tiny she would blow away in a good wind. If only there were some way to bring her back so we could spend our last years together . . ."

The war was equally difficult for those whose religious principles prevented them from serving as soldiers. There were many, many cases involving violence against the young men who refused to bear arms but were willing to perform necessary public services during the war, such as the Mennonites and Hutterites who worked in mental institutions and in the forests as the first smoke jumpers. They were never shown any appreciation for this work; smoke jumpers did their jobs without benefit of accident or death insurance. They were cannon fodder for the home front.

Some religious groups, especially the Jehovah's Witnesses, appeared intent on making themselves martyrs to the wrath of patriots. Their refusal to serve in the armed forces in any capacity and, perhaps worst of all, refusal to salute the flag made them instant targets in this country and in Nazi Germany, where many were executed shortly after Hitler's armies began marching across Europe and North Africa.

In the middle of Kansas where many Mennonites settled, a group of six Mennonite youths were sent to Fort Leavenworth to be inducted into the army. Once there they would have to declare themselves conscientious objectors, which they dreaded, but it was the trip there that caused them the most grief:

"There were six of us in a group of between thirty-five and forty, and one fellow was put in charge of us six COs, and we all sat together on the bus. It was some kind of double-decker with a separate tractor pulling it; I haven't seen one since.

"I think the others spotted us because we went to a high school that was largely Mennonite, and there was a local boy in the group who wasn't Mennonite. However it happened, they knew right away that we were COs. I don't remember just how it got started, but they started heckling and name-calling. After a conference or something they decided to come walking past our section and spout off a few things.

"It kept getting rougher and rougher, and there was one boy from Hutchison who tried to stick up for us. Finally they got mad at him and told him point-blank, 'You either bow out or we'll take care of you right now.' But he stayed with it as long as he dared.

"Along the way we had to stop for a meal, and that's when one of the fellows went out and bought a pair of scissors. As soon as we got back on the bus, they started haircutting procedures. The bus had sections to it, so they took us to the front part of the bus, one at a time, to threaten us and to say that when we got to Leavenworth we would change and tell them we didn't want to go CO, that we wanted to go straight army.

"So they took us up there and forced us to do different things, forced us to smoke a cigarette, you know, because COs weren't supposed to smoke, they thought. Then one of them had a heavy western belt and they took that and beat on us a while. Their point still was to get us to change our classifications. They called us yellow all the time and would see how much beating we could take before we broke down, or started bawling. But there really wasn't that much of a problem because you can take a heavy belt like that and they are whacking you across the back or arm with that thing, and after about ten whacks you don't feel anyhow, you get numb.

"I don't remember if it was an individual thing like the

beating, or if they just came down to our group and started whacking hair off. They just lobbed it off like you would with scissors, all chewed and notched up.

"When we got to Leavenworth they had already heard about it. Apparently the Associated Press had picked us up at one of our stops. I wasn't worried about my parents' reaction because I didn't think they would know about it until I got home, but the Associated Press had wired ahead to Leavenworth, and they were there waiting for us. Right away we were ushered into a place, and we looked like hicks with our haircuts.

"From then on it was all easy for us because the army, even though they didn't sympathize with us, didn't want anything like this going on again. I guess they really made an example of those guys, gave them a rough time. They interviewed us separately, trying to get us to tell what had gone on and who had done it. There were a few things that you didn't exactly want to mention.

"Then they took us into this room where all these guys were lined up and told us to go down the line and point to each of these guys that did something and to tell them what they did. One of the ringleaders drew back his fist and was going to let us have it, and he just about knocked down an officer. They steered him right out of there.

"Another thing they did: They gave us a haircut the first thing. We still looked bad when we came home, but at least we looked better because they gave us a butch all over.

"One of the fellows practically had a nervous breakdown over it. He was in pretty bad shape when we got to Leavenworth."

Another Mennonite became a smoke jumper and enjoyed the hard, dangerous work because he was doing something useful, wasn't being persecuted constantly for being a conscientious objector, and was with other young men of identical religious beliefs.

"I was sent down to a camp at Boise, Idaho, and all of us were COs except one ex-paratrooper. We had a list, and every time we jumped, our name moved to the bottom of the list. The rest of the time we did work around the camp, building new barracks, repairing the chutes, and working out west of Boise on a ski lift. We also did a little logging and roadwork for the Forest Service.

"The number of guys on a fire depended on the size of the fire and how quick we could get to it. The first fire I jumped was real rugged, down in the Snake River Canyon. A snag was burning there and they flew two of us over and dumped us out to take care of it, and that was that.

"After we put out the fires, we'd hike back out. They showed us where we were going and where the nearest trail was to get out. As soon as we jumped, they sent in a pack train—a string of horses and a packer—to bring our equipment out. I never was on a fire when there was an extra horse, so we always walked out behind the packer. If he wasn't there when we got through, we marked our equipment, piled it up with a yellow streamer on it, and let him go in after it while we got out of there. The longest I was out on a single jump was a week.

"On the bigger fires, as soon as we went out and jumped, they'd send in a ground crew and we'd leave as soon as they arrived. But on the smaller fires we'd work until it was out. One of them kept us going twenty-four hours. I've never been so tired. I'd be sure I couldn't take another step, but there it went, so I kept going.

"There were several injuries, of course. It seemed that backs were worse than anything else. The two main things for injuries were if you hung up in a tree, particularly a dead tree, and then a limb would break off and you would drop because your chute was collapsed. Or you'd land on a rock. I never was injured. They gave us good orientation, and in Missoula they had a house where all the injured men were kept. All these guys with broken jaws and casts made you wonder why you were there.

"When I got home I had trouble getting a job, just because I was a CO. I finally got a job for a produce company and my boss was a Lutheran. He was a very patriotic man, but he was open-minded. I think one of the reasons was because he was in an area where there were a lot of COs, so he couldn't be in business there and be too rough. I think I had worked there about six months when a bunch of businessmen got together and tried getting concerned about servicemen coming back, getting jobs. They went around to all the businesses trying to get them to fire everybody who had a CO classification. They contacted my boss. He got rid of them in a hurry. That thing died out eventually, but they caused a little static for a while. Some guys lost their jobs."

Ralph Lee, a Jehovah's Witness, had an incredibly tough time during the war. His refusal to serve was made suspect by the fact that he had served in the armed forces before he was converted to his new religion.

"They tried me in July 1942, and the story got big headlines in all the papers—there was only one bigger that day and it was a battleship that was torpedoed somewhere out in the Pacific. Of course it was all new then and I was one of the first Jehovah's Witnesses to be tried for refusing to go to war.

"That was the first trial. I served eleven months for that offense, and when I got out of prison they were waiting for me and I refused induction again and they hauled me back to court. Since they couldn't try me for the same crime twice, they charged me with violating another section of the Selective Service Act. This time they put me away until May 1946. But it was essentially the same crime; they just put another name on it so they could get away with violating the Constitution. A case like mine went before the Supreme Court, but it refused to hear it.

"I guess there were reasons other than the war. We wouldn't salute the flag, not only the American flag but any flag of any country. But we respect the flag for what it stands for, and prove that we respect it by leading good lives. Some of the brothers were asked to hoist the flag and lower it in prison camps, and they didn't have any objections to doing that at all; they were careful not to let it drop to the ground. And after I had gotten out of prison I worked for the telephone company and I've been asked several times to raise and lower the flag.

"The reason is in the word 'salute.' According to the Funk & Wagnalls dictionary I have, one of the meanings of 'salute' is that it is an act of prayer or worship, and we pray to and worship only God.

"It was in Hitler's Germany that the Witnesses really got it. There were 6000 Witnesses in concentration camps in Germany alone, and some were killed. Murdered. Hitler had made the remark that this brood must be exterminated because they wouldn't bow to the Third Reich.

"The only Witnesses that went to prison in this country during the war were those of draft age. A few were given exemptions because they were working in some special capacity. The government worked from one of our yearbooks that had the names of all ordained ministers in it, and of course us fellows who had just started getting associated weren't listed. When we went to our draft boards, they would ask why our names didn't appear on the list and they told us they weren't recognizing us as ordained ministers, even though I had a letter of ordination.

"My local draft board had several American Legion

members on it who were hostile to the Jehovah's Witnesses. The chairman was an attorney who was extremely prejudiced, and I still see him once in a while on the street. The vote of the board was unanimous against me, so I told them I wasn't going to report for induction, and that I had given them the last statement, written or oral, they would receive from me, and walked out and headed for a telephone booth. I was going to call the state Selective Service director and try to get an interview with him. But as I came out of the phone booth, the chairman of the draft board and a deputy sheriff rushed me right there and stuck me in jail. That was May 5, 1942.

"I went to trial and the jury deliberated eleven minutes before coming back with a verdict of guilty. The second time it was fifteen minutes, so they went four minutes longer.

"The second time I handled my own defense because I wanted to give my own reasons why I wasn't going. I gave a little presentation to the judge and jury and a whole bunch of people in the courtroom. The place was packed. I was the first Witness to be tried around there. They even had people standing in the halls. I gave them a fifteen-minute discourse at the trial, and on the day I was sentenced I gave them an eleven-minute talk. I gave them the scriptural reasons why I wasn't going in, like John 18:36 where Jesus said, 'My kingdom is not of this world. If my kingdom were of this world, then would my servants fight.' See, the kingdom was that of the Jews. They did fight over that, but then no other nation has actually had God's full favor since.

"They just ignored it.

"The first time they sent me to a road camp, after I'd spent a little time in the federal penitentiary on McNeil Island. It was too dangerous for us there, so they put us to work on the road camp in Fort Lewis. They put me to work in the sawmill pulling logs through the cutoff saw. It wasn't really that bad, but it was just—you know—confinement. You couldn't just get up and walk down to the corner drugstore.

"But the second time I was in was worse. They sent me to where the Hanford Atomic Reservation is now. They had a guard there who I was told had been the sheriff who led a mob against the Witnesses in Rawlins, Wyoming, in 1940. He was an ornery cuss—oh, he was an ornery cuss—and he had selected me and another Witness to try and break down. We were supposed to be working out in the fruit orchards and vineyards, but he put us on his own project. He had us digging a ditch, and when we finished it, he had us fill it in and dig another ditch alongside it, and then we'd fill it up, too. And all the while this guy was standing there making remarks at us. It went on two months, I guess, before he finally gave up.

"The other prisoners were pretty hostile, too. There was a Filipino who was converted to become a Witness and he was in House Number 5. They named that house 'Blood and Guts' for the simple reason that they stabbed him twice trying to kill him in there.

"There was also a big Indian, a half-breed, and he was an ornery guy, too. He was trying to knife this one brother, and the brother got a half-nelson headlock on him and made him drop the knife. This happened in the back of a truck going to camp. I saw the whole thing.

"The reason I got a job with the telephone company after the war was that President Truman gave me a presidential pardon, and I was one of the few who got one.

"The animosity toward us died slowly after the war. There are a few diehards along that line—a few live near me—who have memories like elephants and refuse to forget. But the majority of people don't seem to have any resentment along that line. At least not now, anyway."

While the traditional victims of American society, plus the new ones, the Japanese-Americans, were being subjected to indignities during the war, a curious thing was happening to our avowed enemies, the German and Italian soldiers who had surrendered. They were being treated with compassion. The gentlemanly rules of the Geneva Convention relating to prisoners of war were being honored scrupulously. Except for a very few isolated incidents, the German and Italian POWs were treated as well as our own men in military uniform.

Nearly half a million POWs were brought to this country and Canada, the survivors of the Afrika Corps in North Africa and the first prisoners taken in the Italian campaign. Rather than keep them in Europe or Africa, they were brought to North America to keep them as far away from the war zone as possible should the Germans launch a massive counterattack that could free the POWs to fight again. Another reason for bringing them here instead of the British Isles or elsewhere was the severe food shortage in Great Britain. It was simpler to bring them to the source of food than to ship the food to them. They also could be used to supplement the labor force in America.

They were placed in camps throughout the United States and Canada, some 360 such camps in the United States alone. The government kept them on a low profile for their own safety, although Americans accepted their presence more readily than they would have Japanese POWs simply because they looked like the dominant Caucasian society.

Many of the POWs liked this country so much that they returned as citizens as soon as possible after the war. Some 200 escaped and blended so well into the fabric of American society that even at this writing something like two dozen remain unaccounted for. One former Italian POW was found two decades after the war working in a federal building in Chicago.

More or less typical of the German POWs was Bernard W. Hoetr, a lieutenant in the Italian campaign. He was captured in Sicily in 1943 and taken down to North Africa to join the more than 300,000 prisoners captured there when

Rommel's Afrika Corps ran out of fuel and ammunition and had to surrender.

"I had been out of Germany since 1939, and in 1943 was stationed in Sicily as a navigator with the night fighter units. We left Sicily ahead of the Allied invasion and went up to southern Italy. But the Americans didn't come as fast as we expected, and they asked for volunteers to go back to Palermo to destroy our radar equipment we'd left behind. I was twenty-two and very adventurous, and I went. They flew us into Palermo and gave us motorcycles to go back to our installations and save what we could, and destroy the rest. We worked about a week behind the lines, then tried to reach German lines again.

"It was during the attempt that I was captured. I was riding a tank because I knew the roads and where our mine-fields were, so I was leading the tanks out on an unmined road. We came to a little village, and there was not a sign of the Americans. We checked the streets and didn't see anything. But the American boys were sitting there in a door and got off a bazooka shot at about twenty or thirty feet. The tank blew up. I was sitting on top in the open turret and was thrown away. I woke up in an American field hospital, where I was in shock and bruised, but nothing serious.

"The Americans had not anticipated the amount of prisoners they would take. Most were, of course, Italian. At that time the Italians just didn't want to fight anymore. They just said, 'The war is finished,' and threw away their weapons. There were big compounds with one little strand of barbed wire strung around it, no blankets or tents. There we got our first experience with American plenty. We got K-rations—cans, cans, cans of it. We got, for the first time in our lives, Nescafé. We didn't know what to do with it, so we opened the cans and poured water in them.

"But we didn't have enough food and water. I can't

blame anyone, because they just didn't anticipate the mounds of prisoners they got. So the first two weeks south of Palermo were rather hungry times, not only hungry but thirsty. It was a hot July and there wasn't enough water.

"Then we were put aboard big landing crafts and taken down to North Africa. There we were handed over to the French, and after another two or three months we marched to Oran, where a most fantastic thing happened. While the Americans had not figured they would capture so many prisoners, they had anticipated much higher casualties. So they had hospital ship after hospital ship in Oran, and they were beautifully equipped. So we went to America in the hospital ships.

"We came out of the desert and I didn't have shaving blades, so I sported a beard. I didn't have a spoon, so I had carved one of wood. I didn't have a mess kit, so I had an old can with a wire handle. And we marched up to this big ship.

"There were some colored stewards at the gangplank and they told us, 'Officers to the left, please.' Our first reaction was that they were up to the old trick of separating the officers from their men and would abuse us. So we told the steward we were staying with our men.

" 'Gentlemen,' the stewards said, 'officers get separate rooms.'

"Ooh, this is even worse, we thought. We did not believe him. Finally he got some MPs, who said we'd better go. What could we do? We had to face our fate, and went on our way while the enlisted men went their way.

"We walked up the stairs and they said, 'Lieutenants four to a cabin, captains two to a cabin, and majors and colonels get cabins by themselves.'

"We couldn't believe it. The first thing we did when we got in our cabins was turn on the water taps. Cold running water came out. In the desert we had been rationed to a pint a day, half of which was taken into the kitchen. So we got half a pint a day and were supposed to shave with it, wash with it, and drink the rest.

"We had white linen on the beds. We couldn't believe it. Then we heard a bell ring—bing-bong, bing-bong—and the stewards told us to get ready for chow. We got our little mess kits and stood in the corridor. A steward in a white jacket came along and told us to please follow him into the dining room.

" 'Dining room?' we said. 'What's going on?'

We were led into the dining room, where we saw women for the first time in six months, American nurses who were sitting on the left with American officers. We were kept separated by a corridor. I spoke some English and got myself the spokesman's role. The waiter came with a menu and asked what we would like.

"I looked at the menu and said, 'Boys, we can't lose.'

" 'Can we have soup?'

" 'Four soups,' the waiter said.

"I looked at the menu again and saw steak. What could they do but throw us out?

" 'Can we have steaks?'

" 'Four steaks.'

" 'Ice cream. Can we have ice cream?'

" 'Four ice creams.'

"We still didn't believe it. This world is crazy, I thought.

" 'Can we have four cigars?'

" 'No,' the waiter said. 'Cigarettes and cigars you have to buy yourself.' At this stage we had three cigarettes a day or one cigar a week, which wasn't enough for an active smoker.

"Then someone asked for a second helping of ice cream, and the waiter said, 'Of course.' Unbelievable.

"A week later we landed in New York, and the wealth of the United States was a tremendous psychological shock to us. A few of the old diehards among us told us not to believe what we were seeing because it was all propaganda. 'The governor of New York must have ordered all the cars in the state to come down to the harbor for us to see,' he said when we saw cars driven by ordinary people. In Germany all cars were either official or military.

"The first thing was a stop at Ellis Island to be deloused. We came into those little shacks and the Americans told us to put our valuables in a little bag because we would be stripped and deloused, and the bags would be returned to us. We refused, saying it was the oldest trick in the world. We knew they would take the things away from us. There was a very nice little old white-haired colonel who said, 'Do you dare to say that Americans would steal wristwatches?'

"There was an outburst of laughter and everybody lifted their empty left arms and somebody shouted, 'Where do you think these wristwatches went?'

"It seemed that even before an American soldier took side arms, they stripped you of your watch, which they considered a souvenir. Some of us knew it was a big fad with the Americans and had hidden our watches.

"From New York they took us by train to the South, first to Alabama, then to Florida. Later, after the war, people said Florida was the best part of the United States, but we were picking peanuts and the mosquitoes there were as big as butterflies. It was very, very hot, but not too unpleasant after we got used to it.

"We worked with colored people and we had stakes to pick. Each stake of peanuts would be about eight feet high, and we were supposed to pick three or four a day. Some of the boys laughed and said they could do eight a day, but it was hot work and backbreaking for someone unaccustomed to the work.

"So the POWs quickly unionized. We were paid $1 a

day, and the farmer had to pay $5 a day for us. So we said that if he would throw in a pint of ice cream we would add another stake a day. Or we worked in teams for a carton of cigarettes, which I believe sold at that time for $2 on the market.

"There was no bitterness among the farmers we worked for. None at all. They talked to us about their sons, some of whom had been killed, but there was no personal hate at all. The ordinary soldier who guarded us didn't associate us with the hate propaganda, either. They were under orders to say 'yes' or 'no' and nothing more to us. Just official words.

"The only private contact we had was with the men from the Salvation Army, who came into camp and asked if we had everything we wanted. We told them we were treated well, but that we would like to have a piano.

" 'Why don't you ask for one?'

"Ask for a piano? We were incredulous.

" 'I'll get you an old piano,' he said, and he did. We had musicians and theater groups in the camp and got the material to build stages and scenery through the Salvation Army. They never tried to sell us their beliefs. Definitely not. The Catholic Church did, but that boomeranged. They came in and asked who was Catholic. 'The pope has sent ten cigarettes for each Catholic in camp,' they said. The boys were embarrassed and told the Catholics that we had thousands of cigarettes we could buy. The German Red Cross also sent cigarettes—I believe it was two or three a day—but the cigarettes were so poor that nobody wanted to smoke them. We wanted to destroy them but our consciences wouldn't let us. We reasoned that maybe somebody would want them, so we put them in the latrine. Every morning we saw hundreds of German cigarettes in the latrine because the American cigarettes were so much better.

"I remember when we got our first $10 for the PX and

how everybody ran to spend their money because we were convinced it was a propaganda trick: that they had just stocked the PX for that time and there would be no more after that.

"There were ways of bootlegging women into the camps, but the quality of women was very, very poor. We had a great scare because some POWs contracted syphilis. Some of the women thought it rather exciting to have intercourse with German POWs, and most were harmless Negro women, not prostitutes. We simply did not see any white women.

"The thing that always surprised me was the lack of homosexuality in camp. There was none. It was not condoned. And if you have four or five thousand men, mostly young, in one big camp, it is really surprising. But it was frowned upon in the German Army, wasn't manly. It was a major crime.

"There were some suicides in the camp, but relatively few. A couple occurred before the war ended, and about Christmas 1945, our last Christmas in this country and after the war was over, several committed suicide because it was a very sad time. The pope sent us some Christmas records and I played them over the public-address system and we had some suicides that night.

"Escapes were always great excitement. But when somebody tried to escape, it was a suicidal mission because they'd end up sitting in the swamps of Florida where mosquitoes would eat them up. After about five days they would come back, tired, hungry, and covered with mosquito bites. They would talk for hours about their adventures, but the Americans wouldn't do much to them. They knew all we had to do was look at them and think that if that was what freedom was about, the rest of us would stay.

"There was friction between the newcomers and the old-timers in the camps, and between the Afrika Corps and the

others because the desert fighters considered themselves the
elite. There was also some trouble between the hardcore
Nazis and the others, and a few murders were committed by
the Nazis. But what we saw coming to the camps from France
we couldn't believe—men of fifty-five and older and youngsters of sixteen. We knew then that Germany was really
scraping the bottom of the barrel, and it was very depressing.

"I was sent from Alabama to West Virginia to work in
a logging camp, and was there when the European war ended
and the Allies found the horrors of the concentration camps.
None of us old-timers knew anything like this was going on,
and we found it hard to believe. But the Americans said they
were going to show us how the Germans treated the inmates
of concentration camps. They put us on a 500-calorie ration.

"Before that, we might have 3000 or 4000 calories a day.
There was so much food we couldn't eat it all. Mind you, at
the end of the war there was such an overproduction of cer-
tian items, such as chicken, that we sometimes had eight weeks
of chicken only. At another time there was an overproduction
of brains, so our meat was brains for about a month—breakfast, lunch, and dinner. But it was basically good food.

"But in May of 1945 they said they'd show us how the
Germans starved the Jews and gave us 500 calories. This lasted
for about four weeks. It was very bad, especially for the older
prisoners. We had swollen legs. They stood us in parade for-
mation until some dropped to the ground. And they showed
us films of the concentration camps, which we just couldn't
believe.

"After the camp was very, very hungry, they said they
would then honor the Geneva Convention. They would not
force officers to work, but those who did would be in a camp
where the food was 4000 calories. So everyone volunteered
and went to the next camp in West Virginia.

"This was a big camp where they were training young

Americans to be sent to Japan. I got the job of my life then and was put in charge of the garbage detail. Americans throw everything away. The soldiers going to the Far East were allowed to take only one big barracks bag along, so there was a tremendous surplus of pants, shirts, shoes, radios, guitars, and everything. We were supposed to burn everything in two big incinerators outside the base, but I thought it was a very bad policy to burn these things. So I made a deal with black marketeers and we sold them fifty pairs of shoes for a bottle of whiskey, or fifteen pairs of pants for a carton of cigarettes, and so forth. The truck driver was an Italian POW and he and I would dump the goods someplace along the route for the black marketeers to pick up and leave our payment.

"Before we were repatriated to Germany, the Red Cross gave us permission to send a forty-pound parcel to an address near our homes in Germany. My home near Düsseldorf had been destroyed and my parents had moved, so I used an address in Munich where my sister lived. The Allies kept me until 1946 working on the papers Wernher von Braun brought out. I was in charge of a group of translators at Fort Eustis, Virginia, and later in England.

"When they finally sent me back to Germany, I was convinced that my forty-pound parcel with ten cartons of cigarettes in it would be gone. In fact, German POWs who had those parcels sent to places in France did lose them. But I went to the big military warehouse in Munich and showed my receipt to an American sergeant and asked him if he thought the parcel would be there.

" 'If you've got a receipt, we've got the parcel somewhere,' he said, and went looking for it. Pretty soon he came back with the parcel.

"Those cigarettes were my starting capital in private life in Germany. A carton cost 1000 marks after the war, and I was worth 10,000 marks. They were two years old then and very dry, but they were my starting capital.

"It wasn't necessarily the wealth of America that brought us back. It was the way of life, which we found out through magazines and the radio. We didn't see the very rich or the very elite. But we saw that the farmer was proud and loyal to his country. It was the tremendous amount of freedom that we hadn't even read about. It was foreign to our thinking."

My own conviction is that the war experience was as close as this country has ever come to living the American Dream. Vague though that phrase is, if it means anything at all, it is that America had something for everybody. A wildly heterogeneous nation was more completely united in purpose and spirit than at any time in its history. That in itself is an emotional experience. It gave everybody a vital sense of community . . . it was also as just as a war could be . . . it was a response to a surprise attack . . . it was a war against palpable evil. It was a boon to people's hearts and ideals.

Geoffrey Perrett, *Days of Sadness, Years of Triumph*

Battles are never the end of war; for the dead must be buried and the cost of the conflict must be paid.

James A. Garfield

CALCUTTA, India, May 6, 1945—(AP)—A bomber pilot who knew what to do when his flaming ship exploded over Japanese-held Burma and how to cope with captivity for 18 months does not know what to do now— his wife has remarried after he was declared officially dead by the war department.

"I thought I could take anything," said Lt. Harold W. Goad, 27, of Portsmouth, Ohio, liberated in a Rangoon hospital. "But this is rougher than anything I've been through."

9

Victory

V-Mail

M y darling:
  Your voice—it was so calm on the phone last night
that I can still hardly believe it was you, after all you've
been through. And silly me wasting your money—make
that our money—by blubbering like a baby. I'm so sorry
and so terribly happy.
  I'll make this short because I want to save everything
else I have to say until you get here. Call me, wire me or
whatever when you arrive, and don't you dare sneak in on
me because I want everything to be perfect when you get
here.
  You're back. I still can't believe it.
                    With all my heart and soul,

T WAS THE biggest party in the history of the nation, a spontaneous eruption of emotion. It was New Year's at Times Square raised to the 10,000th, a generally pleasant form of mass hysteria, a Rose Bowl victory and a Super Bowl and World Series all rolled into one. It was an orgy of drinking and kissing and screaming, and occasionally praying, that swept the nation without need of confirmation by mass communications. Shipyards and aircraft plants locked their gates. Men threw away their lunch buckets, and women their shipyard coveralls. Servicemen fortunate enough to be within the country's boundaries were treated like conquering heroes for the last time. There were some incidents of pure rioting, of looting and vandalizing and rape, but they were scattered— most people simply wanted to have fun. It was the first time in four years they could do so without feeling guilty because of the men overseas, and the last time within our lifetimes, although none of us had any idea what life would be like within the confines of a superpower that was planning to save the world. How could we know that real social problems and invented personal problems would keep us so unhappy when we were not at war? How could we know that our nation was at its best when it was in an all-out war? How could we know that plenty was never enough, and that happiness can be sold but never bought?

"I was working in a hotel as a waitress when V-J Day came, and everything closed down. A couple upstairs brought down a bottle of whiskey since neither drank—they just kept it for friends—and said they were happy enough already and didn't need a drink. So they gave it to us waitresses. A little bottle among a dozen people wasn't much, but it was really enough. It was just the thought.

"We didn't really need anything either. We were high on excitement. We went out to the street and walked up and down the main drag, five or six of us, and there was a parade forming spontaneously. So we all swung into it and hiked down the main drag, then headed up a side street. Nobody got tired. I heard later they did a lot of wild things in San Francisco. We didn't. It was just a small town celebrating. That's all."

Another woman remembered V-J Day for a more sensual reason:

"V-E Day didn't mean too much to us in the Midwest, but V-J Day was something else! The main thing I remember from that day was it was the first time in years, it seemed, that we felt young men with firm muscle tone. A bunch came to our small town in a jeep they had 'liberated,' and we jumped in with them. You forget how different the muscle tone is between young and old men. We'd get those young, strong arms around us and we just wouldn't know what we were doing.

"One of the fellows had just returned from several months in the South Pacific and hadn't been around white women in quite a while, and he said the smell of a clean American girl almost drove him crazy. He asked me what kind of perfume I was wearing and I told him it was just soap and me.

"He took a deep whiff and sighed, 'Boy, I like that!' "

A nurse was on duty when the radios announced peace with Japan, and the hospital went into an uproar.

"I was on duty until around eleven o'clock that night, and it was about 5:30 when we heard about it. Some of our patients actually got out of their beds and left. I can still see this one guy leaving with only a sheet around him, headed for home and the parties.

"As soon as I got off duty I went back to the nurses' residence and put on my best uniform—the summer cadet uniform—and a bunch of us took off. They had bands playing in the street and people were dancing and I had thirty-seven kisses in one block. I counted them. There were traffic jams, and some cars ended up driving on the sidewalk. A whole bunch of us ended up on the stage of a nightclub singing our hearts out.

"We picked up complete strangers, went to house parties, places I could never find again. When the housemother made the bed checks that night, she found absolutely no girls. I got back just in time for the duty at seven o'clock, and I went back out on the streets again that afternoon.

"It sounds crazy, and it was. But there were no troubles I knew of, no knifings, no rapes, nothing. You couldn't do that today."

Another woman remembered that day because of the problems the cheap dresses made during the war caused her:

"V-J Day. Good grief! I went downtown in a dress that had buttons all down the front, and town was just body-to-body. And, believe it or not, I lost all my buttons on the dress. Every one. It wasn't what you might think; the guys didn't pull them off. We were just so close that the movement would pop them off. And of course the guys were all bombed out of their birds and were screaming and hollering. They thought I was putting on a terrific show. Finally a former classmate came to my rescue and he helped me pin myself back together and took me home. My mother got a kick out of it, but my dad didn't appreciate it much, especially when he saw this young man bringing me home with my clothes torn halfway off my back."

Another found an ingenious way to keep the servicemen at almost arm's length:

"I worked on a newspaper during the war, and being a woman, they of course put me in the women's department. I wrote about those ghastly clubs, teas, luncheons, weddings. . . . This was years and years before women's pages had stories about real things. But it was a living and it helped pass the time while my husband was gone.

"When V-J Day arrived, I was sent out with a photographer—a dear, sweet guy who is still on the same paper. He was a 4-F, which I know bothered him, but there wasn't a thing he could do about it. On V-J Day we were sent downtown to get some photos and quotes on the celebration—the usual roundup story on such events.

"When we got downtown it was absolutely wild. Sailors were running in the streets by the thousands, it seemed, and there was poor little me. The minute we got out of the cab I was surrounded by these wild-eyed sailors. They were trying to kiss me and what-have-you, and I was terrified. The thing that saved me was my silly reaction to the whole thing. I clutched my notebook and pencil to my chest and shouted, 'Stop it! You'll break my pencil!'

"The photographer couldn't get over it. It worked! To this day, when we see each other, one of us has to bring it up and we always laugh."

Times Square in New York, the parks of Washington, D.C., the streets of all cities in America were the scenes of conga lines and liquor bottles brandished wildly and shared with strangers. It was a jubilant riot that swept the nation, and was especially wild in a city noted for its wild parties:

* * *

"I still feel the same excitement about San Francisco as I did during the war years when I worked there, first for an agency and then as a hostess at the Fairmont Hotel officers' club. When I get off the plane there, I wish I could live there. It has a mystery, a charm that no other city on earth has.

"Being in San Francisco when the war ended was like being in the middle of the wildest, craziest carnival you'll ever see in your whole life. They were throwing water bags out of the Fairmont and guys were kissing, and practically raping, everybody on Market Street. Everything stopped dead. They were pulling girls' pants off and sailing them down the street, and when I was going home on the streetcar some navy guy about three sheets to the wind gave me a whole fistful of shoe ration stamps, sort of symbolic of the war's end. And he had about five white [sailor] hats standing on top of his head.

"It took the city about a week to recover from the hangover. A carnival in Brazil couldn't hold a light to it. I doubt if our kids would ever understand how it was that day, and I doubt any writer could ever describe it."

Business ground to a standstill, and people who had grown tired of the war—including those who wanted to work *only* forty hours a week for a change—saw the day as the last chapter of a strange time:

"We had been putting in quite a bit of overtime at the telephone company during the war and were getting tired of it. So when V-J Day came, the whole town went bananas. Everything stopped in its tracks. The foreman told us to knock off early, mainly because people were sneaking out anyway. Another fellow and I went out into the street to see what was happening uptown. People were all over the streets, whooping and hollering.

"We stopped in this little arcade and stood watching the

party, just a couple of businessmen in business suits. A couple of nice-looking girls came up and stopped and looked at us. Then one came over and said, 'Hey, I've kissed a soldier, I've kissed a sailor, and a marine. Now I've got to kiss a civilian for all this war effort.'

"So we strolled back into the building arcade, back by the elevator, and she kissed both of us.

"It was—I don't know—kind of nice."

One woman couldn't partake of the festivities because she was a brand-new mother:

"Just a few days before the war ended, I had a baby. I had gone to see one of Danny Kaye's movies with a friend. He was hilarious and I laughed so hard I literally could not get up when the movie ended. Everybody left the theater and I was still sitting there and just couldn't get up. Finally I made it up and home, but when I got there my husband was out with his father getting initiated into either the Elks or the American Legion—something like that. By dang, this baby was coming. I am certain Danny Kaye was to blame. I called a cab and walked into the hospital under my own power, and *boom*, I had a baby, just like that.

"The doctor wouldn't see me, so I had it in the bed with a nurse helping. At the same time there was a woman screaming and hollering because she was Jewish and the doctor had just automatically circumcised her baby. She was screaming for them to sew the foreskin back on so the rabbi could do it right. But that was that. That kid was circumcised and there was no returning. Hilarious.

"Right in the middle of all this the doctor finally comes in and he looks tired and as if he's being chased by demons. He looks at me and listens to the Jewish mother and he's had it up to here. 'It's a goddamned hatchery in here,' he shouts. 'A goddamned hatchery.'

"I survived and so did my baby, but I've always wondered about the doctor and that Jewish mother."

Within two or three days, life was trying to return to normal, although nobody could quite describe what a normal life would be with the war over and the veterans returning and the uncertain job market haunting everyone.

Some people, however, had certain urges to satisfy before settling down, such as Charlotte Paul in Chicago:

"When the war finally ended, I think we all had two urges: One was to travel and the other was to buy a car. We were able to get a car through a man in my husband's office who had an uncle with an agency. He said we'd have to take whatever model he could get us, and never mind how many cylinders or what color. It turned out to be a very fine car, a white Nash. So we went to New Orleans and it was really fine. We hadn't gone anyplace at all during the war.

"I think we had a great yearning for luxuries. We are such a spendthrift people that when they took the cap off after the war and told us to go on about our lives, some of us went overboard. A lot of people had been making a lot of money in the factories.

"A woman I knew during the Depression had one son and was married to a carpenter. Nobody could afford a carpenter then, or even the wood for him to work with, and she kept them from starving by working at the Italian Balm hand-lotion factory. She earned $5 a week and fed the three on that.

"So fifteen years later this little baby that she took care of is working in a war plant at such wages that he came home wearing a silk shirt that he had paid $20 for. She was shocked. She was a very provident person, a Swede who never wasted anything. Furthermore, she said he wouldn't let her wash it; it had to be dry-cleaned. She said it would ruin him, that he'd never, never be able to take the bad times.

"I think the importance of material acquisitions was very strong then with the people who had never had them. It was only when the hippies came along and said that none of this is important that it began to dawn on us that they might be right. The 1940s and 1950s were a very, very materialistic period.

"Now young people don't seem to pick the work they do by how much they're going to be paid, either. Not very often, anyway. Some of them do, I'm sure, because any generalization has holes in it. But I know in the case of many young people I know, they don't talk about fringe benefits or pay scales. They talk about whether they're doing something valuable or making a contribution."

The day the men came home from the war is another day everyone remembers, except that these dates scattered through the summer and fall of 1945 were different dates for each person:

"I was taking swimming lessons down at the Y and the night he came home he called grandmother, with whom I was living. When I got home that night I was all tired out and my grandmother said someone had called and said they would call back. She didn't tell me who. I went into my bedroom and she told me not to go to sleep because that call would be coming in pretty soon. The phone rang and it was him! My goodness!

"He was in a hospital and said not to worry. He had picked up some tropical things and he was OK otherwise. He couldn't leave the hospital that night, but could the next day.

"After we hung up I called my best friend and she said, 'You're not going to work tomorrow, are you?' and I said, 'He won't be given liberty until the afternoon. And she said, 'You're going to the hairdresser in the morning, aren't you?' and I said, 'Why, of course.' I was in shock.

"He had lost a lot of weight and a lot of hair and he looked older, too. We acted like strangers at first because we'd spent only about a month together before he went overseas for nearly two years."

Not only was it difficult for husbands and wives to get reacquainted, the children had a worse problem, especially those who had never seen their fathers, or were infants when they left. Dorothy Hyatt remembers:

"My husband was gone two years and our daughter was born just after he left. Two years. I know people now who think two days is a long time to be away from their husband. I went for as long as a month without hearing from him, and when a packet of letters would arrive, I would only know that he was still safe, but only at the time he wrote them. What had happened to him since?

"When he finally arrived back in the States, he couldn't get to a telephone so he sent me a telegram. When the Western Union woman started reading it over the phone, she got only as far as 'I'll be arriving . . .' She said, 'I understand, dear,' and started reading it all over again. All the way to the train depot that night I tried to remember what he looked like, how his voice sounded. And when we got home, do you know what we did? We sat in front of the fireplace, all night, just *talking*. Just wanting to hear each other's voices.

"It was tough on both him and our daughter. That night when he came home he wanted to see her, of course, and she woke up when he went into her bedroom. He immediately picked her up and she started crying. He was a stranger.

"He came home to a little girl who was rather spoiled. Her grandparents had been minding her while I sat with my ears glued to the radio news. We let her get away with everything. So he had the rather unpleasant job of having to be strict with her about riding her tricycle too far and so forth. I remember he scolded her for going beyond a particular spot because we were on a busy street. He said he'd spank her if she went farther. She did and he did. Then she went out again and was starting to pedal away and this older lady was walking by. The girl put her head down on the handlebars and was crying, and the lady was glowering at the house because she thought my husband had beat her up. He hadn't. But it almost killed him to spank her."

During the war years, there had been servicemen on the home front, some assigned to stateside posts, others simply coming and going from the war. Like the German and Italian prisoners of war who were stunned by the wealth of this country when brought here, many of the servicemen home on furlough had been shocked at the almost instant wealth the nation had acquired in their brief absence. Since they had been in Europe and the Pacific risking their lives, the resentment some felt toward the good life at home was understandable. Yet there didn't seem to be that many who felt they were being used during the war. It was only after the war, when they came home job hunting, that the bitterness set in, and sometimes the resentment became retroactive. Their battle scars and memories came to represent the down payment on other people's financial well-being.

Maybe those of us left behind on the home front didn't realize that victory neglected to bring happiness as advertised, but the men coming back soon learned that medals and newspaper clippings did not guarantee jobs. We had shared our happiness and grief during the war, but, without that binding agent, peace seemed to send us on our own separate ways. It was almost as if we had been sitting on the sunny side of the stadium while our team overcame a first-quarter deficit and went on to win the championship that balmy afternoon. The game ended, we stampeded to the parking lot, fought our way through traffic, and went home, never to see the people sitting and cheering around us again.

Occasionally, though, over the coming months, and the coming championship seasons, some of us get together and talk about the Big Game, the Good War, the last one that made sense, the one they played before they changed the rules and allowed the platoon system. We know it was better then. We sat there and watched it ourselves. We sometimes look at the men who played in it and wonder why they look so much like ourselves. We wish they didn't. We wish they still wore their tailor-made officers' blouses and their shiny paratroopers' boots and their bell-bottom trousers like Gene Kelly and Frank Sinatra wore in that film. We wish our heroes of our youth didn't have the habit of getting soft and flabby, like us, and that they still acted like heroes. They should be out at airfields flying those few Dauntless dive bombers and Hellcats that are still in the air. They should have all their own teeth; and when they take their caps off, they should have hair on their heads. But that was another game, another war, a long time ago.

For many, the war lasted long after 1945, and the after-effects of it would remain with them for months, years, decades. One example of this is Mrs. Fred Ross, who lost her fiancé, but never knew the details until a chance conversation a few years later:

"My fiancé was on a plane en route home on October 5, 1944, when they ran into a typhoon off Saipan. They turned back and tried to land, but crashed. He was one of twenty-two killed. There were only two survivors, and one died soon afterward and the other ended up in a mental institution.

"I was never able to find out any of this until 1953. In the meantime I had met my present husband—the only one I've ever had—and we were living in a small town in Michigan where my husband had an International Harvester dealership. I worked on the books and could hear about everything that went on in the office.

"One day a group of men were talking about the war and they were talking about some place in the Pacific. I was only half listening until a few key words came to me. I walked out and asked them for more details, and it turned out that one of the men was on the ground crew at Saipan and saw the whole thing happen. He turned white and said, 'I serviced that plane before it took off.' "

Unlike most other Western nations, America has always had a penchant for bringing home its war dead. Other nations tend to leave their dead where they fell in battle, but Americans have always wanted their dead buried in local cemeteries. So shortly after the war ended, plans were put into motion to return the bodies to America under a massive reinterment program. One of the body escorts, Lawrence Rudell, tells what it was like:

"When I came home from the war, three of us brothers went into the industrial-maintenance contracting business in the spring of 1946. We had a big Standard Oil contract to clean up their gas stations; nothing had been done to them in six or seven years. We were paying high-school kids $1.25 an hour sandblasting, steam-cleaning, and spray-painting. A master painter at that time in northern Wisconsin was getting 90¢ an hour. Ohhh, the unions were on our backs! We were paying too much. We even did their work-clothes laundry, paid for their hotel rooms. They had to buy their own meals on the road.

"We worked them from 'can to can't,' from when you can see in the morning until when you can't see at night. Every town we pulled into with the crew, it wouldn't be a couple of hours until we had union pickets walking back and forth in front of the gas station. Yeah. We were paying too well, and we weren't hiring a percentage of local painters. We'd tried that, and when we did give in to them, they'd send us some joker sixty-two or sixty-three years old with a half-pint sticking out of his back pocket. We squirmed out of that because Standard Oil never put us under a bond, never forced us to bond ourselves, so they couldn't pull a contract on us. But we did them a damned good job and got the same contract the following year.

"I got sick and tired of the union, just sick and tired of fighting with them, and I happened to read this article in a paper about the disinterment of the war dead overseas and reinterment stateside, and that they needed people with past military service to reenlist and escort them back home. So I went down to talk to a recruiter, signed up, and went to Fort Sheridan for training.

"They were going to take me back in as buck sergeant, which would be Airman First today, so I went ahead and went through the training course at Fort Sheridan for five weeks, and just before the final swearing-in I went to the personnel officer and said that unless he made me staff sergeant, I was out. He took my service records somewhere, then came back and put an 'S' in front of the rate and said, 'Okay, you're a staff sergeant.' That got me out of all the KP in Kansas City.

"Those five weeks were the best training you could get. They had the best psychiatrists available telling us what to expect when we delivered these bodies back home. They taught us what answers to give to every conceivable question, how to conduct ourselves. There were 147 of us working out of Kansas City: army, navy, Air Corps, marines, Coast Guard—the works. Whatever branch of service the dead man was in, someone from that branch escorted the body.

"They did a good job of organizing the reinterment program. They had special railroad cars built to deliver the bodies to about thirteen distribution centers around the country—

San Diego, San Francisco, Seattle, Denver, Kansas City, Chicago, Nashville, and some East Coast cities. But they had overlooked one thing when building those cars: They were so long that they couldn't make turns in some towns. The railroad would be so close to some buildings that these cars would clip off the corners of them. So they had to plan routes across the country with pretty straight tracks and lots of room on the turns.

"The program was held up awhile when a shipload of coffins went down between France and the U.S., and they had some problems in France because they hired Spanish workers to dig up the coffins and they were opening them and stealing the gold teeth and whatever else they could find. Oh, we had our problems, you bet.

"The coffins they used were just great. They were made of stainless steel and had either forty-seven or forty-eight special bolts holding the cover on. These bolts were specially made for the caskets, and they were almost made for allen wrenches, so you had to have special wrenches to open them.

"When we'd get an order to deliver one somewhere, they'd give us forms with a pink slip and a white slip. We'd have the parents sign one; if I remember right, the pink was for us to stay for the funeral, and the white that they didn't want us to stay. We also carried a ditty bag with all kinds of gear in it we might need, including several kinds of ammo for different calibers of guns in case the VFW or American Legion had old World War I guns for the military salute.

"There was only one case I had when I had to open the casket, and I made seventy-six trips to thirteen states in twenty-three months. There were some close calls, but only one when I had to open it. It was a little farm and the only people left were the father and a seventeen-year-old girl with the mind of about a seven-year-old. She insisted and insisted, and finally the father gave in. So I went out and got the county health director for approval, figuring he would back off, but he didn't. Then I went for the boy's dentist, in case there was some question. I was by God going to convince them that was who we said it was.

"Just before noon the health director and dentist showed up. I had the special wrench and we lifted the lid off. The minute I threw the GI blankets back, the girl reached over, made a fist, and rapped the skull. Boy, that was a tough one. I guess she had always hit her brother that way—they must have been close. Anyway, she was happy. I buttoned him up again and we had the funeral. But I didn't want any more like that one.

"There was another one almost as bad. The family had the casket brought into the house, and the next day, before the funeral, I went to the house and I knew I was in trouble. I knew what the question was going to be. I told the mother that as sure as she believed that Jesus Christ was the Lord, that was her son in that casket. That satisfied her.

"After each trip, we'd get together in Kansas City and talk about our experiences on the last trip so we could learn from each other. They really did a good job training us and preparing us for every emergency. But some things we learned the hard way. A navy chief escorted a body back to an Indian reservation in Oklahoma, and the tribe wanted him to stay for the ceremonies. Their ceremonies lasted forever, you know, and all the Indians came in, crossed their legs, and sat on the floor. The [navy] chief sat in the front row, and pretty soon his legs are killing him. He couldn't stand it anymore, and he had to get up and walk out. Ohhh, you should have seen the letter that came to the commander in Kansas City after that! They put the word out to the rest of us that anyone we escorted with Indian blood, we stayed with them no matter what.

"I had an Indian body to take back to Oklahoma myself once, and it wasn't so bad. I sat with the tribe for their ritual, then they had the funeral director take the casket out somewhere in the rolling plains, then told him to stop. They got out and the last we saw of them they were carrying that casket off across the plains. The funeral director said they'd all gather around the casket at about midnight and paint his face to prepare him for the hereafter.

"A lot of those funeral directors were really something else. There was one who chased women. Oh, how he chased women! Every night. Then he'd come in about dawn looking like he was ready to crawl into a casket himself. But by noon he'd be all business again. I don't know how he did it.

"Down in Arkansas there was a little town I had to go to a couple of times with bodies, and the funeral director was old. He had a young wife. You know the rest of the story. She was a good-looker and made it known she was ready for some diversions. No sooner than I got back to Kansas City, she was there and on the phone to me. I told her I was flat broke, had the duty, and hung up. That kind of trouble I didn't need.

"Not everybody was happy about the bodies coming home, of course. I had a case in East Saint Louis where the widow showed up for the service, and the service only, then got on a train back to California. The boy's parents said she had married him for his $10,000 insurance. I sort of believed them. Some of those gals married as many as seventeen guys, and they would be collecting the allotment checks while they were out hunting another husband, and getting the insurance if they were killed. You'd be surprised how much of that went on.

"But you had to be careful all the time, especially where the boy's parents and friends were concerned. One time up in South Dakota the fiancé of the boy's brother took me on a sightseeing tour of the area, including a big retirement farm run by the Odd Fellows. It was really a layout, and the girl was just being friendly, that's all. Well, her fiancé didn't see it that way, but we managed to get it all smoothed over before the funeral.

"I suppose the wildest trip I was on was out to Thermopolis, Wyoming. One of the other guys had been out there before on escort duty and he warned me not to let the funeral director get me to drink water out of the fountain on the square because it had sulfur in it; it tasted awful, and the funeral director thought it was funny to get us to drink it.

"I was in my hotel room shaving, lather all over my face, when I heard crash-crash-crash-crash on the street below. I poked by head out and saw what had happened. There was a steep grade coming into town and a big, twelve-cylinder diesel with a lowboy trailer had lost his brakes and ripped the rear ends off seventeen cars, one right after another, as he sideswiped them trying to lose speed. There were insurance agents all over the place in ten minutes. And the mother of the boy I was escorting had gotten pinned in her car that was hit. She wasn't hurt bad, so we went ahead with the funeral, 2:30 that afternoon as planned.

"I decided to stay around a couple of days with some people I knew there, and they took me to see the Sunshine mine. I saw a little shack up on the lip of the open pit and asked them what that was. They said it belonged to a religious freak who lived on the edge of the pit by choice, and every sunset and every sunrise he was out there praying for the safety of the men working below. They had him on the payroll because they felt he was the best mining-safety engineer they could get. The miners liked having him there, so they kept him.

"Then I was sent to the town of Ida Grove in Iowa. There was a veteran running a farm-implement agency who had lost a hand in the war. He invited me to come out to the country club that night and we had a great time. I was looking around and saw a big fireplace, all cleaned out, one of those almost big enough to walk into. I always carried dice with me and suggested we get a crap game going. We did, and there was one drunk who really got hot. Then his luck changed and he started losing, and kept losing. He started writing checks, one after another, and his luck changed again and he cleaned us all out. He had money sticking out of every pocket he owned. He tried to get those checks back he'd written, and went to the custodian to open the safe, but they'd zipped that place up tight for the night. He was stuck with a bundle of cash in his pockets and a stack of hot checks in a safe. He was in a hell of a fix.

"He was staying in the same hotel I was, and we went back together. He told the clerk to get him up at 8:30 the next morning at all costs so he could get to the bank and cover those hot checks, and staggered off to bed.

"They got him up, all right, and he got to the bank at opening. Then he went back to work. He was an Internal Revenue Service agent and he was in that county running audits on everybody. He cleaned up there, too, and all over that county were farmers sitting at their kitchen tables writing checks to cover their back taxes, some as high as $17,000. It was a clean sweep no matter how you look at it.

"But I'd describe the general mood during the time as kind of stagnant. There were between fifteen and sixteen million guys coming home, and they all couldn't be treated like returning heroes. It was a hell of a stress on the economy to dump that many humans back on the industrial work force and have no jobs for them. The progress wasn't there. It was slow, like a snail, and some of the guys were pretty bitter.

"Sometimes when you went into a community with the remains for reburial and people from other communities came for the funeral, you'd get to talking to them and you could tell that an awful lot of people felt the whole bloody Second World War was nothing but one big expensive circus. I heard comments that it would take 150 to 180 years to pay this thing off, and they knew what they were talking about. There was some bitterness there, sure, and bringing a body home would bring it up. The pent-up feelings would surface.

"And the unions weren't pushing for their members then. Everything was slow. People were still recovering from the effect the war had on us all. I ran into some bitter Legionnaires and VFW guys, especially those who were wounded and would carry those wounds to the grave. But most of them had made up their minds they were going to make it, like the one-handed Legion commander in Ida Grove.

"Seventy-six trips, twenty-three months, and thirteen states. Quite a time during those two years. But it didn't have any effect on me, walking around and riding trains with all that death. No, it had no effect on me at all. Why should it?"

Lawrence Rudell's twin sister, Florence Rudell Marx, had married during the war, and her husband decided to make a career of the military. Her observations perhaps sum up the whole experience of civilians during World War II:

"We were all lonely and we were all waiting for something or someone. We had a common bond; there was an understanding. We weren't afraid of one another. People were traveling alone so much—young and old and women and men, young mothers headed to camps with small children. There was always someone to lend a helping hand.

"After the war ended, I was going to New York by train with my first child, who was six months old then, and from there I was going by ship to meet my husband, who was stationed in occupied Germany. I had a compartment on the train, and the people in the next compartment partied all night long. When I came out the next morning in New York, one of the men said: 'Were you in there all night long with that baby?' I said I was, and he apologized for the noise and bent down to help carry my luggage out. He dropped the bag, and when he picked it up he spilled baby oil all over his expensive suit. He told me not to worry about it and insisted on carrying the bag for me. People were still helping each other, see?

"But then it was all over. When we came back from Germany in 1949, I couldn't believe the changes. People weren't helping each other anymore. They were so busy with their own lives that they never went back to the old way of living before the war during the Depression. We suddenly got caught up in the hustle-bustle of a growing, growing country with all its new technology learned in the war. We forgot about one another. We forgot about humanity.

BIBLIOGRAPHY

BAILEY, THOMAS A. *Voices of America: The Nation's Story in Slogans, Sayings, and Songs.* New York: The Free Press, 1976.

BLUM, JOHN MORTON. *V Was For Victory.* New York: Harcourt, 1976.

DUNNING, JOHN. *Tune In Yesterday.* Englewood Cliffs, N.J.: Prentice-Hall, 1976.

FUKEI, BUDD. *The Japanese American Story.* Minneapolis: Dillon, 1976.

GANSBERG, JUDITH M. *Stalag U.S.A.* New York: Crowell, 1977.

GARRETT, JESSIE A., and LARSON, RONALD C. *Camp and Community.* Fullerton, Ca.: California State University, 1977.

LEONARD, THOMAS M. *Day by Day: The Forties.* New York: Facts on File, 1977.

LINGEMAN, RICHARD R. *Don't You Know There's a War On?* New York: G. P. Putnam's Sons, 1970.

MANSFIELD, HARVEY, et al. *A Short History of the OPA.* Washington, D.C.: U.S. Government Printing Office, 1948.

ITO, KAZUO. *Issei.* Seattle: Japanese Community Center, 1973.

PERRETT, GEOFFREY. *Days of Sadness, Years of Triumph.* New York: Coward, McCann & Geoghegan, 1973.

PHILLIPS, CABELL. *The 1940s: Decade of Triumph and Trouble.* New York: Macmillan, 1975.

SLOAN, GENE H. *Somewhere in Tennessee.* Nashville: Self-published, 1956.

WEBBER, BERT. *Retaliation: Japanese Attacks and Allied Countermeasures on the Pacific Coast in World War II.* Corvallis, Ore.: Oregon State University Press, 1975.

WEGLYN, MICHI. *Years of Infamy.* New York: Morrow, 1976.